# Business Ethics
## THE STATE OF THE ART

# THE RUFFIN SERIES IN BUSINESS ETHICS
R. Edward Freeman, *Editor*

THOMAS DONALDSON
*The Ethics of International Business*

JAMES W. KUHN AND DONALD W. SHRIVER, JR.
*Beyond Success: Corporations and Their Critics in the 1990s*

R. EDWARD FREEMAN, EDITOR
*Business Ethics: The State of the Art*


FORTHCOMING TITLES TO BE ANNOUNCED

# Business Ethics

## THE STATE
## OF THE ART

❏ ❏ ❏

Edited by

## R. EDWARD FREEMAN

*New York    Oxford*
OXFORD UNIVERSITY PRESS
1991

## Oxford University Press

Oxford   New York   Toronto
Delhi   Bombay   Calcutta   Madras   Karachi
Petaling Jaya   Singapore   Hong Kong   Tokyo
Nairobi   Dar es Salaam   Cape Town
Melbourne   Auckland

and associated companies in
Berlin   Ibadan

## Copyright © 1991 by Oxford University Press, Inc.

Published by Oxford University Press, Inc.,
200 Madison Avenue, New York, New York   10016

Oxford is a registered trademark of Oxford University Press

Library of Congress Cataloging-in-Publication Data
Business ethics : the state of the art /
edited by R. Edward Freeman.
p.   cm.—(The Ruffin series in business ethics)
Includes index.
ISBN 0-19-506478-X
1. Business ethics.   2. Industry—Social aspects.
I. Freeman, R. Edward, 1951–   .   II. Series.
HE5387.B876   1990
174'.4—dc20          90-7372   CIP

9 8 7 6 5 4 3 2 1

Printed in the United States of America
on acid-free paper

# FOREWORD

The purpose of The Ruffin Series in Business Ethics is to publish the best thinking about the role of ethics in business. In a world in which there are daily reports of questionable business practices, from insider trading to environmental pollution, we need to step back from the fray and understand the large issues of how business and ethics are, and ought to be, connected. We need to integrate the teaching and practice of management more closely with ethics and the humanities. Such an integration will yield both a richer ethical context for managerial decision making, and a new set of practical and theoretical problems for scholars of ethics.

During the past 20 years scholarship in business ethics has blossomed. Today, more than ever before, there is a growing consensus among management scholars, ethicists, and business executives that ethics should be a vital part of the teaching and practice of management.

Responding to this need, the Peter B. and Adeline W. Ruffin Foundation in 1987 established a fund at The Darden School, University of Virginia, to create a distinguished lecture series in business ethics. The Ruffin Series will publish these lectures as well as other distinguished books that will be of interest to management scholars, ethicists, and practicing managers. Each of these three audiences is important because only through a sustained dialogue among management thinkers, philosophers, and managers, will lasting progress be made in bringing ethics into the daily business of business.

It is a distinct pleasure to edit the first volume of the Ruffin Lectures. A distinguished interdisciplinary group of scholars gathered in Charlottesville in April of 1988 to discuss the papers of Ruffin lecturers Norman Bowie, Kenneth Goodpaster, Thomas Donaldson, and Ezra Bowen. During the following year a number of scholars undertook the project of developing the themes that these lectures called to mind. The resulting volume can be seen as a series of sketches, an interweaving of strands of thought, that hangs together by virtue of the richness of the field. These scholars have created a volume that will be an exemplar of the state of the art in business ethics rather than some final or penultimate word. Our conversation, begun in Charlottesville in 1988, is ongoing and one which we invite you to experience through these essays.

*Charlottesville, Va.*                                                       R.E.F.
*April 1990*

# ACKNOWLEDGMENTS

This book would not be possible without the help and support of a number of people. First of all the participants in the yearly conversations known as the Ruffin Lectures have given their best intellectual efforts to the volume. Second, The Darden School and its Sponsors have created a wonderful environment for conversations about ethics. Of special note are Dean John W. Rosenblum, Charles O. Meiburg, Robert R. Fair, Charles B. Fitzgerald, and the rest of the administration.

My faculty colleagues at Darden and the University of Virginia are also important conversational partners. Of particular note are James Childress, John Fletcher, Daniel Ortiz, Jahan Ramazani, Michael Brint, Michael Cornfield, Richard Rorty, Diana Harrington, Mark Haskins, and Andrea Larson.

My colleagues at the Olsson Center for Applied Ethics have been supportive and helpful, particularly Henry Tulloch, Karen Dickinson, Patricia Bennett, Alec Horniman, and Tom Donaldson.

The Olsson Center for Applied Ethics would not exist without the generosity of Sture Olsson and the Olsson family, and Edward and Brian McAnaney and the Ruffin Foundation. This book is therefore appropriately dedicated to the Olsson and Ruffin families for making it possible.

# CONTENTS

# CONTRIBUTORS

Ezra F. Bowen
Cardinal Concepts
Westport, Connecticut

Norman E. Bowie
Carlson School of Management
University of Minnesota
Minneapolis, Minnesota

Joanne B. Ciulla
Department of Legal Studies/
    Management
The Wharton School,
    University of Pennsylvania
Philadelphia, Pennsylvania

Richard T. DeGeorge
Department of Philosophy
University of Kansas
Lawrence, Kansas

Robbin Derry
The American College
Bryn Mawr, Pennsylvania

Thomas J. Donaldson
Department of Business
    Administration
Georgetown University
Washington, D.C.

William C. Frederick
Graduate School of Business
University of Pittsburgh
Pittsburgh, Pennsylvania

R. Edward Freeman
The Darden School
University of Virginia
Charlottesville, Virginia

Daniel R. Gilbert, Jr.
Department of Management
Bucknell University
Lewisburg, Pennsylvania

Kenneth E. Goodpaster
College of St. Thomas
St. Paul, Minnesota

Edwin M. Hartman
Rutgers University
Newark, New Jersey

Jennifer Mills Moore
Department of Philosophy
University of Delaware
Newark, Delaware

Lynn Sharp Paine
Harvard Business School
Harvard University
Boston, Massachusetts

Robert C. Solomon
Department of Philosophy
University of Texas
Austin, Texas

# Business Ethics
## THE STATE OF THE ART

# Introduction

The discipline that has come to be known as "business ethics" is hardly new. Since ancient times philosophers and others have questioned the connection between business or commerce and moral life. Today, these questions have become institutionalized through the creation of an academic discipline. Although the nature and status of this discipline is sometimes open to question, its existence is a real fact. The accrediting body of American business schools, The American Assembly of Collegiate Schools of Business (AACSB), has mandated that business ethics, in some form, be taught.

The popular press is full of stories about the latest trespasses of business executives. Ethics experts are quoted routinely in the *Wall Street Journal,* the *New York Times,* the *Washington Post, Time,* and other mass media. Even television has gotten into the act, with the recent Public Broadcasting System's series on "Ethics in America." Management guru Peter Drucker has even started a new wave of thinking by questioning whether there is any such thing as "business ethics."[1]

In a similar vein, the corporate counterparts of business schools have developed a real interest in business ethics. Faced with the fact that fully two-thirds of the American people believe that business executives do a lousy job on ethics, and disasters on a global scale such as Bhopal and the EXXON Alaska spill, executives recognize the need to think clearly about tough ethical matters.

The study of ethics and business has a long history, which has been amply chronicled by others.[2] From Aristotle's equating of profits with usury to Aquinas's discussion of the "just price," business was not seen as an activity outside of everyday life.[3] Naturally, business practice was subject to the same analysis as any other human endeavor. There was no need for a separate field of study. The exchange of goods and services, the creation of marketplaces and town fairs, were responsible for the growth of urban environments, and better lives for many. They were not believed to be inspired by some

3

evil influence. There was little or no competition between ideologies. However, several major trends have combined to give a renewed emphasis to the connection between ethics and business.

The rise of capitalism in the West, the Industrial Revolution, and the emergence of socialism and Marxism fundamentally changed the relationship between business and ethics.[4] The Marxist critique of the industrial world of the nineteenth century raised questions about the moral nature of the dominant business system. The labor movement made these questions real, as owners and workers often resorted to violence to settle their differences.

The shift to managerial capitalism, and the resulting increase in the prevalence of the modern corporation, has raised numerous questions of governance. From Berle and Means's classic treatise adumbrating the separation of ownership from control of the corporation, to more modern discussions of leveraged buyouts, greenmail, and takeovers, there are a host of specific issues that raise the question, "In whose interest and for whose benefit should the corporation be managed?"[5]

Finally, in recent years we have seen a renewed attention to the role of business in society, and specifically renewed interest in management. Witness the fact that Tom Peters and Robert Waterman's *In Search of Excellence*[6] sold over 10 million copies worldwide. At the center of this renewed interest in management are questions about how people treat each other in organizations, questions that are essentially ethical. Peters and Waterman's prescription for corporations could be summarized as a modern-day version of Kant's principle: Treat others with respect and dignity.[7]

These broad trends yield a four-part division of the research questions that comprise the current state of the art in business ethics.[8] At the *Societal* level there are questions of the relationships among the chief institutions of society. Milton Friedman's argument that the proper role of business in a capitalist society is to maximize profits delineates the function of capitalism (at least in Friedman's view).[9] And Andrew Carnegie's argument that the role of the businessperson was to apply the principles of charity to help the poor is another version of the meaning of capitalism.[10] The merits and demerits of capitalism and socialism, the mixed economy, market socialism, and the like are all societal level questions.

One particular controversy is noteworthy because an answer to this question frames a great deal of the debate: the nature of the corporation. Is the corporation to be understood solely as a means to the creation of wealth for stockholders, or can it be understood as a social contract among stockholders, customers, suppliers, employees, and communities?[11] Alternatively, can the corporation, as an institution, be seen solely in structuralist terms, or is there a post-structuralist view as well?

Alternatively, philosophical theories of justice are relevant to analysis at the societal level. One cannot assess the worth of capitalism outside of some framework for the just distribution of goods and services, rights and duties in society. Likewise, philosophical theories of justice are uninteresting absent real discussions about the features of various economic systems. The separation of economics from politics, sociality, and philosophy leads to arid pseudoscience or an unworkable political ideology. So, there is little wonder that John Rawls's *A Theory of Justice* stands as the major intellectual edifice on which answers to societal level questions must stand or fall.[12] Recent work by Alasdair MacIntyre, Michael Sandel, and Richard Rorty has led to a renewed vigor in political philosophy, which is of the first importance to scholars in business ethics.[13] In addition, recent work by scholars in women's studies on the gender bias inherent in the Kantian tradition of justice, in which Rawls and his followers clearly place themselves, has led to new insights and fresh analytical constructs such as Seyla Benhabib's notion of "the concrete other."[14]

Societal level questions are necessarily abstract, but if the method of reflective equilibrium is to be followed, these questions both inform and are informed by judgments about particular cases: (1) corporation-stakeholder relationships; (2) corporation-employee relationships; (3) employee-employee relationships. Because comprehensive theories are intellectually expensive, we can also see these more concrete levels of analysis as standing on their own, perhaps only implicitly informed by concerns of justice.

*Stakeholder* level questions comprise a large body of the literature in business ethics. In general these questions are about the particular relationship between a firm and those external groups that are affected by or can affect it. There are a host of such questions regarding each of customers, suppliers, stockholders, and communities. The following are but a few examples.[15]

Should there be restrictions on the advertising and promotion of products? Who is responsible for proper and improper uses of products? Do concepts such as "fair price" and "fair competition" make sense in a free market? What is the proper mix of customer behavior between "exit," "voice," and "loyalty"? What purchasing arrangements between vendors are proper? In particular, should facilitating payments be made to expedite the handling of goods and services? What is the moral nature of bribery? How much information should be disclosed to stockholders, suppliers, customers, and communities about products or operations of the firm? Is insider trading morally objectionable? How should firms handle externalities such as pollution? What obligations does a company have to the communities in which it operates?

Stakeholder questions have for the most part been approached in the literature as isolated instances. Only recently have scholars sought to work out comprehensive positions on a host of issues that stem from theoretical perspectives, and in particular from perspectives informed by answers to societal level questions.[16]

*Internal policy* questions are about the relationship between the organization as an entity and its employees, both management and non-management. What is the nature of the employment contract, or the psychological contract? Is continued employment guaranteed or is there employment at will? What are the political rights of employees? For example, is there free speech, the right to organize without penalty? What is meaningful work? How should employees participate in the design of their tasks and their work environment? What are the firm's policies on issues such as lie detectors and security, drug testing, employee health and well-being, family well-being, and privacy? What protection, if any, should be afforded whistleblowers?

Internal policy questions provide a rich area of research that is interdisciplinary. Encompassing diverse scholars from organizational studies, psychology, sociology, business policy, economics, and philosophy, the volume of research on these questions has exploded in recent years. Internal policy questions are rarely answered in isolation from governmental policy, or analyzed without understanding the effects on other key stakeholder groups.

Finally there is a large set of questions around the moral life of employees in their relationships with other employees. These *Human* level questions, once again, both inform and are informed by the societal, stakeholder, and internal policy level questions. Some of the human level questions are about the relationships between specific roles occupied by employees. We might break these down into "boss-subordinate," "subordinate-boss," "peer," "network," and "other" relationships. In addition, there is a distinctive human quality to relationships that the language of "roles and rules" cannot capture. Questions of "care" often go beyond specific role obligations. The ability of humans to integrate the diversity of roles that they occupy also transcends the very concept of "role." For instance, should Jones demand that subordinate Smith complete a task when she knows it will conflict with Smith's family obligation? And, how much weight should Smith attach to his role as father versus his role as employee? What obligations do we owe each other every day in our work situations just because we are human? What virtues such as hope, love, trustworthiness, honesty, and integrity need to be exhibited? Is treating each other as mere means ever justified?

There are important connections between societal, stakeholder, internal policy, and human issues. The state of the art in business ethics is in creating frameworks, theoretical edifices, and decision techniques for linking these questions into coherent wholes. The episodic, issue-oriented, sometimes knee-jerk approach is ending. We are seeing business and ethics as tightly connected, rather than at different ends of a spectrum featuring the extremes of "good business" and "good ethics."

The delineation of these four levels of questions is not intended to be comprehensive, but rather as a heuristic to understand the pervasiveness of ethical questions in business. And the essays in this volume should be read as exemplars of the state of the art rather than as encompassing it. Any attempts to encompass either "business" or "ethics," much less their combination, will surely fail. Neither business nor ethics has an essential nature to be discovered. The essays in this volume can easily be read as narratives, about how we see, and might come to see, certain connections between business and ethics. The major lectures that comprise the opening essays in each of the four parts of the book make substantial contributions to the state of the art in business ethics.

In a comprehensive account of the academic discipline of business ethics, Norman Bowie takes on the whole mosaic, articulating a defense of the legitimacy of business ethics. Bowie takes aim at critics of business ethics, from within the academy and within business, and puts business ethics at least on the same par with the other business disciplines. Kenneth Goodpaster works at the internal policy level, focusing on the decision-making process, for the most part, and articulates an ideal of moral leadership and culture that includes a normative core. He coins "teleopathy" as a way to diagnose what often goes wrong in corporate decisions. Thomas Donaldson sketches part of a more comprehensive account of a principled approach to international business. In doing so Donaldson defends capitalism against charges of moral relativism through his use of "fundamental human rights," showing how multinationals do in fact have obligations beyond doing in Rome what the Romans do. Finally, Ezra Bowen delves into the avant garde, the relationship between business and literacy, an issue that is getting increasing scrutiny. Bowen believes that business firms have moral obligations to make citizens more literate and suggests that the concept of "ethical literacy" is behind the current crisis in business ethics.

Each of these essays is rich in theme and plot. Some of these themes have been picked up and developed by other scholars in their contributions to the volume. In summary, we hope to have created a living document that will spur others to enter into and continue the conversation about the connection between business and ethics. There is a great deal of work to be done.

## NOTES

I would like to thank Tom Donaldson and Patricia Bennett for their help with the introductions and the editing of this volume. Without their efforts this book would have been much less timely.

1. Peter Drucker, "What is 'Business Ethics'?" *Public Interest* 63 (Spring 1981): 18–36.
2. Cf. Richard DeGeorge, "The Status of Business Ethics: Past and Future," *Journal of Business Ethics* 6 (1987): 201–11; and L. Preston, "Business and Public Policy," *Journal of Management* 12, no. 2: 261–75 (1988).
3. For an interesting analysis see Robert Solomon's essay in *Business and the Humanities,* The Ruffin Lectures, Vol. 2 (New York: Oxford University Press), forthcoming.
4. For a definitive account see Fernand Braudel, *The Structures of Everyday Life* (New York: Harper & Row, 1981). For a different point of view see Nathan Rosenberg and L. E. Birdzell, Jr., *How the West Grew Rich* (New York: Basic Books, 1986).
5. Adolph Berle and Gardiner Means, *Private Property and the Modern Corporation* (New York: Macmillan, 1932). For an analysis of these trends in more modern form see a special issue of *The Journal of Law and Economics,* June 1983, n; for a different view see Oliver Williamson, *The Economic Institutions of Capitalism* (New York: Free Press, 1985).
6. Thomas Peters and Robert Waterman, *In Search of Excellence* (New York: Harper & Row, 1982).
7. For an argument to this effect see R. Edward Freeman and Daniel R. Gilbert, Jr., *Corporate Strategy and the Search for Ethics* (Englewood Cliffs, NJ: Prentice-Hall, 1988).
8. This four-part division of business ethics is often used as an organizing principle. There is nothing particularly novel about its use here. For an example see the introductory text, James Stoner and R. Edward Freeman, *Management,* 4th ed. (Englewood Cliffs, NJ: Prentice-Hall, 1989), Chapter 4.
9. Milton Friedman, *Capitalism and Freedom* (Chicago: University of Chicago Press, 1962).
10. Andrew Carnegie, *The Gospel of Wealth and Other Essay* (New York: Doubleday, Page and Co., 1906).
11. For an incisive discussion see Thomas Donaldson, *Corporations and Morality* (Englewood Cliffs, NJ: Prentice-Hall, 1982). For two different views see Oliver Williamson, *Economic Institutions,* Chapter 12, and R. Edward Freeman and William Evan, "Corporate Governance: A Stakeholder Approach," *Journal of Behavioral Economics,* in press.
12. John Rawls, *A Theory of Justice* (Cambridge: Harvard University Press, 1971).
13. Cf. Alasdair MacIntyre, *After Virtue* (Notre Dame: Notre Dame University press, 1981); Michael Sandel, *Liberalism and the Limits of Justice* (New York: Cambridge University Press, 1982); and Richard Rorty, *Contingency, Irony and Solidarity* (New York: Cambridge University Press, 1989).
14. Seyla Benhabib, "The Generalized and the Concrete Other," in S.

Benhabib and D. Cornell, eds., *Feminism as Critique* (Minneapolis: University of Minnesota press, 1987), pp. 77–95.

15. For a more comprehensive view see Archie Carroll, *Business and Society, Business Ethics, and Stakeholder Management* (Dallas: Southwestern Publishing, 1989).

16. The best recent example is Thomas Donaldson, *Ethics and International Business* (New York: Oxford University Press, 1990).

# I
# BUSINESS ETHICS AS
# AN ACADEMIC DISCIPLINE

Norman Bowie looks at some longstanding objections to the teaching of business ethics in the business schools. He observes that academic skepticism about the professionalism of business has been matched by the business faculty's skepticism concerning the validity of ethics as part of the business curriculum. While the business school has been viewed as a vocational school by some, and has had to fight for its inclusion in graduate professional education, so too, the history of the business ethics curriculum has been turbulent.

Business faculty have received the teachers of ethics as unequal partners in education. Ethics teachers who are not trained in business are suspected of lacking a proper sense of the bottom-line nature of business. If trained in business, the ethics teachers were often seen as merely providing anecdotes on ethics or leading discussions of cases that would have little practical application in the business world. There has been a prevalent notion that ethics is a soft, impractical discipline.

Bowie treats the criticism that business ethics is an unscientific discipline by comparing it to other parts of the business curriculum that are purported to be scientific, such as accounting or marketing. Although ethics cannot purport to be scientific, accounting and marketing are not strictly scientific either, and yet their validity is not called into question for that reason.

Bowie considers the issue of objectivity, as against "soft, mushy" thinking, as a required characteristic of a discipline. He concludes that objectivity does not constitute a part of the criteria used to include or exclude other courses and is thus an irrelevant consideration. The liberal arts nature of business ethics is precisely what, along with rigorous moral reasoning, business ethics requires to afford both the sensitivity and thinking functions necessary to solve ethical dilemmas.

Bowie argues that disciplines rest upon metaphysical choices that underpin theories of human nature. He urges that a distinction be understood between the nature of theory in the natural sciences, which can be empirically based, and theory in the social sciences, which is based upon models of human behavior. Bowie observes that while agency theory and general equilibrium theory are accorded credibility as safe assumptions concerning human behavior, they do not so easily provide empirical evidence of human actions.

Finally, Bowie looks to Kant and Adam Smith for evidence that basing actions on a sense of altruism and enlightened self-interest has strong support from both of these philosophers. Far from splitting business ethics off from a humanitarian perspective, Kant and Smith rely upon that perspective as an unassailable given upon which they postulate their theories. Bowie insists that this perspective will serve to inform the business ethics student in the most complete manner.

Richard DeGeorge questions the worth of business ethics becoming legitimate. The very success of the attention focused on ethics in business has threatened the nature of the academic discipline. DeGeorge points out that the success of business ethics as a discipline, or the legitimacy of business ethics, depends upon the quality of research done in the field and on its success as a liberal arts subject, not on its effectiveness in changing the ethics of business practice.

The *critical* function of business ethics is jeopardized by the popular success of business ethics consultants and by the trendiness of the subject in public opinion. It has become fashionable to be concerned about ethics in business. The popularity of the subject has outstripped the availability of trained teachers of ethics.

The expectation placed on business ethics curricula that they influence the businessperson can lead to disillusionment of the public with the field as a whole. There is some feeling that the business school has caused many of the excesses found among entrepreneurs and Wall Street financial executives, and that business schools, by teaching ethics, can put a stop to these excesses. Again, there is a fundamental confusion over what is the academic discipline of business ethics and what is ethics in the practice of business.

DeGeorge notes the popular opinion that we all really know what is right or wrong, and the task of business ethics is to enforce these notions in business education. However, it is clear from interviews with perpetrators of the more scandalous incidents that there is no agreement on what is right and wrong. In fact, the establishment of such a consensus is a large part of what business ethics tries to accomplish.

Furthermore, DeGeorge asks whether the teaching of ethics in the corporation will be unhampered by the firm's own ethical preferences. He notes the emphasis on the case method as an indication of the bias toward problem solving on the individual level, rather than a discussion of the larger issues considered by ethical theories. He further suggests that what is likely to happen in corporate ethics programs is an inculcation of the firm's conventional morality, its credo, rather than the development of critical thinking skills. Thus, the proliferation of ethics consultants and the use of business schools as a service for businesses is a challenge to the critical function of business ethics in the academy.

Business ethics is not only legitimate, according to William Frederick, it is essential in the business curriculum. Frederick refers to some popular arguments against the inclusion of ethics in the graduate business school curriculum. The first is the claim that ethics education should be part of the liberal arts program at the undergraduate level; the business school is not the place to teach ethics. The second argument is that the ethical habits of students are already formed by the time they reach the business school and trying to change these habits is not likely to be fruitful.

Frederick points out that the acceptance of ethics as a valid course in business school is desirable, but the possible co-optation of ethics as a means of legitimizing a company's culture is a real threat to academic courses in ethics. The process of inculcating corporate values is risky, and the companies that see ethics as a legitimizing label for company indoctrination are doing a disservice to the discipline. Again, it is imperative that ethics education not become a fad and thereby miss serving its essential function: inquiry into the nature of ethical dilemmas in the practice of business.

As a response to Bowie's remarks on empirical research in business ethics as being somewhat at odds with the normative work being done, Frederick contends that a "bridging between the philosopher's evaluative insights and the empirically verified data base of the social scientist" needs to be effected in order to provide meaning for empirical data as well as verifiable grounding for theoretical analyses.

Jennifer Moore's reflections on Bowie's lecture point to the erosion of the liberal arts base of business ethics as indicative of the erosion of liberal arts education in general. The present vocational approach to education encompasses a view that the liberal arts are valuable only to the extent that they enhance a career education, that they enrich marketable skills.

Moore examines the differences in a liberal and a vocational education. She notes that where the vocational curriculum prepares a student to pursue certain goals, the goals themselves are seldom scrutinized. Liberal arts, on the other hand, examines the goals themselves. Second, the role orientation of vocational education tries to produce a skilled professional, whereas the liberal education tries to produce a good person, a good citizen. And last, vocational education is narrower in nature, with the teaching of skills and a body of knowledge its primary offering, while a liberal arts education is broader, more general, and tries to develop judgment and autonomous rationality.

By contrasting the corporate bureaucratic rationality, which puts truth in service to the fluctuating political culture of the corporation, autonomous rationality recognizes ends in themselves and organizes means around those ends. Eventually, in an environment that is at the mercy of short-run planning, even the firm itself is a means to an end and its well-being is jeopardized by leaders whose allegiance is to their own desires. Moore sees a need in the business community for individuals to construct means that satisfy fair and rational ends, and she sees the liberal arts education as providing a process to develop those individuals.

Lynn Paine tackles Irving Kristol's assertion that educators have no business trying to form character in their graduate students. She disputes his claim that the job of ethics teachers is to help students "identify the logical inconsistencies in systems of moral propositions constructed by other ethicists." Kristol believes that ethics educators cannot change conduct or character at the graduate school level, and therefore ethics does not belong in the graduate business school curriculum.

In responding to these observations, Paine notes that some ethicists avoid trying to develop character in students and hope, rather, to arm their students with the "tools" of ethical analysis. She notes that a teacher who purports to develop students' moral character is inviting criticism of her own character and is risking failure at a subjective and elusive task.

Although students need to learn how to apply moral theories, they also need to have access to reliable character traits within themselves that they can draw upon for the many decisions they will have to make. Paine accepts Kristol's view that ethics education should contribute to the formation of character in students, but she asserts that it can do so at both the undergraduate and graduate levels.

Seeing character change as possible and gradual, Paine develops a concept of positive influence of the educator upon the student. Citing Aristotle's idea of the acquisition of a virtue by the imitation of one who possesses it, Paine suggests that the increase of ethical integrity must begin with personal resolve and be supported by actions grounded in convictions.

Paine advances the idea of a program for ethics education and describes it as comprising the development of four key elements: ethical sensibility, an ability to detect ethical considerations in situations; ethical reasoning, a deliberate and conscious approach to working through situations: ethical conduct, the evidence of moral judgment; and ethical leadership, the ability to be accountable for not only one's own conduct but also that of subordinates.

# 1

# Business Ethics as a Discipline: The Search for Legitimacy

## Norman E. Bowie

Business ethics has become a real problem for business schools. The general public wants it taught. So do many businesspersons, although many of them don't like the name "business ethics." However, few business faculty are trained in ethics. The so-called experts in the field are philosophers and theologians whose loyalty to the free enterprise system is suspect. Even if the loyalty of some individual philosophers and theologians isn't suspect, business faculty allege there isn't anything else in the business curriculum they can teach. Moreover, most business faculty don't want another "soft" course in the curriculum. The AACSB wants ethics addressed, but they have lots of other demands as well. What's a business dean to do?

Where does business ethics stand today? Despite the clamor for it, its legitimacy as an academic discipline is suspect. I take as my theme this crisis of legitimacy. Unless this question of legitimacy is addressed, and to some extent answered, the future for business ethics is not bright. I will argue that business ethics is a discipline and that it should be a legitimate course in business education. But I wish to go further. Unless business ethics is a part of the business curriculum the legitimacy of the business curriculum itself is suspect.

### I

Perhaps the place to begin is with the history of business education. Higher education has been dominated by the Colleges of Arts and Sciences and the faculty of those colleges have long looked askance at vocational education. Vocational education didn't belong in the

17

university. Some of this elitism was eroded by the Morrill Act, which
created land grant universities. In addition, professional schools,
particularly law and medicine, have always been accepted. Even if
professional education was practical, at least it was *professional*. What
are business schools? Are they professional schools or trade schools?
The suspicion of many on the Arts and Sciences faculty is that business schools were like trade schools, that business education was vocational education, and that business faculty really didn't operate on
the traditional research model. Business faculty weren't scholars.
Professors of economics have always considered themselves scholars
in the traditional sense, and even today most economics departments
remain as departments in Colleges of Arts and Sciences rather than
departments in Colleges of Business. Well into the 1960s the legitimacy of business education was very much in question.

To combat this perception of inferiority, schools of business have
argued that business education is professional rather than merely
vocational. But is it? To answer that question we need to know the
distinguishing marks of a profession.


## II

The classic definition of a profession was given over 70 years ago by
Abraham Flexner, an aide to the Rockefeller and Carnegie foundations, in a speech entitled "Is Social Work a Profession?" To qualify
as a profession an occupation had to

1. Possess and draw upon a store of knowledge that was more than
   ordinarily complex.
2. Secure a theoretical grasp of the phenomenon with which it dealt.
3. Apply its theoretical and complex knowledge to the practical solution of human and social problems.
4. Strive to add to and improve its stock of knowledge.
5. Pass on what it knew to novice generations not in a haphazard
   fashion but deliberately and formally.
6. Establish criteria of admission, legitimate practice, and proper
   conduct.
7. Be imbued with an altruistic spirit.[1]

The classic professions were considered to be medicine, law, teaching, and the ministry.

The professions have had their greatest success meeting the first
five of Flexner's criteria. Indeed, Walter Metzger, addressing the
question "What Is a Profession, "argues that" the paramount function of professions . . . is to ease the problems caused by the relent-
less growth of knowledge."[2] This is what specialization and the growth
of large firms permit.

Business schools began to address the vocationalism issue most seriously during the 1960s in response to two 1959 landmark studies of business education.[3] As a result of these reports,

> [t]he often unsubstantiated descriptive content of earlier business school curricula and research has been replaced by quantitative description based on rigorous data collection, computer-assisted mathematical modeling, and the foundational concepts of science—testable hypotheses (or, at least, testable networks of hypotheses), correlated observations, and causal explanations.[4]

There is little doubt that business education succeeded in being more academic and that business professors could argue that business education now meets the first five criteria for being a profession—the epistemological criteria as I shall call them.

But professional status is not achieved by academic sophistication alone. The 1959 studies also pointed out that business education should address the legal, social, political, and economic environment of the firm.[5] Moreover, Metzger casts the epistemological problem of the growth of knowledge in *moral* terms. In a progressively complex world, people become increasingly ignorant of the information necessary to run their lives. The job of the professional is to protect the client from his or her own ignorance. It is worth quoting Metzger at length.

> I subscribe to these interlinked propositions: that, as the amount of knowledge increases, so too does the relative amount of ignorance, for each man can know only a decreasing fraction of what can be known, that knowledge, as it grows more specialized, also tends to grow more potent, more capable of being used for ill or good; that, as a consequence, there comes into being not a mass society but a lay society—a society, that is, in which each is potentially at the mercy of someone more thoroughly in the know; that these mutual dependencies grow more dangerous as knowledge, which had once been held by holy men, kin and neighbors, passes into the hands of strangers, and as the customary means of assuring its benign uses—parental love, communal sanctions, religious discipline—tend increasingly not to work. It is to avert a Hobbesian outcome that society urges occupations to tie their expertise to honorableness, to accord even ignorance moral claims. In that urging the professional ideal is born.[6]

In these interlocking propositions, he spells out the relation between professional knowledge and the altruistic spirit of a genuine profession. The chief function of a professional is not to use her specialized knowledge to maximize her income, rather it is to use her specialized knowledge to protect ignorant clients from being exploited by others.

Business has clearly made great strides in meeting Flexner's epistemological conditions. Each of the disciplines within business has developed a complexity, has claimed that it is theoretically grounded, has applied the discipline to the solution of human problems, added to the store of knowledge, and through undergraduate and graduate programs passed that knowledge on to the next generation.

But what about conditions six and seven? These conditions cannot be met by a rigorous course in finance or accounting nor by a new, more sophisticated course in organizational theory. Standards of proper conduct and altruistic spirit is the stuff of business ethics. If business education is to take its legitimate place in the academy, it must be professional in nature. It can only be professional if it includes an ethical component. Therefore, a business curriculum without an ethics component is not professional and hence not legitimate.

### III

Some of you may believe that I have proven my point by verbal sleight of hand. Suppose one challenges the definition of "professional,"or suppose one denies the traditional view of academic legitimacy that restricts legitimacy to liberal education and professional education. Such responses are appropriate. Controversial issues shouldn't be settled by verbal fiat.

However, we don't get anywhere if one definition is simply replaced by another. Definitions are open to debate, and there are criteria for saying that one definition is better than another. A definition can be richer, more precise, more inclusive, more consistent, more refined, or more in accord with experience than another. One of the strengths of the traditional definitions is that they do provide a means for discrimination. Universities can't and shouldn't have a department for everything that can be taught. Should there be a college of plumbing, a college of auto repair, etc., in all the major universities? The traditional definition keeps professional education distinct from merely vocational education.

But suppose someone said all you need are Flexner's first five conditions. The difference between professional education and mere vocational education is that the former is more theoretical and complex. Such a response wouldn't do. Airplane mechanics and the training of chefs for first-class restaurants could qualify even if barber schools couldn't. Moreover, without conditions six and seven, there is no way to keep certain practices that are legal but immoral out of the curriculum. Do the business schools really want courses that would teach students in labor relations the most effective way to break unions and in sales or marketing courses the most successful techniques to sell frills to the poor? If the only reason for a marketing course is to maximize the potential for professional success, why not? Because, in fact, business schools accept an implicit ethic.

To prove my point, consider the reaction to the disclosures about West Virginia University's course Marketing 321. Students in that course were assigned field research projects. Two student groups worked for Caterpillar heavy equipment dealerships. Their assignment was to do research on competitors. The students received valuable information from competitors because they identified themselves as West Virginia students and did not announce their affiliation with the Caterpillar dealerships. The professor, who was a consultant to Caterpillar, defended the students' actions. However, many other students, faculty, and business executives thought the professor's reasoning was morally flawed. People let their guard down when they are talking to students; the competitors had been misled.[7] Corporate espionage is unethical in both the corporate world and in academia.

In another well-publicized case, Columbia University Adjunct Professor Asher Edelman offered a prize of $100,000 to the student in his class who came up with the best plan for a corporate takeover. Edelman was forced to withdraw his offer on the grounds that such an offer was subversive of academic values.[8] Within the business school, market values must be subordinate to academic values. Otherwise business education should not take place within the university.

The best way to get a sense of these academic values is to examine the purpose of a liberal arts education. Here are a few 1987–88 statements of purpose from well-known liberal arts colleges and universities.

### University of Virginia

Purpose: The central purpose of the University of Virginia is to enrich the mind by stimulating and sustaining a spirit of free inquiry directed to understanding the nature of the universe and the role of mankind in it. Activities designed to quicken discipline and enlarge the intellectual and creative capacities, as well as the aesthetic and ethical awareness of the University, and to record, preserve, and disseminate the results of intellectual discovery and creative endeavor serve this purpose.

### University of Chicago

What kind of education can you secure in the College? It is an education designed to give you access to the entire world of human knowledge and some appreciation of the possibilities of human achievement. At the same time it is an education that develops your individual powers of judgment and expression, one that equips you to ask fresh questions and to pursue them on your own. It challenges you not only to acquire the tools of learning but also to raise questions about the ends for which they should be used.

The teaching provided by the College serves three major purposes: liberal education, specialized training in the academic disciplines, and preparation for entrance into professional schools. Liberal education is the oldest and still most important concern of the American liberal arts college. A liberal education is one that prepares one not for a career but for life. Such a course of study should ideally lead to the mastery of those bodies of knowledge and the acquisition of those intellectual habits that will enable the student to participate creatively in the civilized life of his or her contemporaries and to become an intelligent and effective citizen.

What do those statements of purpose tell us? The central purpose of an education is to understand human nature and our place in the world. Moreover, each person has ethical responsibilities in addition to vocational ones. Sometimes liberal education is explicitly justified on the grounds that its purpose is to produce civic-minded leaders.

What eliminates courses of study from the curriculum or rescues them from second-class status is the fact that their aim is altruistic rather than purely vocational and that they are taught in a manner respectful of academic values. Hence, my argument is *not* based simply on sleight of hand. It is buttressed by a tradition that is steeped in ethics. Of course, one can challenge a tradition. But you pay a price and the price is that any course based on complex knowledge is a legitimate candidate to be put in the university curriculum. Moreover, the values of the discipline being taught could overrule academic values. Most business educators seem unwilling to pay that price.

## IV

The critic of business ethics might employ a different strategy. She might agree that the business curriculum could address business ethics so that business education was professional in the required sense. However, she could argue that business ethics as practiced is not a genuine discipline—that business ethics as a discipline doesn't meet Flexner's knowledge conditions. She could charge that business ethics isn't theoretical or complex.

But what evidence exists that business ethics courses fail these tests? Some say that business ethics courses are nothing more than a series of anecdotes or intuitions, that ethical judgments are simply matters of individual opinion, that they aren't scientific, that they aren't verifiable. In other words, these critics could argue that ethics courses are soft and mushy, lacking any objective basis. Sound familiar?

Although the soft and mushy criticism sounds like one argument, it is really a collapsed version of several logically distinct charges. The first charge, that business ethics courses are nothing more than a series of anecdotes and intuitions, is simply false. No business ethics course taught by an ethical theorist would consist of such material. If these courses exist, they are most likely taught by business faculty without training in ethics and should be abolished as unprofessional. So much for the first charge.

What about the claim that business ethics courses aren't scientific? Well, that claim is true. What is suspect is the implication that because a course isn't scientific it lacks objectivity. Accounting courses aren't scientific the way physics and chemistry courses are, but they surely aren't formless. In fact, I would argue that almost no courses in the business curriculum are scientific in the full sense of that term. Business courses don't have a body of theory the way physics and chemistry do.

Critics are likely to grant this point but redefine "scientific" to mean "empirical." There is an annoying tendency for some business faculty to label *any* course that deals with empirical statements as scientific. But what about the claim that ethical judgments aren't empirical?

Unraveling that claim is exceedingly complex. First, the claim that ethical judgments aren't empirical is itself controversial. Although logical positivists of the 1940s held such a view, the philosophy of the logical positivists has been completely discredited; there are hardly any professional philosophers who subscribe to logical positivism in its original form. Logical positivism of the more naive variety is chiefly held by business faculty and social scientists—possibly to help separate themselves from their origins and to buttress their claims to scientific status for their disciplines or to avoid having to make normative judgments at all. Some might even argue that the pretense to scientific objectivity is used by some to mask the fact that business education assumes pro-capitalist normative goals.

Given the movements in the philosophy of science, e.g., Kuhn, Lakatos, and Feyerabend, the positivist view of science seems quaint at best. In the 1980s the objectivity of science itself is what is in question. The real issue is not the empirical status of ethical claims, but whether ethical claims are significantly less objective than other claims—the claims made in traditional business courses, for example.

Before turning to the objectivity issue, a few more comments should be made about the empirical status of ethical claims. First, there are some who argue that ethical claims are empirical. Admittedly these people are few in number. There are others who claim that ethical judgments can be derived from empirical claims, that the gap between is and ought can be bridged. Again the number of philosophers supporting this view is relatively small in number.

However, this leads to a second point. The debate about the empirical status of ethical claims is itself a debate within philosophical ethics. That debate is a central issue in what used to be called "meta-ethics." Meta-ethics has fallen out of fashion in part because many philosophers believe all epistemological claims are value-laden and that the dichotomy between value-free meta-ethics and traditional ethics was a false dichotomy. In any case business faculty can't simply *assert* that ethical judgments aren't empirical. They have to argue for it. In other words, they have to do some ethical theorizing.

Now let's return to the question of objectivity. There are two ways to handle that issue. First, we might examine the traditional business curriculum in order to challenge the scientific objectivity of its courses. In so doing I submit that we will discover that despite the development of more unified disciplines with a large collection of data and testable hypotheses, teaching and research in business disciplines are not and cannot be scientific in the fashion of teaching and research in the natural sciences. If my argument is correct, business educators accept an account of objectivity that is broader than that found in the natural sciences.

Second, we might examine the curriculum of the liberal arts college and look at the various disciplines that are included within it. After all, chemistry, English literature, history, mathematics, foreign languages, economics, psychology, art, and philosophy are paradigms of accepted university courses. What makes each of them a discipline? Why are they accepted whereas other courses like palm reading, auto mechanics, and hair styling are not permitted? Can each of the accepted courses make claims to objectivity that the others can't? Perhaps the traditional courses accept a notion of objectivity that is accepted by business educators as well.

When these two lengthy discussions are complete, I think we can conclude that the charge that business ethics is soft and mushy in ways that other business courses aren't is itself soft and mushy.

## V

In his provocative article in the *Academy of Management Review,*[9] Thomas Mulligan argues that two cultures exist in business education, the humanistic and the scientific. However, the scientific has generally driven out the humanistic. Although it might seem reasonable to have the two cultures coexist and contribute to business education, Mulligan contends this is impossible because the two cultures have different philosophical assumptions.

Although I concede that many business professors view their courses as scientific and view themselves as members of the scientific community, I think they have more in common with the humanistic culture than they realize. Many of the standard courses aren't scientific at all, and even the most scientific contain humanistic elements even if they aren't recognized as such.

Let's begin with accounting. After all, students often refer to accounting as the mirror opposite of ethics. Ethics is subjective, whereas accounting is objective. What is the status of accounting theory? A rather standard definition of a theory is the following: A theory is a systematically related set of statements, including some lawlike generalizations, that is empirically testable.[10] Accounting texts do speak of accounting theory. Let's start with a simple single theory approach. Vernon Kam describes accounting theory as follows:

> The theory of accounting envisioned here is an elaborate deductive system consisting of three distinct levels of statements of decreasing generality. . . . The first level, at the top, consists of the most general statements. These are, first, the postulates or basic assumptions of accounting. . . . Definitions are also at the first level. . . . The objectives of accounting are also included at this level. The second level consists of the principles or standards of accounting, which are not as general in scope as the statements on the first level. . . . The last level is composed of the statements on the specific procedures of accounting, such as straightline depreciation. . . .[11]

But this accounting theory is neither scientific nor, despite the claims of the author, truly deductive. A scientific theory also has observation statements at the last level. If P then Q, If Q then R, If R then O, where O is some observation statement. Kam's theory implies no observation statements.

Moreover, the theory is not truly deductive. Kam doesn't argue that the basic assumptions logically entail the principles. For Kam, what accounting theory seems to amount to is an elaborate classification scheme.

Moreover, the purpose of the "theory" is not scientific. Kam continues:

> [The FASB] argues that a generally agreed upon, comprehensive theory can generate certain benefits to the profession. Such a theory can:
>
> 1. Guide the body responsible for establishing accounting standards;
> 2. Provide a frame of reference for resolving accounting questions in the absence of a specific promulgated standard;
> 3. Determine bounds for judgment in preparing financial statements;
> 4. Increase financial statement user's understanding of and confidence in financial statements; and
> 5. Enhance comparability.[12]

If Kam's view of accounting is accurate, the generally accepted accounting standards are not like generalizations in chemistry. "Put blue litmus paper in acid, it will turn red" is different from "Put 'good will' in the asset column." The latter is more like a rule of baseball than a rule of chemistry. Such rules are called constitutive rules. They tell you how to play the game. If you are to play the game of baseball, the batter has three strikes. If you are to do accounting, put "good will" in the asset column.

There is another way in which accounting is not scientific in the traditional sense. Accounting theory does not enable us to make discoveries. Accounting is objective but in a conventional rather than a scientific sense. That is, accounting is objective because accounting rules are generally accepted. They can be evaluated and changed. Indeed, distinguished members of the profession are arguing that they should be changed. Note that you can't change the litmus test rule in chemistry if it isn't convenient. So if ethics is less objective than accounting, it is not because accounting rules are scientific and empirical and ethical rules are not. Rather, if the charge is true, it would have to be that there is far less conventional agreement about the rules of ethics than there is about the rules of accounting. Of course, if the ethics profession had an FASB with that authority and power, ethical principles would be as objective as accounting principles. The difference is one of power not of logic.

Mention should be made of at least one view of accounting theory that more closely resembles the traditional view of what constitutes a scientific theory. That theory is called the predictive theory of accounting.[13] The purpose of the theory is to help accountants decide which rule, among possible competing rules, should be adopted in a given situation. For example, "An accountant should choose the accounting technique that most accurately predicts the firm's earnings." But ethics can be scientific in this sense as well. "A society should choose that principle that maximizes the greatest good and we predict that teaching and following principle X will in fact produce the greatest good."

Moreover, if one listens to professional accountants, it seems as if the predictive model hasn't worked well in general. There is still no agreement. For example, William D. Hall, retired partner of Arthur Andersen and Company, says:

My greatest frustration with accounting theory and practice centers on the profession's glacial slowness in developing—or even seeming to sense the need for—an effective conceptual framework. . . . Thoughtful persons increasingly question the usefulness of present standards developed pragmatically over the years. . . . Often the profession cannot apply a clear, logical solution to a new transaction because it would be inconsistent

with established practice that governs another aspect of the same transaction or other similar transactions. So yet one more square peg is forced
into still another round hole. . . .[14]

Hall's remarks are hardly accolades to scientific predictability. What
Hall is saying is that the rules are inadequate for the practice of
accounting today—in part because they rest on an inadequate conceptual framework and in part because they give inconsistent solutions.

Let us move to another seemingly scientific discipline, marketing.
Marketing might be a plausible candidate because the following experiment can easily be imagined. One can scientifically determine
whether, other things being equal, e.g., price, people are more likely
to purchase goods in red boxes rather than blue ones. Indeed, scientific marketing theorists could try to identify all the variables that
go into a purchasing decision. Then they could run a series of experiments, holding certain variables constant while one is being ma-
nipulated. They could then use causal modeling theory to determine
the strength of the variables. That kind of data should enable them
to predict whether a new product would be a success. In fact, marketing theory is supposed to accomplish something like this. However, it has been a remarkable failure.

The British conglomerate Beecham Inc. sued the market research
firm of Yankelovich, Skelly & White for $24 million.[15] The suit
charged Yankelovich with negligence, misrepresentation, and breach
of contract on the grounds that Beecham Inc., was told its cold-water
wash product, Delicare, could outsell the market leader, Woolite. The
American Marketing Association has begun a series of seminars on
the liability issue, and Joseph Seagram and Sons has said it will require all data suppliers to sign detailed performance agreements.

If marketing really is a science, such performance agreements and
liability suits seem quite in order. However, *Newsweek,* confirming an
earlier *Wall Street Journal* story, announced that 70 to 90 percent of
all new products fail. Normally theories with such a failure rate don't
count as scientific. And in cases where high failure rates are tolerated, in certain medical cases, for example, the failure rates themselves can be explained by the scientific theory.

Of course the marketing faculty do have a comeback. They can
claim that although marketing is not yet a science—it's too new and
there are too many variables—at least it has a scientific methodology.
The strategy described earlier, where marketing theorists try to discover the strengths of the various variables that go into a purchasing
decision and then use this information to predict how a product will
do, is what marketing science is all about. That's an interesting response. But could such an enterprise succeed? Suppose the object of

study—consumers—do not behave like the objects of study in the traditional sciences. To examine that possibility, let's look at another course in the business curriculum—organizational theory.

The first thing you learn in Jeffrey Pfeffer's *Organizations and Organizational Theory* is that in organizational theory there is not one theory, but a number of theories. The first sentence of that book reads as follows: "The domain of organization theory is coming to resemble more a weed patch than a well-tended garden."[16]

Even more important is the fact that the debate about perspectives on action is fundamentally a debate about human nature—the very grist of the philosopher's mill. As Pfeffer says, "The three perspectives seen in the literature are (1) action seen as purposive, bounded or intendedly rational, and prospective or goal directed; (2) action seen as externally constrained or situationally determined; and (3) action seen as being somewhat more random and dependent on an emergent, unfolding process." The view of human nature chosen determines the theory developed. But is that choice a scientific one? After all, Pfeffer's first two perspectives reflect a choice between two classic positions in the metaphysical debate about free will. Indeed, with some molding, one might classify Pfeffer's three choices as choices among indeterminism, determinism or behaviorism, and compatibilism (the view that free will and determinism are not contradictory). Whether that choice is a scientific issue or not is itself extremely controversial. Social scientists have generally opted for determinism because they believe that's the only view that is consistent with science. However, a choice made for that reason is based primarily on narrow disciplinary grounds. I need that choice so my discipline is perceived as scientific. Of course the choice might be wrong. If marketers, for example, adopt the deterministic model as part of their scientific methodology and it's the wrong choice, no wonder the error rate is so high. It's not the complexity of variables, it's bad metaphysics.

To focus on textbooks in various standard business courses may not address the real issue. After all, a textbook is a pedagogical tool rather than a research tool. To fully understand the rigorous nature of academic business research, we need to focus on a discipline that serves as a foundation for that research and look at some standard theory that unites the various disciplines. The fundamental discipline is economics.

One theory that has received considerable attention the last several years is agency theory. Agency theory is frequently used in courses in accounting and finance—among others.

It seems to me that agency theory is based on a fundamental assumption of economics that all individuals are personal utility maximizers. An agency problem can be represented in any case where

one individual is supposed to look after the interests of another—
even when that goes against his or her own interest. If people are
always looking after their own interest, then a principal (the party to
whom the agent owes the interest) can be sure that the agent will
sacrifice the principal's interest for his own interest whenever their
interests conflict and the agent can get away with it. The principal
must then figure out monitoring devices so that his interest will be
protected. Certified public accountants help perform this function
for principals (stockholders) with respect to their agents (managers).
However, these monitoring devices are costly. Agency theorists provide elaborate mathematical models to determine the most efficient
monitoring devices.

But how scientific is agency theory? Is it a theory at all? It assumes
that people are egoists—that they will maximize their interests at the
expense of others if they can get away with it. But suppose people
are altruists—or at least partial altruists. If partial altruism correctly
describes human nature, a model based on egoistic assumptions consistently overstates the need for monitoring devices and hence gives
inefficient results.

Now agency theorists have a quick reply. They indicate that they
could modify their assumption and proceed as before. They could,
but in practice they don't, in spite of the fact that there is some
interesting research both speculative and empirical being carried on
by others.[17] Some economists are involved in this research, and the
conclusion seems to be that there is a strong altruistic component in
human behavior. I shall return to this issue later.

The trouble is that most professors in business schools who use
agency theory don't draw a distinction between an empirical claim
and a heuristic axiom adopted for purposes of convenience. Students take the egoistic assumption as a fact about human nature. By
the time a business ethicist gets a student, the damage has been done.
If a student believes that everyone looks after her own perceived
best interest, then ethics that argues that people sometimes ought to
put the interests of others over their own is impossible. Ethics would
be asking people to do what they can't do. No wonder the student
finds ethics unscientific and useless. It takes a long time to convince
the student that egoism is not scientifically established as a fact of
human nature.

If one of the fundamental postulates of agency theory is not scientific and if that postulate is itself one of the fundamental postulates of economics, specifically general equilibrium theory, then the
scientific status of economics itself is in question. In point of fact, the
extent to which the fundamental theories of economics are scientific
is a matter of great debate—both among philosophers of science and
among business writers in the popular business press.

The heart of economics is general equilibrium theory. General equilibrium theory asserts that the maximizing behavior of consumers and producers brings the amount of any good demanded into equilibrium with supply. General equilibrium theory is often criticized either because its assumptions are so unrealistic it can't apply to the real world or because the existence of disequilibria in the real world shows the theory to be false. For example, consumers do not have perfect information. But as contemporary discussions point out, general equilibrium theory cannot be dismissed so easily.[18]

Criticisms of the same logical type could be made against various scientific theories. In the natural sciences, when such charges are made, the natural scientist has a number of strategies she can adopt. They include (1) explanation by inexact laws that appeal either to ceteris paribus clauses or statistical approximations or (2) the use of models and idealizations. What troubles the critics of scientific economics is that economics alledgedly cannot correct for these deficiencies in the way that natural scientists can. The issue is far too complicated for a full discussion here. A lengthy quotation from Daniel Hausman illustrates the point with respect to the charge that the assumptions of general equilibrium theory are obviously false.

> Some . . . will falsely assert that all individuals have perfect information concerning the prices and availability of commodities and concerning the production possibilities. . . . Many will falsely assert that the preferences of all consumers are transitive. To conclude, without further analysis, that general equilibrium models can have no role in explanations would be to misapply pedantically the deductive-nomological model. . . . Consider what happens when natural scientists attempt to deal with complicated everyday phenomena. Take the trite example of the path of a leaf's fall. In what sense can it be explained by physicists? Precise deductive-nomological explanation seems out of the question. Scientists cannot get exact information concerning all relevant initial conditions and cannot do all the complicated calculations that would be necessary if they did have the pertinent data. If the only stumbling blocks were these problems of knowing the initial conditions and of calculation, physicists would have what I shall call "an explanation-in-principle" of the leaf's path. . . . Explanations in principle appear to be genuine explanations. . . . Scientists have good reason to believe they know all the relevant laws when, with simplifications concerning initial conditions, they can make roughly correct predictions concerning falling leaves and are able to cite the factors responsible for any appreciable errors. . . . Economists certainly cannot explain in principle local or overall characteristics of real economies. Not only are the purported laws of economics difficult to confirm—perhaps because of the difficulties of setting up simplified experimental situations—but theorists know these "laws" are inadequate. Economists are ignorant of many relevant laws. They leave out of account significant causal factors.[19]

In the chapter from which the above quotation was taken, Hausman then shows how inexact sciences can be explanatory in principle but that the general equilibrium model fails that test as well.

What conclusions can be drawn from this discussion? First, none of the business disciplines nor the discipline of economics that underlies so many other business disciplines have achieved the status of sciences the way natural sciences have. In Mulligan's terms the business disciplines already contain significant humanistic elements. The two culture split exists in the minds of business school faculty; it does *not* exist in the course content. The business curriculum cannot be purged of epistemological, metaphysical, and ethical assumptions. Hence, I believe there are greater possibilities for reconciliation than Mulligan does. Business faculty need to recognize the humanistic issues in their own disciplines.

## VI

Perhaps there is something fundamentally wrong about deciding matters of discipline legitimacy solely on the basis of whether or not the content is scientific. The notion that a discipline be scientific or even strictly empirical should not function as a necessary condition. In a liberal arts college or in a College of Arts and Sciences in any university, disciplines are accepted in part because they contribute to the overall educational mission—specifically to produce a well-rounded, integrated, socially responsible individual. The purpose of a liberal arts education is to produce a Kantian person—a rational, autonomous, moral agent who can take his or her place in a moral community. A necessary condition for a discipline is that it contribute significantly to the development of such a person. The educational mission provides a normative condition for objectivity. There must be a fit between the discipline and the purpose of a university education.

If the purpose of a university education is to produce well-rounded, integrated, socially responsible individuals, a proper question to ask is: What skills and attitudes should university courses embody? It is commonly held that courses should develop the skill of critical, independent thinking and create a sensitivity to new ideas and an imaginative sympathy with the experience of others.[20]

Suppose one now asks why people should develop these skills and attitudes. Exponents of the traditional liberal arts view have usually answered as follows. Such an education has three desirable outcomes. One is vocational. Young men and women are equipped with the general skills and techniques and the specialized knowledge that will make it possible for them to do productive work.

And such an education also produces a certain kind of person. As Sidney Hook says, "it provides those inner resources and traits of character which enable the individual, when necessary, to stand alone." In other words, it develops individual autonomy.[21]

Third, it develops a sense of civic responsibility—especially in a democratic society. Liberal arts education should develop autonomous individuals who are socially responsible.

The thinking and sensitivity aims of a liberal education allegedly make this possible. Critical thinking tempered by sensitivity and an imaginative sympathy with the experience of others is necessary for the survival of a democratic society. Steven Cahn puts the point this way.

> In a democracy where all adult citizens are supposed to participate in the decision-making process, each individual's education should be of equal concern. A democracy that neglects the education of some will pay a dear price, for the enemies of freedom feed upon ignorance, fear, and prejudice. Thus if an individual should complain his democracy is providing too much education for too many people, he reveals his ignorance about the very nature of democratic process; indeed too little education and there may soon be no democracy.[22]

The contribution of critical thinking to the preservation of democracy is obvious: citizens should be able to recognize trends toward authoritarianism and despotism and be able to thwart them. The role of the sensitivity function may be less obvious; however, there are three areas where its development is especially important. First, in this era of rapid technological change, there must be receptivity to new ideas. We must learn to adjust to technological advance by adopting its benefits and resisting its burdens. Sometimes we respond by changing vocations. Other adjustments—to the energy crisis, for example—may require changes in lifestyle. Second, in a heterogeneous democratic society, there must be understanding of different heritages and lifestyles. The end that best captures this kind of sensitivity is tolerance. Third, there must be recognition of values. There is no invisible hand that creates a good society out of competing interest groups. Everyone pays lip service to the public good, but we must strive to determine what really is in the public good and then seek to achieve it. As I am sure you are aware, this kind of sensitivity is important in the business context as well.

Up to this point, if a discipline is to be accepted at a liberal arts college it must meet two necessary conditions. First, it must be consistent with the purpose of a university education. Second, it must contribute to the development of the whole person—especially in developing the thinking and sensitivity skills just discussed. The natural sciences constitute one area, but the social sciences, the humanities, and the fine arts also have their contribution to make. More specifically, within the humanities, philosophy has always had a central role. Moreover, ethics courses can be especially effective because they address both the sensitivity and thinking functions.

A third necessary condition is that it be a true discipline with a complex body of knowledge. Ethics also meets the third necessary condition because it is a discipline in the traditional sense. It has a definitive subject matter with a long history and a body of authentic texts. Its subject matter is not covered by other disciplines nor is it likely to be. There is less likelihood that ethics can be reduced to any other discipline, such as sociology or psychology, than there is that biology will be reduced to physics. After all, the concepts of ethics have logical characteristics that irreducibly distinguish them from the concepts used in the social sciences. Sociologists can tell us what people think is right or wrong. Ethics studies that data and considers the additional question of whether what people think is right or wrong really is right or wrong.

The discipline of ethics uses at least two major theories, utilitarianism and deontology, and a number of concepts that make sense of the phenomena of moral experience—such as obligation, right, wrong, good, bad, rights, and virtues. Other ethical concepts are then analyzed in terms of these fundamental concepts—e.g., courage, deception. Work in the discipline progresses through conceptual analysis, the "testing" of theories in wider areas, and the revising of theories.

In addition, there are the administrative trappings of a discipline. There are refereed journals, recognized classic works, standard textbooks, and organized societies. Business ethics is a branch of ethics with all the above characteristics including the administrative ones. Business ethics is the discipline of ethics taught in the business school setting.

Ethics also meets the second necessary condition for a subject area to be accepted into the liberal arts curriculum. It substantially contributes to both the thinking and sensitivity aims of a liberal education. Ethics pursues the same fundamental questions that are asked in other philosophy courses—questions of meaning and questions of justification. So do courses in business ethics. Asking such questions promotes the thinking function of the liberal arts.

In the same way ethics fosters the sensitivity function. Business ethics is one of the few business courses that questions preferences. Are some preferences morally wrong? Students are asked to consider the moral status of the environment and of non-human animals. They analyze loyalty in terms of whether long-term suppliers or employees deserve special consideration in business dealings and what loyalty requires if the boss asks an employee to do something contrary to the employee's conscience. Using Kant's second categorical imperative, business ethics broadens the student's ability to extend respect to other human beings. Most important, business ethics tempers egoism by making students aware of how certain business decisions have a negative impact on the interests of others. This sensitivity function is central in business ethics, and to the extent that students are genuinely moved, their behavior will be affected. I am quite willing to argue that courses in business ethics should change student attitudes and behavior. In this respect, business ethics contributes to business education in the same way as the study of art and literature. It sensitizes students to what it means to be a member of the human community.

Finally, ethics meets the first necessary condition of an objective discipline because it is consistent with the purpose of a university education. Business ethics simply brings the discipline of ethics to the business school setting. Within the liberal arts context, the disciplinary status of ethics has never been administratively challenged.

## VII

The critics of business ethics might concede that if business is to be a profession in the traditional sense, then ethics should be studied, and they might concede that ethics is a discipline the way literature, art, and history are, and they might further concede that disciplines like literature, art, history, and ethics are necessary if students are to be fully developed, responsible persons. However, critics might contend that business shouldn't be a profession and that business students shouldn't be liberally educated. I wish to argue that such a response fails on two grounds.

At a rather elementary level, the successful practice of business requires that its students be liberally educated. If they are not they will not be successful businesspersons. This type of appeal has become more popular lately. Some critics have urged managers to adopt the long run point of view and to end the traditional adversary relationship with employees. Japanese management styles have been urged as a model in that regard. Peters and Waterman argued in *In Search of Excellence* that economically excellent companies paid attention to their customers and treated their employees well.

Put another way, business activity consists of a complex set of relationships among human beings—employers, employees, stockholders, customers, and suppliers. To succeed in business you need to understand the full nature of these relationships and the complete context in which they occur. A manager who forgets that her employee has a family and that weekend meetings can create internal conflicts that negatively affect the employee's productivity will be a less successful manager. As a practical matter the critic of business ethics cannot argue that business students should not be liberally educated.

Lately some business people and educators have recognized that business students lack liberal arts skills and have urged reforms in business education itself—reforms that would at least supplement if not decrease the emphasis on science. As William D. Hall said about accounting education:

> Most accountants are not broadly educated. . . . They don't read widely. At least subconsciously, they consider time spent in abstract thinking to be, at best a luxury—at worst a waste of time. . . . This pinched outlook often handicaps an accountant's performance. It restricts his vision; it hampers his reasoning.
>
> Accountants do not generally think in conceptual terms. . . . How difficult it is to make them wonder why rather than just what. It takes several weeks for the better students to cast off the shackles and develop any interest in challenging current practice; initially they tend to probe no deeper than in some authoritative pronouncement for the answer to how we should approach a particular problem.
>
> The role of both accountants and auditors is to tell it as it is; where integrity is concerned, there is no place for gamesmanship or corner cutting. . . . Integrity is not innate; it is an acquired quality that requires careful nurturing. . . . An accountant needs a good basic grounding in philosophy and ethics. . . . The accountant who has reinforced his personal code by a thoughtful study of philosophy and ethics is best fitted to deal with the questions and face the temptations that inevitably confront each of us. He knows himself, he has an abiding sense of values and self-worth; he has a perspective on life that gives him confidence in his judgments.[23]

Up to this point my argument has been prudential. Business schools should teach business ethics because such courses might succeed in providing future businesspersons with skills and attitudes that would increase their likelihood of success in business. But the issue is more complex than that. The critic of business ethics can't exclude the study of business ethics from the curriculum, because business practice itself rests on a moral base. If you overlook that base, as is currently being done, capitalism will collapse. Business ethics in this sense is necessary to the survival of capitalism itself.

A first appeal can be made to the philosophy of Immanuel Kant. Kant argues that a requirement of morality is consistency in action. Suppose that someone were to advocate lying. To be consistent, that person would have to advocate that others could lie to him. Presumably, he would not be willing to be lied to, and hence consistency in action requires that he not lie to others. Morality requires that you not make an exception of yourself, that you not engage in practices or follow rules that you could not recommend to everyone.

But suppose one were to reply to Kant as follows: "I don't care if other people try to take advantage of the rules by making exceptions of themselves. If they can get away with it, more power to them." In the business context, such a person would be willing to participate in a business environment in which deception is expected. Suppose the way in which one wants to be treated is immoral in itself—suppose one doesn't care if others try to deceive him or her. Such a businessperson could be consistent in action and still behave unjustly. How could Kant reply?

Kant has a ready answer. Some contemplated actions would be self-defeating if they were universalized. Lying is just the kind of action Kant has in mind. Kant's categorical imperative says, "I ought never to act except in such a way that I can also will that my maxim should become a universal law." To use one of Kant's examples, consider whether a businessperson should tell a lie. If the businessperson were to make the principle of her action a universal law, namely, "Lying is permissible," the act of lying would be self-defeating. For if lying were universally permitted, people would never know whether an assertion was true or false, and hence the purpose both of telling the truth and of lying would be defeated. Lying is possible only when it is not made universal.

Kant's point can apply specifically to business. There are many ways of making a promise. One of the more formal ways is by a contract. A contract is an agreement between two or more parties, usually enforceable by law, for the doing or not doing of some definite thing. The contract device is extremely useful in business. The hiring of employees, the use of credit, the ordering and supplying of goods, and the notion of warranty, to name but a few, all make use of the contract device. Indeed, the contract is such an important part of business operation that it is often overlooked. This is a serious blunder. I maintain that, if contract breaking were universalized, then business practice would be impossible. If a participant in business were to universally advocate violating contracts, such advocacy would be self-defeating, just as the universal advocacy of lying was seen to be self-defeating.

Kant's position gets surprising support from Adam Smith, although not the Adam Smith of the conventional wisdom. The conventional wisdom says that Smith advocates a brand of ethical egoism that supports utilitarian results. Because each person is the best judge of his or her interest, each person should look after his or her interest rather than worrying about the interests of others. As a result an invisible hand operates to coordinate these individual pursuits of individual interests so that the greatest good results.

Actually Smith's moral philosophy is a good deal more complicated. He believed that human beings possessed an innate sympathy
for other human beings and that this capacity for sympathy is of
greatest value for all of us.

> As society cannot subsist unless the laws of justice are tolerably observed,
> as no social intercourse can take place among men who do not generally
> abstain from injuring one another; the consideration of this necessity, it
> has been thought, was the ground upon which we approved of the en-
> forcement of the laws of justice, by the punishment of those who violated
> them. Man, it has been said, has a natural love for society, and desires
> that the union of mankind should be preserved for its own sake, and
> though he himself was to derive no benefit from it. . . . He is sensible,
> too, that his own interest is connected with the prosperity of society, and
> that the happiness, perhaps the preservation of his existence, depends
> upon its preservation.

> All members of human society stand in need of each other's assistance,
> and are likewise exposed to mutual injuries. Where the necessary assis-
> tance is reciprocally afforded from love, from gratitude, from friendship,
> and esteem, the society flourishes and is happy. All the different members
> of it are bound together by the agreeable bonds of love and affection,
> and are, as it were, drawn to one common centre of mutual good of-
> fices.[24]

Notice where we are in the argument. Adam Smith says that as a
matter of fact we are not always motivated to act in accordance with
our perceived best interest. Sometimes people act for the good of
another or for the good of society. Of course people benefit from a
society where altruism exists. However, people don't act altruistically
because they will benefit. Smith does not reduce altruism to enlightened egoism.

Neither does Kant. Obviously a world without universalized contract breaking is better for everyone. But that is not why a Kantian
wouldn't break a contract. A Kantian wouldn't break a contract out
of respect for the moral law—i.e., the categorical imperative that forbids contract breaking. Every person is better off in the Kantian ideal
kingdom of ends (moral community), but that is not why an individual is motivated to behave morally.[25]

Of course an enlightened egoist would be unconvinced. She could
deny the factual claim that people are moved by sympathetic altruism. A more profitable reply would be to advocate ethical egoism.
The ethical egoist would argue that everyone ought to pursue her
own perceived best interest and remind Kant that not everyone breaks
contracts.

The contemporary economist Fred Hirsch shows that the enlightened egoist's rejoinder to Kant is a failure. The enlightened egoist

can only succeed in achieving her perceived best interest if she behaves altruistically. The attempt by egoists to live in a world where others act altruistically and the egoists only act altruistically if it is in their interest to do so is ultimately self-defeating. Free riding is socially unstable. As more people act egoistically, a prisoner's dilemma is created, which can be avoided by having everyone acting altruistically. People get what they want only if people adopt the strategy of "as-if altruism." [26]

Hirsch says, "mutual standards of honesty and trust are public goods that are necessary inputs for much of economic output." [27] However, honesty and trust, like all forms of cooperative activity, have a significant public goods component. As Hirsch argues:

> The rational individualist, in situations of social interdependence knows that he does best when everyone *else* cooperates and he does not, for example, in ducking his contribution to a community project; he is then a "free rider," carried along on the cooperation of others. He does worst when only he cooperates, that is, when everyone else is trying to free ride. It follows that in the absence of coercive or self-enforcing arrangements to impose the cooperative lines of action on everyone except himself, or as a second best on everyone including himself, he will take the third best course, of noncooperation; this being individually rational (because it is superior to the fourth best outcome when only he cooperates), even though socially irrational. [28]

The recognition that a society where each person really tries to maximize his or her individual self-interest is inherently unstable and collectively irrational is occurring in a number of diverse disciplines—political science, decision theory, anthropology, sociology, psychology, and philosophy.

One illuminating example is provided by the anthropologist Mary Douglas. Her interest is in group solidarity, or how it is that people manage to sacrifice their own interests for the public good. Douglas contends that market behavior cannot be based on completely self-regarding motives.

> There is the normative commitment to the market system itself, the needful fiduciary element sustaining prices and credit. Some equivalent analysis of thought style is needed to explain why forms of cheating do not destroy the market processes. Again, in a complex hierarchy, a combination of coercion, multiple cross-ties, conventions, and self-interest explain a lot, but not everything about the commitment of individuals to the larger group. [29]

Her argument, oversimplified here, is that the individual doesn't calculate as general equilibrium theory requires. An individual identifies with other individuals in an institutional setting. We take on the thoughts of others and they take on our thoughts. An institutional culture develops. An individual in a business situation does not maximize his individual self-interest but rather makes the decision from both individual and institutional interests.[30]

### VIII

We can bring this complicated discussion to a conclusion. I have argued that the most plausible attempt to make business courses scientific is to firmly ground them in economics. Of all the business courses, economics is the one that has the most plausible claim to be constituted a science. However, it seems that economics is not a science the way the natural sciences are.

Moreover, economics has as one of its fundamental theories the postulate of egoism. Despite its methodological convenience, I believe it must be given up. The problem of reconciling egoism with the directive to maximize shareholder wealth has already been noted.

Certainly one of the greatest contributions that business ethics could make to the education of business persons is to show how egoism in theory and in practice is destructive of business itself. Think of the revolutionary changes that would occur in every course in the business curriculum if the operating assumption was that each participant in business transactions is motivated by altruistic concerns as well as self-interested ones, the view that Adam Smith actually held. One of the central tasks of business ethics would be to determine when businesspersons should behave self-interestedly, when they should behave altruistically, and how business practice might maximize the coincidence of behavior that is both self-interested and altruistic. Sometimes the invisible hand coordinates individualistic egoistic behavior to the public good. But sometimes strong doses of altruism are needed. Business ethics courses should teach that the concept of cooperation is as important as the concept of competition. As any football coach knows, individual team members must cooperate with one another if they are to compete successfully.

Some economists are disciplinary imperialists. They believe that every policy issue is at heart an economic issue. Should one vote? Some economists answer that question by calculating the cost of voting against the likelihood that your vote will make a difference. From that perspective nearly always it is economically irrational for an individual to vote. Therefore, from that perspective, democracy requires that each individual usually behave irrationally for it to survive. But perhaps the issue of voting is just one where economic analysis doesn't belong. Voting is rational in a non-economic sense of rational.

One of the most fashionable trends in law is to analyze legal decisions in terms of economic criteria. But should a legal system historically rooted in a tradition of individual rights be looked at from the economist's perspective?

Perhaps a task of business ethics is to bring a halt to this economic imperialism. Perhaps it is time to argue that economics has an ethical dimension and hence so does nearly every business discipline. Even if the critic of business ethics doesn't care if business is a profession or that business people are liberally educated, the critic ignores the ethical foundations of business at her peril. As a discipline, business ethics is interdisciplinary and it could well be enriched by the contributions of all the social sciences. But business ethics is a discipline with a crucial contribution to make in the education of businesspersons. That academic ethicists desire to teach and do research in schools of business should be welcomed rather than scorned.

## NOTES

I have benefited greatly from comments provided by my University of Delaware colleagues in Philosophy and the College of Business and Economics, and by responses from participants at the Ruffin Lectures, University of Virginia, April 7–9, 1988.

1. Abraham Flexner, "Is Social Work a Profession?" as quoted in Walter P. Metzger, "What Is A Profession?" in *College and University* 52 (1976): 42–55.

2. Metzger, *College and University*, p. 51.

3. See R. A. Gordon and J. E. Howell, *Higher Education for Business* (New York: Columbia University Press, 1959); and F. C. Pierson et al., *The Education of American Businessmen* (New York: McGraw-Hill, 1959).

4. Thomas M. Mulligan, "The Two Cultures in Business Education," *Academy of Management Review* 12, no. 4 (October 1987): 593.

5. This point was called to my attention by William C. Frederick, School of Business, University of Pittsburgh.

6. Metzger, *College and University*, p. 51.

7. Clare Ansberry, "For These M.B.A.'s, Class Became Exercise in Corporate Espionage," *Wall Street Journal*, March 22, 1988, p. 27.

8. John W. Rosenblum, "From the Start, the Rules Weren't Clear," *New York Times*, November 22, 1987.

9. Thomas M. Mulligan, "Two Cultures," pp. 595–96.

10. Richard S. Rudner, *Philosophy of Social Science* (Englewood Cliffs, NJ: Prentice Hall, 1966), p. 10.

11. Vernon Kam, *Accounting Theory* (New York: John Wiley & Sons, 1986), p. 34.

12. Ibid., p. 37.

13. Ahmed Belkaoui, *Accounting Theory* (New York: Harcourt Brace Jovanovich, 1981), pp. 44–54.

14. William D. Hall, *Accounting and Auditing: Thoughts on Forty Years in Practice and Education* (Chicago: Arthur Andersen & Co., 1987), pp. 43–44.

15. Annetta Miller and Dody Tsiantar, "A Test for Market Research," *Newsweek*, December 28, 1987, pp. 32–33.

16. Jeffrey Pfeffer, *Organizations and Organizational Theory* (Marshfield, MA: Pitman Publishing, 1982).

17. See, for example, George Akerlof, "A Theory of Social Custom, of Which Unemployment May Be One Consequence," *Quarterly Journal of Economics* 94 (June 1980): 749–75; Arthur Okun, "The Invisible Handshake and the Inflationary Process," in *Economics for Policy-making: Selected Essays of Arthur M. Okun* (Cambridge: MIT Press, 1983), pp. 119–30; Roy Radner, "Can Bounded Rationality Resolve the Prisoner's Dilemma?" in W. Hildenbrand and A. Mascolell, ed. *Contributions to Mathematical Economics in Honor of G. Debreu* (Amsterdam: North-Holland, 1986), pp. 387–99; Robert Solow, "On Theories of Unemployment," *American Economic Review* 70 (1980): 1–11; and Lester Thurow, *Generating Inequality* (New York: Basic Books, 1975).

18. See, for example, Allan Gibbard and Hal R. Varian, "Economic Models," *The Journal of Philosophy* (1978): 664–77; Daniel M. Hausman, *Capital, Profits and Prices* (New York: Columbia University Press, 1981); Alan Nelson, "New Individualistic Foundations for Economics," *Nous* 20 (1986): 469–90; Alexander Rosenberg, "The Explanatory Role of Existence Proofs," 97 *Ethics* (October 1986): 177–86; Alexander Rosenberg, "The Puzzle of Economic Modeling," *The Journal of Philosophy* (1978): 679–83.

19. Daniel M. Hausman, *Capital, Profits, and Prices* (New York: Columbia University Press, 1981), pp. 118–19.

20. See for example Sidney Hook, *Education For Modern Man* (New York: Humanities Press, 1973).

21. Ibid., p. 55.

22. Steven M. Cahn, *The Eclipse of Excellence* (Washington, DC: Public Affairs Press, 1973), p. 3.

23. William D. Hall, *Accounting*, pp. 16–19. The recent Treadway Report on Fraudulent Financial Reporting (1987) has made a similar if somewhat muted recommendation.

24. Adam Smith, *The Theory of Moral Sentiments* (New York: Augustus M. Kelley Publishers, 1966), pp. 124, 127.

25. This discussion ignores some of the objections made against Kantianism. Obviously there are legitimate exceptions to the rule against breaking a contract—although I think these exceptions to be few in number. The contemporary Kantian argues that an exception is legitimate if it passes the Kantian test, i.e., can the exception be universalized without being self-defeating.

26. Fred Hirsch, *Social Limits to Growth* (Cambridge: Harvard University Press, 1976).

27. Ibid., p. 141.

28. Ibid., p. 135.

29. Mary Douglas, *How Institutions Think* (New York: Syracuse University Press, 1986), p. 42.

30. A view in the spirit of both Hirsch and Douglas can be found in Amartya K. Sen, "Rational Fools: A Critique of the Behavioral Foundations of Economic Theory," *Philosophy and Public Affairs* 6 (Summer 1977): 317–44.

# 2

# Will Success Spoil
# Business Ethics?

## Richard T. DeGeorge

As an academic field, business ethics came to the fore from a marriage between philosophical ethics and management education. Like the marriage of Romeo and Juliet, neither of the parent disciplines was pleased with the union. But unlike Romeo and Juliet, the union has thrived and borne fruit, and the offspring are tolerated—if not adored—by both sets of grandparents. During the past 15 years business ethics has become a well-entrenched academic field.[1] More than twenty-five textbooks serve the over 500 business ethics courses taught in business schools around the country. There are two professional journals dedicated to the topic, and other journals publish articles on business ethics with some regularity. The Society for Business Ethics is thriving. Thus business ethics is an established academic field, whether the parent disciplines like it or not.

Despite the success of business ethics courses, however, there is still a good deal of ambiguity concerning just what business ethics is. Ethics has been appropriate in business since the beginning of business as a human activity. Some people equate business ethics with ethics in business and see its aim as making people in business behave more ethically than they would otherwise. Many who envision business ethics in this way see nothing unique or special about it. We are all supposed to behave ethically in all aspects of our lives and business is no exception. Moreover, they assume that we all know what is right and wrong, and the only difficulty is acting as we know we should. Hence, many people who construe business ethics in this way are thus rightly puzzled by what those who claim to be engaged in the *field* of business ethics are doing. The latter seem to be charlatans who have nothing to sell or contribute but pretend they do; or they are sophists who will give arguments in defense of anything business wants to do—depending on who pays them or which action will yield other rewards—publication, fame, royalties, or the like; or contrariwise they are anti-capitalist critics who attack anything business does.

I shall briefly defend two claims. The first is that there is an academic field of business ethics, which is broader than ethics in business, even though the latter is part of it. The second is that what is gaining such success and popular attention is not business ethics in the academic sense, but ethics in business; and this success threatens to some extent, if not the field of business ethics, then its possible salutary social effect.

## I

Business ethics as an academic field includes discussions of and aims at promoting ethics in business. But it is not restricted to these. As an academic enterprise business ethics is a systematic study of business from an ethical point of view. As such it is concerned not only with *individual* behavior in business. Because those in business ethics as an academic field approach business on all its levels, they appropriately carry out their ethical analyses on the level of economic systems, on the level of corporations, and on the level of individual action. They see these three levels as interrelated, and the interrelations as well as the components on each level are subject to ethical investigation. Thus on the systematic level those in academic business ethics seek to ethically evaluate economic systems both in their theoretical formulation and in their actual operation. Ethical evaluation *of* the system is distinguishable from ethics *in* the system. Within the system, e.g., of American free enterprise, they then seek to ethically evaluate corporations as such, their ideal and actual structures, their effect on the society in which they operate, and their impact on people affected by their operations. A distinction between the ethical evaluation *of* the corporation and ethical practices *in* the corporation parallels the earlier distinction. The third level of analysis considered the activities and practices of individuals within the corporation and in non-corporate business generally. The task at each level is threefold: first, descriptive; second, evaluative or critical; and third, normative or prescriptive, with justification given for both evaluations and prescriptions. As a systematic study academic business ethics aims to be objective and neither pro-business nor anti-business. As systematic, it also seeks to operate with some justifiable methodology, the justification for which it seeks to provide.

The analysis involved in this systematic study includes uncovering presupposition at each level, and clarifying and evaluating terms and practices. Hence, such key notions as profit, competition, just wage, efficiency, and so on, all become candidates for discussion and evaluation. Those engaged in business ethics as an academic subject do not claim to know all the answers, and do not claim to know in every case which actions or practices are ethically justifiable and which are not. The task is to uncover and develop the arguments that support one's claims that certain practices or institutions are ethical, or that a preferable (from an ethical point of view) alternative is available. New business practices are constantly evolving, the ethical nature of which is not always or immediately clear. Neither corporations, nor managers, nor academics in business ethics have any privileged position from which to judge these practices. The practices should be submitted to ethical scrutiny, and if their ethical status is unclear, the arguments for and against their being ethical should be developed until sufficient clarity is achieved that an ethical consensus emerges. This is the aim of ethical debate about such practices as greenmail or golden parachutes. Such objective debate, if fruitful, may in turn provide the basis for social action, legislation, or corporate policy.

Those with a philosophical interest in business ethics have also turned their attention to the interrelation of business ethics and general ethics. They have been concerned, for instance, to clarify the status of corporations from an ethical point of view. There is a developing literature on the question of whether or not corporations are moral agents, and whether, if they are, they have moral rights and responsibilities. Involved in this discussion is the question of whether concepts such as responsibility, conscience, shame, and blame can appropriately be attributed to corporations and whether the terms mean the same thing when applied to corporations as when applied to individuals.

If business ethics is conceived in this broad systematic way, then what is taught in a business ethics course corresponds to these topics. Clearly such a course does not consist simply of teaching students what is right or wrong in business, or of sensitizing them to issues they will have to face, even though it may also do these things. As an academic subject it aims not to preach what is right in business but to argue what is right in business. Its emphasis is on helping students learn how to deal with ethical issues in business, rather than with dogmatically telling them what they must or should believe about the issues. In this way a course in business ethics is a liberal arts course and not a technical course. As such, the courses are sometimes attacked as fuzzy, even though the level and stringency of argument and analysis that they can demand are as rigorous as that demanded by any other subject.

Those who assume that business ethics is the same as teaching ethics in business sometimes imagine a business ethics course to be one in which a teacher preaches his moral predilections or prejudices to a captive student audience that is required to memorize and regurgitate them. Courses of the latter type have no place in either a business school or a liberal arts college. Nonetheless, the onus of demonstrating the academic respectability of courses in business ethics falls on those who teach them. The reception has been mixed on both the part of departments of philosophy, which sometimes tend to look down on them as having too little philosophical content, and on the part of schools of business, which sometimes tend to look down on them as lacking rigor or business content.

Although courses in business ethics have not been universally well received in business schools, especially in MBA programs, they have not been completely rejected—as the large number of courses taught in business ethics shows. But the legitimacy of business ethics as an academic field does not depend on its being accepted by business schools, any more than it depends on being effective in changing the climate of business in the United States. As an academic field it stands or falls on the quality of the research done in it, on the body of knowledge developed, and on its success as an academic, liberal arts subject.


## II

Despite its initial success, the field of business ethics is in jeopardy and its future is somewhat in doubt. It is in jeopardy not because it has not been accepted but precisely because of its popular success.

Business ethics, as I have described it, is strictly speaking a philosophical field, a division of applied philosophy, in this instance of applied ethics. As I have indicated, the field as so envisioned has as part of its task a critique or evaluation from an ethical point of view of business, of its presuppositions, of its practices, and of its aims. This critical aspect is essential to it as a liberal arts subject and as a philosophical area of inquiry. This view of business ethics is admittedly a philosopher's view, and the one that has dominated over the past 15 years as business ethics has developed as an academic study. It is precisely this view that is being slowly overwhelmed and submerged the more successful business ethics becomes.

The threat to business ethics as thus conceived is fourfold: (1) the threat from diluted competence; (2) the threat from unfulfillable expectations; (3) the threat from co-optation; and (4) the threat from the replacement of critical by descriptive ethics.

1. Although those who toiled early in the vineyard of business ethics might be pleased at the success of what they in some sense

started, there is also cause for dismay. Since there was scarcely a course in business ethics 15 years ago, those who taught the first course were usually self-trained. Introducing a new course meant they had to read a great deal outside their usual areas of competence in order to develop the new course material that was by its very nature interdisciplinary. They also had to fight an uphill battle to prove that they knew enough to teach the course. To their business colleagues they had to show that the business content was adequate and informed; to their philosophy colleagues they had to prove that the ethical content was sufficiently rigorous.

The pioneers in the field wrote and compiled the first texts in the area. Many of those who followed quickly on their heels introduced themselves into the area through the newly appearing texts. In many cases the texts rather than the specific competence of the teacher were used to justify the content of the course. Demand swelled and courses proliferated more quickly than those competent could teach them and more quickly than people who had an interest in teaching themselves could do so. The inevitable result of the great initial success of business ethics courses was an almost immediate dilution of the quality of instruction.

Moreover, although business ethics has become institutionalized in the sense that it is widely taught, there are few programs that have been developed to train people in the field in such a way that they know both theoretical ethics and the basics of business. Almost all those in the field are primarily teachers of philosophy or theology, who may or may not have learned something about business, or teachers of business, who may or may not have learned something about ethical theory. Those who have a good grasp or firm foundation in both areas are relatively few. Nor is there any leading program that has set the standard to which other universities might aspire.

One result is that there are no criteria that anyone must fulfill to be recognized as a practitioner in the field. Courses are being taught by those who agree to do so—because of interest, because they are told to do so by their departments or schools, because that is where there is student demand, or for any number of other reasons. The same is true in the area of publication. Although the respectable journals are refereed, referees do not always know what criteria to apply, and the result is the publication of articles of very mixed quality. There are also journals of business ethics that make no claim to being scholarly and publish whatever the editor wishes. The result is some confusion between the scholarly and the popular, the objective and the vested interest, the preachy and the argued.

One argument for the continued development of business ethics as a field is that only in this way can one hope to promote programs of study that will serve the needs of those academics who wish to work in the area. This is also one of the best ways to establish criteria and to distinguish the scholarly from the popular, the argued from the preachy, the objective from the vested interest. There is nothing wrong, and much right, with popular journals on ethics in business. But business ethics as a scholarly field includes more than ethics in business and the two should not be taken to be synonymous. A danger of the two becoming confused is that the field may be judged by inappropriate criteria and some of its tasks undermined. Teachers with insufficient training in business and ethics, inadequate graduate programs to train those interested in the field, and the lack of accepted criteria for judging research all pose threats to business ethics as an academic field.

2. One of the reasons for claiming success for business ethics is that it has become part of the accepted vocabulary in the academic world, the business world, and the popular press. Business ethics is no longer easily or playfully dismissed as a contradiction in terms. Government has mandated that business ethics be taught in some firms that have been found guilty of fraud and price-gouging on government contracts. As the Levine-Boesky scandals emerged, letters to the editors and editorials in the *Wall Street Journal,* the *New York Times,* and many local newspapers called for courses in business ethics in the schools of business. The AACSB added as one of its accrediting requirements some work in business ethics and values. John Shad gave the major portion of $20 million to the Harvard Business School for business ethics—a magnificent gift that *could* make Harvard a true leader in the field of business ethics.

While a general raising of popular and business consciousness about ethical issues in business has occurred, this success carries with it a twofold danger for business ethics. The first is the raising of expectations that cannot be met. The second is the reinforcing of the notion that ethics in business is equivalent to adopting conventional morality in business practices.

The popular call for more courses or instruction in business ethics increased as a result of the 1987–88 insider trading scandals. This call expressed two implicit and false beliefs. The first was that the immorality that surfaced on the business scene was in some way linked to business schools, and may even have been fostered by the business schools. Although many—if not most—business schools may have been, and may still be, at fault for not teaching business ethics, one can hardly place the blame for the insider trading scandals on the business schools. The people involved were not fresh out of business school, and some of the principals never even went to business school. Implicitly placing the blame on the business schools served a dual role. First, it identified a scapegoat and a rationale for the immoral conduct of those involved. Second, it implicitly exonerated the business community itself from any blame. Hence it tended to preclude too close a look at the climate of Wall Street and of the large firms operating there, and it tended to obviate the necessity of asking whether the activity of Boesky, Levine, and company was a reflection of the practices and pressures, opportunities and outlook, status and structures of the financial community itself.

The other implicit false belief was that a course in business ethics, or the integration of business ethics into the business school curriculum, could have prevented Levine and Boesky and their ilk from doing what they did. Both Levine and Boesky knew that their actions were illegal—whether or not they even considered them from an ethical point of view. The proof is the lengths to which they went to cover up their activities. To believe that a course in business ethics would have changed them sufficiently so that they would not have succumbed to temptation is to expect more from a course or program in business ethics than any course or program is capable of delivering.

The claim here is not that business ethics courses are of no use in helping those who wish to act ethically in business do so. Instruction in business ethics can certainly sharpen one's awareness of and sensitivity to ethical issues. It can provide guidance in how to resolve ethical problems. And it can give students some ideals to live up to and hence help reinforce their personal ethical values and motivate them to behave ethically in business as well as in other areas of their lives.

But instruction in business ethics cannot make ethical people out of unethical ones, and it should not be seen as a panacea for the unethical behavior that keeps emerging on the business scene. If business ethics instruction is equated with producing ethical business people, then it can be appropriately judged by this criterion. If after five or 10 or 15 years of teaching business ethics we do not find the ethical climate in business any better than before, we can correctly say that business ethics has failed in its task. If business ethics is the cure for unethical business practices, then the cure is correctly judged by whether the illness for which it is prescribed is cured or arrested. Given this test of success, business ethics is doomed to failure. For it is not a panacea, and those who view it as such fail to understand just what business ethics as an academic area is and what its limitations are.

If business ethics is judged by this implicit criterion, then its failure to measure up to that criterion will undermine the aspects of business ethics as an academic field that do not relate directly to inculcating ethical values in students or to motivating them to act ethically in business.

The second way in which the call for more instruction in business ethics may endanger the field comes from another assumption made by those who issue the call. Editorial and letter writers often express the view that we all know what is right and wrong, ethical and unethical in business as well as in the ordinary realms of everyday life, and that the only problem is how to induce students in business schools to act on this knowledge when they enter the business world. The implicit belief is that conventional morality—what we all know to be right and wrong—is correct and is what is to be taught and reinforced in the business schools. The difficulty with this view is that it reinforces the status quo with all its possible defects—ethical as well as other. Business ethics as an academic subject should not simply be the inculcation of conventional morality or the reinforcement of socially accepted norms. Business ethics can and at its best should have a critical component. It should help the student ask whether accepted business practices are ethically justifiable and defensible. If so, how are they defended and justified; if not, how are they shown to be unjustifiable? Ethical thinking should not be reduced to learning by rote prescriptions of what is right and wrong. Nor should business ethics at its best be strictly and only descriptive of what society says is ethical or not. There can be no externally imposed or prescribed limits to ethical inquiry, and no strictly descriptive approach will produce ethically perceptive practitioners.

Instruction in business ethics as an academic subject aims to produce critical ethical thinkers. But this is not what many who call for business ethics courses want. They do not want the financial industry, for instance, subject to ethical scrutiny and possibly to a great many new restrictions on its activities. Critics like Felix Rohatyn want business schools to produce investment bankers who observe the old rules of the game as established by seasoned practitioners.[2] The danger to business ethics as an academic field is that if business ethics instruction is effective in calling into question established business practices, its success will undermine its growing acceptance from and its possible salutary effect on the establishment. But if business ethics is tailored to the wishes of established business, then it will become the inculcation of established norms, a handmaid of business's vested interests, and it will cease to have the objectivity and the critical function that justifies it as an academic field.

Moreover, the claim that we all know what is right and wrong in business undermines the legitimate task of attempting to determine whether certain practices are right or wrong. The way to determine, e.g., whether insider trading—which we know to be illegal in the United States but not in New Zealand—is unethical is by discussing the ethical nature of insider trading. The way to determine whether it is ethically justifiable for multinational corporations to pay the going wage in less developed countries, even if this is barely enough for subsistence, is by clarifying the nature of exploitation and of a just wage. The way to determine whether equal pay for comparable work is ethically required is by investigating what is involved and the basis for the claim that it is unethical to do otherwise. On these and a host of other issues it is not true that we all know what is right and wrong.

Those in business ethics can contribute to our developing greater ethical insight through public, published, informed debates on these issues. They can thus help provide a basis for arriving at an ethical consensus. Such debate is different from students' discussion of these issues in classes. For although each student may come to a personal conclusion, not all conclusions are equally good or ethically defensible. The same is true of companies. These are not issues that each company is free to decide for itself, as if one may choose one side or the other and both will be ethically justifiable. Whether equal pay is ethically demanded for comparable worth is not simply a matter of opinion; just as it is not simply a matter of opinion whether discrimination on the basis of sex or race is ethical. American society has arrived at a consensus on the latter. By debating ethically controversial business practices, those in business ethics hope to shed light on them. The assumption that we all know what is right and wrong implies that there is nothing for those in business ethics to do in this area, that each company is to decide for itself, and that any decision companies arrive at is ethically appropriate, even if different companies arrive at mutually contradictory decisions. The belief that we all know what is right and wrong thus undermines one of the tasks of business ethics. By defending the status quo the belief implies that corporate ethical decisions are to be made only by the corporations involved, and it tends to inhibit rather than promote much needed discussion and clarification of new, complex, and controversial business practices. The defense of the status quo is once again a defense of descriptive ethics and a rejection of the legitimacy of critical ethical thinking about business by those in business ethics.

3. In the spring of 1988, Arthur Andersen and Company, in Chicago, announced a five-year, $5 million program to promote the teaching of business ethics. Part of its announcement emphasized the firm's wish to train teachers to integrate business ethics into their courses, rather than to teach business ethics as a separate course. The $5 million program promotes developing courses and training teams of business teachers in accounting, economics, finance, management, and marketing from business schools across the country. Who can complain about such an endeavor? Who can fault any company for providing $5 million for such an effort?

Yet despite the nobility of the undertaking and the fact that it once again shows the success of business ethics, the Andersen program poses three dangers to business ethics, even while obviously supporting it. The first is simply another instance of the dangers already cited. Can a two-day seminar sufficiently train business professors to teach business ethics? Is the applying of cases enough to enhance the teaching of business ethics? Will the program promote or alleviate the threat of diluted competence, and will it raise expectations that cannot be fulfilled?

The second danger is the danger of co-optation. In the present instance this may not in fact be a danger. But when business ethics was a course or a program of instruction developed and taught in the universities, there was some hope that it would be objective and that the academic community would supply the pressures necessary to keep it so. When the material to be used and the training of instructors in business ethics is not only directly funded but is carried on by a corporation, even with the best of intentions, the appearance of objectivity must be compromised. A normal and immediate reaction is that no company would pay $5 million to have itself, for instance, accused of unethical practices or to have the system of free enterprise attacked as unethical and in need of radical change. Because this outcome is at least possible if business ethics is an unbiased inquiry, outsiders will be skeptical about whether a company-run program really teaches critical ethics or whether it is structured to present conventional morality as the norm to be inculcated into students and employees.

The third danger comes from the fact that the company has leaped into two academic debates with a $5 million investment on one side of the debates. One debate is whether business ethics should be taught as a separate course or should be integrated into all or many of the courses in the business curriculum. A third possibility, of course, is that there be a separate course in business ethics and that ethics also be integrated into all or many of the courses. Duane R. Kullberg, Arthur Andersen and Company's chairman and CEO, says, "Too often courses are put in the philosophy or religion schools, places where it is isolated as though it were a separate consideration." His point that ethics should not be seen as separate from business is well taken; but his probably unintentional attack on separate course in business ethics, especially if taught in places other than a business school, is symptomatic of the danger. Mr. Kullberg implies that courses in business ethics are not the way to go and the firm is putting up $5 million to develop cases because the schools have done too little.[3]

Arthur Andersen and Company thus enters the other debate as well, namely, whether ethics should be taught via the case method or whether business ethics should be taught as a discursive subject in which students learn ethical theory as well as applications. Once again, it is possible to teach ethical theory and to use the case method.

Yet $5 million has been placed on the side of the case method. Why say this is a danger?

The reason stems from the conception of business ethics as an academic field and its proper scope as such. Because in its critical aspect business ethics studies business on three levels, the economic system, the corporation, and the individual, it must be free to ask: Is capitalism ethically justifiable? If so, how? If not, why not? Is socialism ethically justifiable? If so, how? If not, why not? Is one preferable to the other? Is there some preferable third alternative? Is any given instance of a social-economic system, e.g., that of the United States, ethically justifiable? Are there ingredients that are unethical, even if it is on the whole ethically justifiable? Is there a system of international capitalism? Is the international order ethically justifiable or is there an ethical need for a new economic order? Should there be international organizations that enforce ethical practices and codes, and what should these practices and codes be?

These are all questions that are appropriately addressed and debated by people in business ethics. They are large questions, and the answers are not clear, even though many people have already made up their minds about the answers. Do corporations want these questions raised and discussed? Some at least do not. And if corporations take the lead in teaching teachers what to teach and in developing course material, there is at least the danger that these issues will not be raised.

On the second level, the level of the corporation, business ethics must be free to ask: Are corporations ethically justifiable? If so, how? If not, why not? Are there structures within the corporation that from an ethical point of view should be changed? Is some particular corporate structure more conducive to ethical behavior than others? What are the ethical arguments for and against plant closings without advance notification? For and against AIDS, drug, and other testing, whether mandatory or not? What rights do workers have from an ethical point of view that have not yet been written into law? What is the ethical status of greenmail, leveraged corporate buyout tactics, golden parachutes, and other similar practices? These are issues to be debated and discussed. They are issues on which there is no clear consensus. Teaching students to work with these issues helps them learn how to deal with gray areas of business ethics and how to think through problems. If in some instance it turns out that what is ethical leads to a company's demise, so be it. The number of companies that are willing to teach this to their employees is an open question. But there is a well-founded fear that not many companies are willing to spend millions to teach their employees to raise questions and follow their consciences even if it means the demise of the company.

The third level is the level of the individual. This is what most companies are interested in. At this level many companies want their employees to be ethical—where this means not pilfering company goods, obeying company rules, and bringing ethical concerns to the legal department to be decided there. Some companies admittedly go beyond that and, believing the company is ethical, want their employees to act ethically, where this means not only the above, but raising ethical concerns about company practices and structures and ethically questioning corporate actions and the actions of top management. The latter approach is a commendable one, and one that is consistent with critical ethics and with ethics as a field. The only criticism that can be placed here is that the emphasis on this level often precludes any attention to the ethical issues on the other two levels.

The exclusive emphasis on the case method approach poses a danger to business ethics as a field. Cases typically involve the discussion of action on the individual level. Hence the question arises, if the only method of instruction is the case method, and if ethical issues are raised in standard business courses together with other material, where will the other two levels of business ethics be discussed? Where will issues be discussed that are not resolved and that cannot be resolved by simply dealing with cases? The advantage of a separate course is that the first two levels of business ethics, the economic system and the corporation, can be dealt with systematically and objectively, even though they are not brought out by specific cases and are not really appropriate to any of the standard sub-areas of the business curriculum. It is because they are not appropriately parts of management or accounting or finance or marketing, but are presupposed by all of them, that they may be ignored if not raised in a separate business ethics course. It is because they are not easily raised by cases that there is justification for discursive teaching as well as case discussion. It is because unresolved issues and practices are best resolved by marshalling the arguments for and against them in print that discursive writing in the field is necessary, and that cases are insufficient.

These constitute some of the arguments for a separate course of business ethics, in addition to integrating ethics throughout the curriculum, and for the use of something other than the case method. Five million dollars for a program that openly opposes independent ethics courses puts a great deal of weight and influence on one side of an academic debate. That this constitutes a danger is clear, even if the danger can be averted. It is one more instance, however, in which the apparent success of business ethics may threaten its continued success as a critical, objective, academic field.

4. Business ethics has thus come to mean two related but very

different enterprises. One is the academic, objective, critical field of
business ethics. The second, which I have referred to as ethics in
business, is primarily the inculcation of conventional morality in
managers and workers. Businesses, on the whole, are not interested
in the academic field of business ethics. Many of them *are* interested,
however, in inculcating conventional morality in their employees. A
growing number of *Fortune* "500" firms have in-house programs in
business ethics. A 1988 Business Roundtable study of business ethics
in a number of prominent firms considers the codes of these firms,
their credos, their corporate culture.[4] In general the companies are
presented as ethical firms, and their ethical beliefs and norms are
spelled out in their self-defined and self-established codes. What is
worthy of note is that the Business Roundtable Report is completely
descriptive. It raises no question about the ethics of any firm and
implicitly presents the companies examined as ethical models. The
models it gives us are models of the status quo, of firms that attempt
to embody and inculcate in their employees conventional morality.

There is nothing wrong with conventional morality. But conventional morality is not the same as critical morality, and the critical
investigation of the American system of free enterprise, the critical
examination of one's own company, and the critical yet objective
evaluation of other companies is not the same as what the Business
Roundtable understands as business ethics. The Business Roundtable's understanding of business ethics, however, is very close to if
not identical with what most of those in business want taught in business ethics courses.

Accordingly, this approach to business ethics is that taken by the
growing number of ethics consultants, some of whom are professors
of business or have been trained in business schools, some of whom
are lawyers, and some of whom have no apparent training in ethics
or business. In ever increasing number and force would-be consultants have seen the market for business ethics and have responded
by developing their own approach, which in many ways is very unlike the philosophers' approach. Since the consultants are primarily
trained—if trained at all—in what they conceive of as empirical research, business ethics consulting is becoming more and more restricted to descriptive rather than critical ethics. The aim is frequently to determine what the practices and values of a particular
company are, often with the implication that the accepted norms are
the proper ethical norms.

Based on this approach, a growing number of ethical consultants
are entering companies to help them inculcate in their employees
those aspects of morality desired by top management and included
in the company's credo. The consultants do not seem to question the
credos. That is not their job. They may help formulate a credo; but

the developing practice is to find what the implicitly held values of various members of the firm are. In reply to the question of who is the client of such consultants, the answer is clearly the firm, and one knows one does not bite the hand that feeds one.

A truly critical approach to any business might raise issues, question structures, pose questions that the business would rather ignore, leave unexamined from an ethical point of view, or not answer. The point is not that a company cannot develop critical ethical material, but that the fact that the company develops it makes the material suspect because of the company's self-interest. The academic community is supposed to be objective, in the sense of having no particular axe to grind either pro- or anti-business.

Can business ethics consultants maintain their objectivity when being handsomely paid for their advice? The answer is surely yes. Yet the temptation to defend or rationalize what a company wishes to do or is doing, to say what the company wants to hear, or what it can live with, to define business ethics as ethics in business is surely a temptation that should be acknowledged. The fact that business ethics is becoming popular among companies means also that many people who have no scholarly interest in the field and no interest in or competence in critical ethics are consulting on ethics issues. The results are fairly predictable. Companies will tend to hire consultants who they believe are friendly toward business and the way it operates rather than those who may be critical, and companies will attempt to construe ethics as something that should be taught to their employees, rather than something that might also be used to evaluate corporate policies and structures. The results are not necessarily bad. But they do mean that business ethics in this way can be and already is being co-opted by business. The more this is so, the more business ethics will be seen by employees and eventually by the general public as a tool used by management to control its employees, prevent internal losses, and increase its profits. Such a use of ethics will in turn reinforce the skepticism of some who continue to believe that ethics and business do not really mix, and that in a conflict the bottom line will win out over the ethically right action.

The descriptive approach to business ethics, moreover, is what is gaining increased attention not only in business but in business schools. To the extent this is so, a real danger to business ethics is not that it is not respected for its humanistic qualities but that it is being taken over, some of its practitioners are being co-opted, and the enterprise to some extent is being changed (some would say corrupted) from within. A danger exists that business schools may teach business ethics not as a critical subject but as one that provides a service sought by businesses. Ironically, if that happens, it may undermine the field as an objective area of study. The real danger is thus not that busi-

ness ethics will not be accepted and will be forced to remain a suspect gadfly, but that it may become an accepted child, molded to the
image of those who wish to make use of it.

In these and similar ways, the growing apparent success of business ethics may spell its failure as an academic discipline. Scholars
who see the subject matter as critical may still pursue their research.
But the impact that they had in the beginning of the field may well
be overwhelmed by the ethics in business and conventional ethics
approach. And if that approach becomes discredited, as I have suggested it might, business ethics as an academic field might be discredited and so make it impossible for academic business ethics to
continue to influence business structures and activities.

As a critical, objective, academic field, business ethics has an un-
popular edge. It remains a possible, if not an actual, threat to the
status quo, the establishment, and business as usual. If business ethics is to remain objective, it must retain that edge. If it is to be aca-
demically respectable, it must also retain that edge. The role of ethical gadfly should endure. That aspect of business ethics may not be
sought by corporations, but it should be nurtured at least at the universities, and encouraged, not stifled, at the better schools of business.

## NOTES

1. See Richard T. DeGeorge, "The Status of Business Ethics: Past and
Future," *Journal of Business Ethics* 6 (1987): 201–11.

2. Felix Rohatyn, "The Blight of Wall Street," *New York Review of Books,*
March 12, 1987, p. 21.

3. Sallie Gaines, "Arthur Andersen Making Case for Ethics in Business
Classroom," *Chicago Tribune,* March 11, 1988.

4. The Business Roundtable, "A Report on Policy and Practice in Company Conduct," *Corporate Ethics: A Prime Business Asset,* February 1988. See
also The Conference Board Research Report No. 900, *Corporate Ethics,* 1987.

# 3

# Commentary on Business Ethics as a Discipline: The Search for Legitimacy

## William C. Frederick

Norman Bowie's central message is important and should be given an attentive reception by all business schools. He argues, not only that business ethics is a legitimate academic discipline worthy of the same pedagogical status that is accorded to standard business topics of instruction, but that its inclusion in the business school curriculum is the sine qua non of professional legitimacy itself.

Bowie's position will not be welcomed in all quarters of the business school faculty, for reasons cited in his lecture. Beyond those factors that he describes are others that are somewhat less sophisticated but often more typical of the kinds of obstacles one encounters in faculty dialogues about the place of ethics analysis in the business curriculum.

Some business faculty members who are quite ready to acknowledge the importance of ethics inquiry simply believe that this part of a student's educational experience either has been already "taken care of" in the liberal arts college or, if not, it should have been. The central task of the business school, they believe, is to build beyond that earlier and broader educational experience by teaching students the specialized bodies of information that comprise so much of the business landscape. In this view, it is simply not the responsibility of the professional business school to teach ethics.

A second argument sometimes found is that precious little can be done to inculcate an ethical awareness or an ethical attitude in students at a time when most of their values and ethical habits of mind are more or less "in place" and relatively stable. This point of view is particularly compelling when only one ethics course, and that one an elective, is to be found in the entire business school curriculum.

Those ethics advocates who then say that ethics should suffuse *all* business courses often must admit to themselves and to their colleagues that this curricular ideal is difficult if not entirely impossible to achieve because the typical professor of accounting or marketing or finance or computer science has little professional knowledge of ethics theory or of how to relate it to these business fields. Even if this kind of insight were to be developed through special educational and training efforts, it becomes difficult to find a place for it in courses already overburdened with an expanding array of new "functional" knowledge

Counterarguments may be advanced against each of these positions, an experience that many of us who are hearing these Ruffin Lectures have had on our own campuses. My point is that it is these rather less sophisticated obstacles that tend to frustrate the entry of business ethics into the business school curriculum. One could almost wish for the day when business school faculty members were prepared to do battle with Bowie concerning the disciplinary and professional bases of business ethics when considered (and challenged) as a legitimate field of academic inquiry.

When that day arrives and when ways might have been found around the more mundane curricular problems mentioned above, a more serious threat may loom than the question of whether business ethics is a legitimate discipline deserving full status and acceptance in the professional business school. Institutional and ideological co-optation is a real and distinct possible outcome of including ethics in the educational experience of business students. One already hears an ever more popular view that simple awareness of a company's values is the first step toward insuring "excellent" corporate performance. Little or no attention is given by those holding this view to the nature of those embedded corporate values, to their effect on the lives of employees and external stakeholders, or to the broader consequences that those value-driven corporate decisions might have for the larger portion of humankind. As someone has written, this is not a search for *moral* excellence. In this ethically cramped conception of corporate behavior, ethics instruction (whether in one course or several) might become little more than an indoctrination into "how we do things around here." If ethics becomes this kind of "tack-on" exercise, it will have fallen short of its fuller potentialities as a normative field of inquiry that probes the meaning and place of business in society. The faddish enthusiasm for ethics now current in business circles is a worrisome sign that neither the academic community nor corporate practitioners are yet ready to explore the full potential significance of ethics inquiry as a way of judging business performance.

One emphasis in Bowie's lecture is troublesome for those scholars who have undertaken empirical research into ethical phenomena within corporate settings. In attempting to show that empiricism by itself is an insufficient qualification for identifying one's discipline as a scientific one, and in further arguing for the inclusion of both normative and altruistic components in the definition of a profession, Bowie may have unintentionally denigrated the importance of empirical research into business ethics and values. It may be both an unfair and an inaccurate interpretation of his lecture to say that it occasionally seems to reflect a latent, implicit suspicion of or even a hostility toward empiricism. Certainly, it can be agreed that many empiricists, in their zeal for empirical verification of their hypotheses, have ignored, overlooked, or denied the normative implications of their findings. In this sense, positivism is alive and well in business school circles, although it may have loosened its hold on the professional philosopher's mind.

Rather than to emphasize the gap that exists between empirical studies and normative analysis, the better course may be to search for common elements that allow a bridging between the philosopher's evaluative insights and the empirically verified data base of the social scientist. Just how that bridging might be accomplished is suggested by Bowie himself when, near the conclusion of his lecture, he says, "As a discipline, business ethics is interdisciplinary and it could well be enriched by the contributions of all the social sciences." It is this perspective that might well serve as a beacon for those empirical (social science) scholars who wish to find the normative meaning of their data, as well as for those philosophers of business ethics who strive to ground their analyses in a verifiable base of human experience.

# 4

# Autonomy and the Legitimacy of the Liberal Arts

## Jennifer Moore

In his lecture, Normal Bowie argues not only that business ethics is a legitimate discipline, but that business education itself lacks legitimacy if it fails to include business ethics. Bowie's models for a legitimate discipline include the traditional profession such as medicine, the law, and the ministry, but his primary model for legitimacy is the liberal arts. Business education will be legitimate, he argues, only if it includes a "link" to the liberal arts,[1] and it is precisely this link that business ethics provides.

I find Bowie's arguments most persuasive. However, I believe that the crisis in legitimacy is even wider than he suggests. It is not simply business ethics that lacks legitimacy, but the liberal arts curriculum itself. Because this is true, Bowie's argument is not likely to persuade business deans or business faculty who are not already convinced of the importance of liberal education.[2] What is needed is a closer examination of the legitimacy of liberal arts education in general. Bowie provides a take-off point for this enterprise in the "defense" portion of his paper, where he states that the purpose of the liberal arts is to develop "a Kantian person—a rational, autonomous, moral agent who can take his or her place in a moral community."[3] I want to develop the theme of the Kantian person, and his or her significance for business, a little further.

There is little doubt that the legitimacy of the liberal arts is eroding. Once taken for granted as the core of a fine education, the liberal arts today are on the defensive. Students do not seem much interested in liberal arts courses any more. They want courses that contribute directly to a specific career, and they do not believe that liberal arts courses do this. Liberal arts faculty increasingly find themselves explaining to students, administrators, and colleagues how their courses provide skills that help students succeed in the "real world." The American Philosophical Association *Proceedings,* for example, continually publishes data on the salaries and jobs philosophy majors attain when they graduate (Carl Icahn is one), and reports studies that suggest that a major in philosophy can enhance performance on standardized tests, in law school, or in upper management. Liberal arts faculty of all disciplines point to skills like effective communication, the ability to get along with people, or expertise at analyzing and solving problems that are furthered by study of the liberal arts.

There is no question that a liberal arts education does, or at least can, provide such skills. This is not really at issue. The point I wish to make here is that the legitimacy of the liberal arts has shifted ground. It has become derivative. The liberal arts are now valued for the contribution they can make to professional or vocational education. Some people think that this is a good sign, and believe that the only alternative is a liberal education that is virtually useless. But because this new, "vocational" approach to the liberal arts is a significant departure from their traditional justification, it is worth asking some questions about it: Are various marketable skills really the most important contribution of a liberal education? Is a liberal education best regarded as a means to such skills, or does regarding it in this way obscure some more important, more essential goal?

Traditionally, the liberal arts were not valued primarily for the contribution they could make to a person's career, but "for their own sake." Indeed, a liberal arts education was frequently defined against or in contrast to vocational or professional education. Vocational education was a means to an end; liberal education was an end in itself. This was not seen as a defect of liberal education, but as its virtue, and as part of its very essence. The view that a liberal education is valuable for its own sake goes back as far as Aristotle. That a liberal education was an end in itself, however, did not mean that it had no purpose or no ultimate "payoff." Rather, it meant that the purpose of liberal education was thought, somewhat mysteriously, to be best pursued by valuing that education for its own sake.

Alasdair MacIntyre's useful distinction between "internal" and "external" goods helps explain this apparent paradox.[4] A good that is "external" to a particular human practice, MacIntyre explains, is one that is related to it merely accidentally or contingently, as making money, say, is to playing football. There are always other ways to obtain an external good in addition to engaging in the practice, for an external good is not embedded in the practice itself, but is a mere by-product of it. An internal good, in contrast, is *essential* to a given practice. Engaging in the practice is the only way to obtain the good. An internal good can only be described in terms of the practice, and it can only be recognized by those who have actually participated in it. A person may engage in a practice simply to obtain one of its external goods. Fitness is one of the external goods of playing squash, for example, and I may play squash merely to become fit. In this case, squash is a mere means for me. I do it only for the sake of something else. But I may play squash because I love the strategic element peculiar to it, the different shots, and the feeling of the ball connecting with the racquet—its internal goods. In this case, squash is no longer a means for me. I play it "for its own sake." Engaging in a practice for the sake of its internal goods is what it means to do it "for its own sake." The claim that liberal education ought to be valued "for its own sake", then, does not mean that it is purpose*less*. It simply means that it ought to be valued for the purpose or payoff that is essential to it, rather than for its external goods. What is the internal good of a liberal arts education?

To find out, it is helpful to look at the ways in which liberal education has traditionally distinguished itself from vocational or professional education. It is here that the notion of liberal arts as an end in themselves is most strong, and hence where internal goods are most likely to emerge. Three of these distinctions in particular appear so often that we can regard them as essential to the traditional understanding of liberal arts education.

1. Vocational education prepares the student to pursue certain fixed goals. These goals are given in advance, and although they can change over time, it is generally fair to say that in vocational education, the goals themselves rarely become objects of scrutiny. The purpose of vocational education is not to question one's goals, but to see how best to achieve goals that have already been chosen. Liberal arts education, in contrast, encourages the examination and assessment of goals, and presents students with quite different views of the good life in order to assist this process.

2. Vocational education is role oriented. It attempts to produce skilled carpenters, or doctors, or engineers. Liberal arts education attempts to produce good human beings. (Hence the terms "humanities," "humane studies," etc.) It is interested not in people as performers of roles, but in people as such. If liberal education makes reference to any role, it is to that of the "citizen." But in our liberal democratic society, it is precisely as citizens that we are most nearly people as such. It is as citizens that we are expected to transcend our narrow roles and act for the good of the community as a whole.

3. Finally, vocational education is narrow, whereas liberal education is broad and general. Vocational education seeks to develop par-

ticular skills and to transmit a specific body of information. The liberal arts attempt to cultivate a certain habit of mind.

The main aim of liberal education, then, seems to be to develop a certain type of rationality, a type quite different from that which is prevalent in vocational training. We may call the latter means-end or *instrumental rationality*. The primary feature of instrumental rationality is that it does not choose ends, but accepts them as given and looks for the best means to achieve them. In instrumental rationality, reason is subordinated to and placed at the services of ends outside itself. In the rationality cultivated in liberal education, in contrast, reason is free ranging. It is not the servant of any end. Rather, it subjects every end to its *own* standards of evaluation and criticism. Because it is obedient, not to ends outside itself, but simply to its own laws, we may call it *autonomous rationality*. Significantly, autonomy is one of the most frequently cited goals of a liberal arts education. It is also the key feature of the "Kantian person" described by Bowie.

As Kant understood it, autonomous rationality has both a theoretical and an ethical component. On the one hand, those who have developed it are capable of independent, critical thought. They are liberated from the "prison" of prejudice, fixed ideas, and the arbitrary conventions of popular culture. (That liberal education "liberates" is one of the most important elements of its traditional justification; it recurs frequently.) This theoretical component is what Bowie refers to as the "thinking aim" of the liberal arts. But for Kant, the moral dimension of autonomous rationality—what Bowie calls the "sensitivity aim"—is even more important.

In autonomous rationality as Kant describes it, reason is subject not to any end, but simply to its own laws. Autonomous agents faced with a choice will thus ask not whether their proposed action serves a particular goal but whether it passes the *rational* tests of consistency and universal validity.[5] Consistency demands that we act only on principles that we are willing to have others act on as well. If we are to act on consistent principles, we must not break rules that we are not willing to allow others to break, and we must not place others on a lower footing than ourselves, treating them as mere means to our ends. According to Kant, autonomous agents thus accord others the same respect they grant themselves; they do not treat others as means or instruments, but, as he puts it, as "ends in themselves."

Moreover, Kant believes that autonomous rationality is a necessary condition for the "moral community" mentioned by Bowie. For it is only when people act on universally valid and consistent principles that they will treat each other as "ends in themselves" and live together in harmony. The Kantian moral community is a world in which each person freely pursues his or her ends within the bounds of respect for others. Principles that are inconsistent, or that defeat themselves when universalized, lead to strife and conflict, and make such a world impossible.

While a liberal arts education can promote communication skills, the ability to get along with people, or expertise at analyzing and solving problems, these seem to be its external, rather than its internal, goods. They are not the primary purpose of liberal education, and there might well be other ways of achieving them. The *internal* goal of liberal arts education is the development of autonomous rationality. To say that such an education should be pursued for its own sake is to say that it should be pursued for the sake of this goal.

It is easy enough to see that a healthy supply of autonomous rationality is good for society at large. It is, as Bowie points out, essential to a successful democracy and necessary for a stable society. But is it good for business? Bowie argues yes. Adherence to the rational norms of consistency and universal validity is as important in the practice of business, he claims, as in any other human endeavor. The conduct of business is governed by rules that must be upheld if business is to be possible at all. A businessperson who breaks these rules— who fails to uphold a contract, deceives consumers, or bribes to secure a deal—undermines the practice of business and contradicts him or herself.

Bowie's arguments make it clear that autonomous rationality is necessary for the business community as a whole, and for the practice of business in general. But what about the individual business firm? Does autonomous rationality have any place here? At first glance, it may seem as if the answer is no. Corporations, after all, are bureaucracies. Surely they need, not autonomous Kantian persons, but "team players," "good old boys," people who "fit in." Indeed, bureaucracies are often described as institutions dedicated to the application of instrumental rationality. This view of the corporation emerges particularly strongly in *Moral Mazes,* a study of the mores of corporate managers by Robert Jackall.[6] According to Jackall, the following traits are typical of the American corporate bureaucracy:

1. Managerial decisions are invariably made with the short-term rather than the long-term in mind. Managers will thus decimate important departments or "milk" plants to cut short-term costs, even though they know that these actions are irrational in the long run. Every practice and structure of the corporation is calculated to reward this behavior.
2. Truth in the corporation is infinitely flexible, determined by the whims of authority rather than to any objective standards. After corporate "purges," history is invariably rewritten to suit the aims of those in power in a manner reminiscent of totalitarian regimes.

3. Credit and blame are detached from performance and are assigned on the basis of internal political criteria. While lip service is paid to objective standards of performance, these are not what matter in practice. Credit cannot be earned, only conferred by superiors. Blame is similarly detached from responsibility. Success and failure in the corporation have little to do with performance.

4. What really counts in the corporation is mastering the social and political culture, fitting in, being willing to accept the ideology of the moment. Managers come to see themselves as commodities, packaging themselves and repackaging themselves to meet the changing expectations of the environment.

5. There are no fixed criteria for right and wrong in the corporation. Morality does not emerge from rational principles such as consistency, but from ever changing relationships of dominance and loyalty among managers. As one manager quoted put it: "What's right in the corporation is not what is right in a man's home or in his church. What is right in the corporation is what the guy above you wants from you. That's what morality is in the corporation."[7]

The fundamental, underlying feature of the corporation as Jackall sees it is the crowding out of autonomous rationality by; instrumental rationality or, as he calls it, following Max Weber and Karl Mannheim, "formal" or "functional rationality." Functional rationality is

> activity consciously planned and calculated to attain some goal, any goal. Weber and Mannheim distinguished functional rationality from substantive rationality. The latter refers to a critical reasoned reflectiveness with which one assesses and evaluates particular goals themselves and which guides one's decisions. In bureaucratic settings, which are institutionalized paradigms of functional rationality, technique and procedure tend to become ascendant over substantive reflection about organizational goals, at least among lower and middle managers. . . . Even at higher levels of management, one sees ample evidence of an overriding emphasis on technique rather than on critical reasoning.[8]

The businesses described by Jackall are chilling places that exact a terrible toll on the people in them and on the society in which they operate. But they are also *poorly managed firms*. In an environment in which instrumental rationality takes precedence over all else, no rationality is exercised to evaluate the goals themselves, and all energy is devoted to finding means. Because no rationality guides the selection of goals, no one goal commands allegiance, no one goal has a greater claim to legitimacy than any other. Everything becomes a potential means to an end, *including the firm itself*. Although a firm may be able to survive under such conditions, it is unlikely to do very well. Without a significant measure of autonomous rationality, without the ability to submit goals to rational criteria of evaluation and justification, no firm can truly prosper.

If these arguments are correct, liberal education is legitimate because it is the one place in our society in which autonomous rationality is actively pursued and developed. Autonomous rationality is the "internal good" of liberal education, that good which emerges when the liberal arts are pursued for their own sake. If liberal education declines, or if it comes to be pursued solely for its external goods, we are likely to see the erosion of autonomous rationality. Jackall's work is only one indication that this is already happening. If autonomous rationality is to be preserved, the liberal arts must be repositioned at the center of the curriculum. At the very least, we must stop thinking of them primarily as a means to various professional skills.

It is also clear why business education needs support from the liberal arts. Both business as a whole and the individual firm need autonomous rationality to survive. Business education needs to encourage the habit of submitting goals to rational scrutiny. It needs to help students develop criteria for the good business and the good businessperson that pass the rational tests of consistency and universal validity. As Bowie suggests, the discipline of business ethics is the one best positioned to contribute to this goal.

## NOTES

1. Norman Bowie, "Business Ethics as a Discipline: The Search for Legitimacy," in R. Edward Freeman, ed., *Business Ethics: The State of the Art* (New York: Oxford University Press, 1991).

2. I use "liberal arts" and "liberal education" interchangeably in this paper. Technically, a liberal education can include the physical sciences and the social sciences, as well as the liberal arts or "humanities." However, the liberal arts are the original core of the curriculum, and the feature that makes it "liberal" or "humane."

3. Bowie, "Business Ethics."

4. See Alasdair MacIntyre, *After Virtue* (Notre Dame: University of Notre Dame Press, 1981), pp. 175 ff.

5. To be precise, Kant says that the autonomous agent asks whether the "maxim" or principle of his or her action (not the action itself) passes the tests of consistency and universal validity.

6. Robert Jackall, *Moral Mazes* (New York: Oxford University Press, 1988).

7. Ibid., p. 6.

8. Ibid., pp. 75–76.

# 5

# Ethics as Character Development: Reflections on the Objective of Ethics Education

## Lynn Sharp Paine

The legitimacy of business ethics education depends in part on success in meeting its objectives.[1] Even if business school faculty accept ethics as a genuine discipline, even if ethics courses are rigorous and challenging, even if ethics comes to be regarded as an essential part of a professional education, ethics courses will not attain a secure plan in the business school curriculum unless their objectives can be defined and met. Management by objectives is a familiar business concept, and business school faculty are used to thinking of success in terms of attaining objectives. Although one might complain that this notion is sometimes taken too far or misapplied in matters of teaching and learning, it is not inappropriate to require that teachers of business ethics have some broad conception of what they are trying to accomplish. Indeed, this is essential if business ethics is going to weather the crisis of legitimacy that Norman Bowie has addressed.

I wish to argue for a particular conception of the objectives of ethics education, a conception that is, I believe, controversial among those engaged in teaching business ethics but accepted by many of its critics. I will take as my starting point the position of a prominent critic of ethics education whose views are, I believe, quite representative of a school of critics. In the course of arriving at this conception I will discuss an alternative conception that has gained some prominence among ethics educators, but that I believe to be inap-

67

propriate. Finally, I will spell out some of the practical implications of adopting the view I favor.


## THE CRITICISM

Irving Kristol asserted in a recent *Wall Street Journal* article that education in ethics has no positive role to play in the process of character formation.[2] The assertion occurred in the context of a commentary on John Shad's gift of $20 million to the Harvard Business School for the purpose of teaching "business ethics." Kristol offered three bases for his conclusion. First, ethics education comes too late: "[t]he moral character of most university students has been formed and fixed before they take a course in ethics." Second, ethics education in professional schools uses the wrong methods: character formation, according to Kristol, occurs by way of precept, example, and the structure of incentives one encounters in real-life situations, and not by the sort of logical analysis that takes place in the classroom. And finally, ethics teachers have the wrong approach: Kristol attributes to ethics teachers a commitment to a "non-judgmental, value-free" approach, which, he says, could not possibly have a tendency to make students more moral rather than less because the approach itself is dedicated to eliminating differences among the moral and the less moral.

One might quarrel with Kristol's factual claims about the methods and approaches used in ethics education in business schools today. Empirical evidence might be marshalled to show that the commitment to value-free inquiry into ethics is the exception rather than the rule as he suggests. Certainly, if he means to imply that most ethics teachers reject the very idea of moral evaluation, he would be wrong. The matter of non-judgmental attitude is something else again. He is probably correct when he says that many ethics teachers adopt a non-judgmental attitude toward students in the classroom. But that is not because they believe that moral judgment is impossible, but because they believe that adopting a non-judgmental attitude toward students is the best way to promote sober evaluation in moral matters.

Empirical study would also demonstrate, I think, that ethics educators in business schools rarely see their job as teaching students to "identify the logical inconsistencies in systems of moral propositions constructed by other ethicists." Certainly ethics educators expect students to adhere to canons of rationality in argument. But the subject of argument is more likely to be a practical business matter than "systems of moral propositions constructed by other ethicists." Study of the actual state of ethics education in business schools shows that

a good deal of time is spent in the discussion of case studies centering on ethical decisions faced by business practitioners—a form of
education by example that Kristol approves.[3] Many courses take up
the very issue he identifies as central to character formation: namely,
how the structure of incentives in a business organization can affect
the character of employees and their tendency to act in ways that are
more rather than less moral.[4]

But even if Kristol's factual assumptions about ethics education
today could be shown to be false, his indictment would stand largely
intact if it is true that ethics education can have no effect on character or conduct. Kristol raises an important question when he asks
about the effects of classroom education in business ethics on the
morality of future business leaders. Implicit in Kristol's critique is
the assumption that business ethics courses aim or ought to aim to
contribute to positive character formation. Their legitimacy, in his
view, depends on their achieving this objective. It follows quite naturally, given his views on the appropriate timing and methods of
character formation, that ethics has no place in the business school
curriculum.

## ONE RESPONSE: ETHICS AS A TOOL

Some ethics educators respond to this sort of criticism by denying
that influencing students to act more ethically or contributing to their
moral growth is part of their objective. Rather, they say their courses
aim to help students understand ethical issues or to understand the
ethical content of business decisions.[5] The "tool" metaphor is commonly used to explain the objectives of the ethics component in the
curriculum: the ethics course, it is said, will give students the "tools"
they need to analyze ethical issues and to resolve ethical dilemmas.
Some ethics teachers offer students "frameworks" and "models" that
will do the same things the "tools" do: help to analyze issues and
resolve dilemmas.

Reluctance to accept any part of the responsibility for students'
moral growth and development is surely understandable. Given the
myriad influences that affect people's behavior, it would seem the
height of folly—or arrogance—to expect a few hours in the classroom to make much of a difference. There are great personal risks
involved in saying that one hopes to contribute to students' character
development. There is the risk of failure: it is much easier to succeed and to know that one has succeeded if one aims to give students
tools of analysis. Students can be examined on their understanding
of the tools and their ability to apply them in hypothetical situations.
Failure to contribute to character formation is, moreover, a more

serious failure than failure to convey an analytic framework. It is likely to be regarded not merely as a technical failure implicating the teacher as an instrument for transmitting knowledge, but as a moral failure implicating the teacher as a person.

A teacher who openly states that she hopes to contribute to students' character development runs the risk of being seen as "holier than thou." Ethics teachers understandably want to avoid presenting or seeming to present themselves as morally better than their students. Such a stance not only smacks of arrogance but also invites an uncomfortable degree of scrutiny. Conduct that would normally be excused, or at least tolerated, in another person becomes an indicator of the ethics teacher's hypocrisy or unfitness. Anyone holding herself out as a moral educator runs the risk of having her own moral failures scrutinized, publicized, and criticized. She must be prepared continually to subject her own life to moral criticism and to strive to be a better person. These risks can all be avoided by limiting one's objectives to imparting information and analytical tools, models, and frameworks.

Moreover, this way of thinking about objectives fits in well with other subjects taught in business schools. As social sciences, many business school subjects depend on the construction and application of models or ideal types. Frameworks, too, are familiar stuff. Students are taught to apply various frameworks in settling on a competitive strategy or analyzing the business environment. A professor outside the ethics field will nod approvingly when she hears that the ethics course, too, provides students with a framework or tool for analyzing ethical issues. Many business school professors who wish to integrate ethics into their courses on marketing or organizational behavior seek a framework or model for discussing the ethical questions that come up in their courses.[6]

The tendency to think of the objective of ethics education rather narrowly in terms of providing analytical tools is not driven solely by risk avoidance and business school culture. The orientation toward problem solving and decision making reflected in the "tool" metaphor is found within ethical theory itself.[7] At stake is a conception of human choice that emphasizes the moment of choice and the explicit deliberative processes through which one arrives at a decision. The habits of thought, the concerns, and the commitments that lead one to see a situation as requiring action or decision play no role in this picture of choice, which focuses on deliberative rationality.

As pointed out by the philosopher Joel Kupperman, ethical philosophy has provided two very different models of choice and action.[8] In one, the agent tests available alternative actions against a rationally derivable theory. The theory, which may be Kantian, utilitarian, or contractarian in nature, serves as the tool or standard for evaluating possible choices. A persistent problem for this conception is the gap between deliberation and action: the connection between the application of moral theory and the decision to do what theory prescribes. Even if the theory is correctly applied, ethical conduct will not necessarily follow unless the agent wishes to comply with the theory's prescription. The theory, like a tool, is external to its user. It sits on the shelf until it is needed to perform the task for which it is designed.

In the other model, many actions and choices are seen to flow naturally from the agent's character—her habits of thought and action, and her commitments and concerns—without the interjection of consciously applied theory. Both Confucius and Aristotle stress the extent to which settled traits of character obviate the need for deliberation and conscious decision in particular cases.[9] Consequently, they see the cultivation of virtue rather than the application of decision criteria as the core of morality.

Grossly oversimplified, the first model of moral choice asserts the primacy of conscious deliberation, while the second emphasizes character. As Kupperman and others have noted, these two models of choice are not necessarily rival models.[10] Reflection would suggest that character is an important determinant of much conduct, but that certain situations require conscious decision. Even persons of the highest integrity must engage in conscious deliberation when they meet with moral conflicts, for example. Within ethical theory, important questions arise about the relation between the two models: whether there is a relation of logical or conceptual priority between them; when each is most appropriately applied.[11]

The inadequacies of the first response to Kristol's criticism may be apparent. First, it is not clear what objective might be served by giving students tools and frameworks for ethical deliberation if they are not contributing to decisions and actions that are morally better than they would otherwise be. Surely, ethics educators who respond in this way do not mean to say that their courses are simply mind-stretching activities with no objective beyond the mental exercise gained through applying the analytical tools. If the response is an indirect way of saying that the desired result—morally better decisions—cannot be guaranteed, it is an unnecessarily misleading way of communicating that message. The response also suggests a rather mechanical model of ethical thought, one that places exclusive emphasis on deliberation in the context of already defined choices, and ignores the importance of character for both ethical thinking and ethical conduct.

It is not that analytical tools and frameworks have no place in ethics education, but that these tools must be seen in the context of an overall conception of character. Moreover, only someone who cares to use the tools, who recognizes when they are appropriate, and who wants to do what they recommend will benefit from careful instruction in how to use them.

## ANOTHER RESPONSE: ETHICS AS CHARACTER DEVELOPMENT

The better response to Irving Kristol's charge is to accept his view that ethics education should contribute to positive character formation, but to reject his claim that it is incapable of doing so at the university and graduate school level. This reply, if it is to be convincing, must rest on a conception of character that recognizes change and permits judgments of degree, and on a description of how ethics education could affect character.

### Character Change

According to a widely held conception of character, one accepted by many critics of ethics education, character is more or less fixed in the very early years of life—as early as age five or six according to some proponents of this view. After the early years, in which attitudes are formed and habits and dispositions adopted, there is very little that can be done to affect the basic orientations and ingrained habits that define a person's character. According to this view, people beyond the formative stages either have or do not have "character" in the narrower sense of integrity or moral strength. Integrity is an all-or-nothing affair: mature people are either ethical or unethical. Neither personal effort nor external influences can have a tendency to affect character in either the broad or the narrow sense after its initial formation. Because moral and immoral actions flow from the presence or absence of integrity, conduct, too, is pretty much unalterable according to this view.

The static view of character is not universally accepted. Confucius, for instance, emphasized the power of a moral leader to influence others to act morally.[12] This would not be possible if character were static. He believed that moral maturity could be achieved only in old age when doing what was morally right would come naturally, without the effort of deliberation often required earlier.[13] Aristotle, too, believed that moral development was possible. He said that one could become truly courageous—with the right attitudes and motives—by acting in ways that a courageous person would act.[14]

A more fluid conception of character is reflected in the words of George Eliot, who said that "character . . . is a process and an unfolding."[15] She described Lydgate, the 27-year-old Middlemarch doctor, as a man with "both virtues and faults capable of shrinking or expanding."[16] Although she did not explain how this shrinkage or expansion could occur, it is reasonable to think that both personal effort and fortitude as well as external influence could affect the process. Stanley Milgram's well-known experiments on authority, for example, suggest that willingness to inflict deliberate harm on others increases in the face of orders issuing from an authority figure.[17] One might conjecture that repeated subjection to such a figure over time could effect a change in character as well as conduct. The expectations of one's social community, as well as formal rewards and penalties, also appear to encourage the shrinkage or expansion of virtues and faults. On the personal side, reason, reflection, and effort can play a role in the character "process."

The more fluid conception is, I believe, the more accurate one, although there are undoubtedly limits on the extent to which and the speed with which deeply ingrained habits of thought and action can be modified, especially in the absence of coercive pressures, external incentives, or strong personal desire. Since habits become more firmly entrenched with the passage of time, modifications become more difficult with age. This is the element of truth captured by the static conception.

Our very language cuts against rapid character changes. The word "character" is sometimes used to refer generally to the pattern of qualities, attitudes, and dispositions a person exhibits rather consistently over time. "Honest," "reliable," "just"—these are traits we are willing to ascribe to character only if they are exhibited over a period of time in a person's conduct, attitudes, judgments, and deliberations. We will not withdraw a judgment of honesty on the basis of a single falsehood, or even several falsehoods, provided there are circumstances that will permit us to regard the conduct as "out of character." Likewise, we are unwilling to attribute a positive moral quality to a person's character on the basis of only a few instances, unless those instances demonstrate particular strength or resistance in the face of temptation.

Given the usage of the word "character," we do not attribute to someone a new character trait, especially one inconsistent with a trait we have come to expect, until it has been exhibited consistently over time, even if, in some sense, the person has actually changed rather rapidly. Thus, the very concept of character is such that it precludes rapid changes in traits that have come to be expected on the basis of past conduct. Whether it is a fact about children, or a fact about the language, that precludes children's acquiring a character until they have been around awhile is an interesting question. Nevertheless, there would appear to be some truth to the notion that deeply ingrained habits of thought and conduct cannot be replaced quickly or easily even if very much desired. Still, if they are to occur at all, they must begin with some action or judgment or thought characteristic of the new trait. Following Aristotle, we become courageous by acting as a courageous person would act.

The idea of character change seems less extraordinary if we think, not of dramatic changes involving the loss of traits or the acquisition of new ones, but the strengthening or weakening of existing ones. Qualities of character can be strengthened so that they are more regularly or consistently demonstrated, especially in the face of pressures to act otherwise. The tendency to speak truthfully may become stronger, for example, through an experience of speaking truthfully in a situation where self-interest would dictate misrepresentation. Or a more consistent harmony between one's own conduct and judgments about others may be brought about. Someone who exhibits concern for injustices committed by others but who sometimes acts selfishly in her own dealings exhibits the quality of justice imperfectly. Such a person can become more just; the quality of justice can become stronger. We might also say that character traits can become deeper or more secure as we become more self-aware and confident of their importance.[18] The reaffirmation and reordering of values that occurs through child rearing is this sort of deepening experience.

If traits of character can become stronger, they can also become weaker as opportunities to exhibit them are foregone or become scarce through change of circumstance. We speak of the erosion of character that can occur as one small departure from a pattern leads to another and another until the earlier pattern is no longer characteristic at all. Breaking the second commitment, for instance, is often easier than breaking the first and can, in some cases and if unchecked, lead to a pattern of unreliability.

### Degrees of Integrity

As already noted, the word "character" is often used broadly, as in the phrase "a person's character," to refer to whatever pattern of attitudes, dispositions, and qualities a person exhibits. In this sense, no one is without character—even if it is an eclectic or unpredictable one. "Character" is also used more narrowly to refer to a certain core group of positive moral qualities. A "person of character" is, in this second sense of character, an ethical person, someone who exhibits the qualities associated with the idea of integrity. Typically, a person of character is someone in whom those qualities are thought to be particularly strong and consistent—sometimes to the degree that the person seems to radiate a distinctive aura that has the capacity to influence others. In this narrow sense of "character" as integrity, a person may be totally lacking in character, or may exhibit it to a greater or lesser degree.

Let us say that a person of character is, at a minimum, an "ethical person." An ethical person conducts her life in accordance with the requirements of fundamental ethical principles calling for honesty, fairness, fidelity to commitments, respect for persons and property, and proscribing intentional deceit, unjustified harm to others, theft, and violations of law.[19] Adherence to these principles involves more than simply acting so as not to violate them. An ethical person will, in addition, have certain dispositions and attitudes that reflect the principles. She will treat the principles as binding, use them as reasons for and against acting, feel guilty for her violations, take steps to repair infringements, and be concerned when others violate them. Integrity, even in this minimal sense, requires a certain level of concern for others. Without the ability to identify sympathetically with others—to put oneself in their shoes—it is doubtful that successful compliance with the principles of fairness, honesty, and avoidance of harm could be achieved. Someone who would violate these principles if only he could do so without being caught is not an ethical person. An ethical person's intentions and objectives need not be noble, but they must be—at least most of the time—consistent with these familiar moral guidelines.

We do not regard as ethical someone who says he wishes to follow these principles but does not in practice do so. There must be some degree of correspondence between what the ethical person says and does regarding these basic principles.[20] Perfect correspondence is not required: the ethical person is not expected to resist every pressure or temptation or to be unduly focused on avoiding infringements. But someone who claims to be an adherent and yet fails to resist routinely present temptations and pressures to compromise the principles, like someone who fails to give sufficient attention to the ethics of her conduct, would probably not qualify. Repeated failures in compliance suggest an insufficient attachment to the principles. They indicate that the appropriate dispositions and emotions are not firmly established. Similarly, the absence of the dispositions, intentions, and emotions involved in adherence to the principles negates any moral credit that might otherwise be given for conduct in compliance with the principles.

A person of integrity in this minimal sense must appreciate fundamental ethical principles, recognize situations in which they apply, and be able to resist the normal, routine pressures and temptations to compromise them. That is to say, an ethical person regularly and consistently exhibits the character traits associated with these principles: she is honest, fair, reliable or faithful to her commitments to others, trustworthy, and careful not to harm others. These traits are reflected in her judgments of herself and others as well as in conduct in compliance with the underlying principles.

Beyond the minimum, a person of character may exhibit integrity to a greater or lesser degree. A higher degree of integrity is exhibited in a strong sense of responsibility and a willingness to be held accountable for the more remote, as well as the immediate, effects of one's choices and actions.[21] A person of integrity in this more demanding sense does not merely refrain from intentional violations of basic moral principles. She is careful to consider the more distant effects of her actions to insure that she does not *un*intentionally mislead or harm others. She is concerned to see that her conduct does not put others in ethically awkward situations or pressure them to act in ways that are ethically questionable. Greater integrity is linked with special conscientiousness in this regard. This sense of responsibility extends to responsibility for the present as well as the future. That is, a person of integrity acknowledges that present choices flow, to a large extent, from past choices.[22]

As Gabrielle Taylor emphasizes in her essay, a person of integrity is capable of evaluating the course of action available to her and the desires and traits of character she might cultivate.[23] She must possess a certain degree of self-awareness and engage in a certain amount of self-assessment. She does not just act on whatever desire is strongest at the moment.

Courage and fortitude to resist the greater and more unusual temptations and pressures to compromise fundamental values are also marks of superior integrity. An ethical person is, at a minimum, someone who resists the routine opportunities to betray a trust or violate a principle for some small personal advantage. When a person speaks truly or stands by a commitment at great cost to himself, however, we speak of integrity—even of great integrity.

Great integrity or strength of character is also associated with strong commitments to persons, causes, and ideals beyond the core of basic ethical principles.[24] These commitments give a person's life a particular definition or shape. They both obviate the need for conscious deliberation about many choices and also determine that certain choices, which to others may be rather routine, will present themselves as of great importance. A commitment to family or to the environment, for example, can have these effects. Derived from the Latin *integritas,* the word "integrity" suggests wholeness, a sense of being "together." There are many senses in which a person of integrity exhibits wholeness or integration: through identifying commitments that provide continuity and unity through the course of life; through conduct that reflects espoused principles; through self-assessment and self-control.

The objective of ethics education must be seen in light of a conception of character that allows for change—for improvement, for degeneration—and that permits judgments of degree—of greater and lesser integrity. Ethics education at the university level should aim, in my view, to contribute to character development by strengthening and deepening those positive qualities associated with the idea of integrity. At the very least, ethics education should aim to prevent the deterioration of those qualities. For business students, this will involve reflection on their own developing characters as well as awareness of the special responsibilies that go with participation in the business enterprise and exposure to the characteristic problems and choices they will face in the business world.

## A PRACTICAL PROGRAM FOR ETHICAL EDUCATION

It is useful to think about ethics education in business schools from the perspective of the individual student who will become a manager or an executive. What will enable that person to achieve higher levels of integrity or at least to maintain the level at which she enters professional life? Although the environment in which she works will be an important influence, there are certain personal capacities that are critical: the capacity for ethical sensibility; the capacity for ethical reasoning; the capacity for ethical conduct; and the capacity for ethical leadership. These capacities are the backbone of character. But, like muscles, they become stronger with use. In the average person, they flourish in an environment that encourages their exercise; otherwise, they atrophy.[25] Most students entering business school have these capacities to some degree. Ethics education can strengthen and refine them, and in so doing, strengthen character.

As with any educational endeavor, learning and growth occur most readily when students care about the subject at hand. Fortunately, most students do care about ethics, though they may be unsure about the importance of ethics in business. Part of ethics education is reassuring students the it is appropriate to care about ethics in business. This can be done in a variety of ways: by appeal to reason, through examples of managers and executives who do care, through opportunities for relationships with business practitioners who are willing and able to discuss the importance of ethics in business. Serious treatment of ethics in the business school curriculum is, in itself, an indication to students that ethics matters.

### Ethical Sensibility

Ethical sensibility is reflected in the capacity to impose ethical order on a situation—to identify aspects of the situation that have ethical importance. A person lacking in ethical sensibility will be insensitive to the ethically important features of a situation and thus very vulnerable to acting in ways that, from the ethical point of view, are improper or less than optimal. Like the connoisseur whose trained and experienced eye picks out the distinctive features of a work of art, the person of keen ethical sensibilities seems to intuit the presence of ethical considerations and to recognize subtle nuances among situations and relationships. Ethical sensibility is not the same as the ability to apply general rules to particular cases, though sensibility might be trained through exercises of this sort. Nor is it just concern for others. While sympathetic concern for others is both an aspect of and a necessary condition for ethical sensibility, sensibility is better described as the ability to see the general ethical category in the particular situation at hand—to see, for example, that an action would be a betrayal of trust or cause serious harm to an innocent party or be unfair or misleading.

A rich vocabulary of ethical categories and concepts would appear to be a prerequisite for an active ethical sensibility. Equally important is experience in using those categories and concepts to describe one's world. The student of artistic styles or of law, for example, first learns the concepts of those disciplines through attention to illustrations of the concepts as well as the concepts themselves. Over time, seeing a style in a work of art or a legally cognizable pattern in a fact situation comes very naturally without an effort of deliberate application or analysis. The cultivation and refinement of ethical sensibility is similar.

One task of business ethics education is to refine students' ethical sensibilities by enriching their vocabulary of ethics and by giving them practice in using that vocabulary in business situations. Developing a working knowledge of ethical concepts will help avoid unethical conduct that arises simply because issues and problems go unnoticed.[26] It can also strengthen integrity by bringing greater consistency to the use of ethical concepts and to the substance of ethical judgments.

Many students have a strong intuitive sense of honesty, fairness, trust, right, and wrong as these concepts relate to situations they are familiar with. Ethics education can build on this foundation by giving students a clearer understanding of the value of these ideas for the individual and for the communities of which she is part. It is essential to give students practice in using these familiar concepts in characteristic situations they are likely to encounter in their business careers. Ethics education can also introduce general ethical concepts that may be less familiar as well as special ethical concepts that are particularly important in the business world. The notion of fiduciary responsibility and the closely related idea of conflicts of interest, for example, may be wholly new to some students.

Much of business school education is conducted in the language of economics: actions, practices, policies, and strategies are evaluated in terms of profitability. Ethics educators should keep this in mind as they present and encourage students to use the language of ethics. Exploring the similarities between these perspectives as well as their points of divergence can be an effective way to highlight the distinctiveness of ethical concepts and to heighten ethical sensibility.

### Ethical Reasoning

Recognizing the ethically important features of a situation is the first step toward dealing with them appropriately. Indeed, in some cases, recognition and resolution go nearly hand-in-hand. Recognizing, for example, that proposed advertising copy contains false or potentially misleading claims about a product should lead rather directly to revising the ad or sending the copywriter back to the drawing board with perhaps more explicit instructions about what is acceptable. Similarly, if a bank loan officer recognizes that a personal relationship will cloud or appear to cloud her judgment about a loan application, she should ask someone else to review the application. The loan decision should be made by someone whose judgment is and is seen to be objective.

In other cases, though, an active ethical sensibility may create puzzlement, if not paralysis. The manager who discovers that the production line presents hazards to the reproductive health of female workers as well as to their offspring, but who also realizes that removing women from the line may be unfair, faces an ethical conflict. The principle of fairness—equal employment opportunity—appears to rule out what the principle of avoiding harm requires. Dealing with ethical conflicts is one type of situation requiring deliberation or conscious reasoning, the second capacity that should be developed through ethics education.

The ability to reason about ethical matters is closely linked with the tools and analytical frameworks that some have thought to comprise the whole of ethics education. This capacity can be developed in part through the application of various approaches or frameworks for making ethical decisions in situations of conflict or in other situations where the alternatives are discrete and well defined. The most commonly invoked approaches involve some device for securing an impartial perspective, for universalizing and generalizing the competing principles of action, and for taking into account the rights and interests of various affected parties.

Students should also become familiar with the patterns of reasoning involved in bringing particular cases under general principles. For example, choice may depend on whether a particular proposed action would fall within a given proscribed category: whether an act would be bribery, or insider trading, or price-fixing. Ethical sensibility may pick out the situation as problematic, but reasoning is sometimes required to determine precisely what categories and concepts are appropriate. Reasoning by analogy—identifying differences and similarities among cases—and reasoning from the larger purposes served by the principle in question may be required to determine whether a particular action should be covered by the general principle.

The situations calling for ethical reasoning are numerous. Resolving dilemmas and choosing among alternative actions are a routine part of the manager's life. Most managers will also be involved in formulating policies that have wide application throughout their organizations. Practice in reasoning about the ethical aspects of a firm's guidelines on competitive intelligence gathering, for example, can help prepare students for their policy-making role and contribute to ethically sound policies.

Deliberation about alternative acts, practices, and policies with a view toward action is important not only for guiding choice and action but also for insuring that actions are justifiable to those who may demand explanations after the fact. Even when ethical sensibility is adequate for guidance, it is not adequate for justification. Students should be able to support their ethical intuitions with arguments and to present and defend those arguments when challenged. Moreover, there is no guarantee that the world will not yield up ethically intricate situations for which our intuitions are not prepared. It is virtually certain that advancing technology will continue to present novel choices whose ethical implications have never before been considered. Most business school graduates will be in positions that require them not only to make and implement decisions in complex and novel situations but also to justify their decisions and actions to others and to evaluate the decisions and actions of those around them.

Another large portion of the ethical reasoning required of an executive or manager involves evaluating the arguments offered for various positions she may be asked to support. Today's business leader must be able to formulate ethically sound positions on numerous public policy issues affecting business. The capacity for this sort of reasoning can be strengthened by examining characteristic patterns and fallacies in arguments and by practice in formulating and defending arguments for various positions.

Strengthening students' capacity to reason about ethical matters can enhance integrity by insuring better decisions in complex cases, by providing a secure foundation for intuitively held ethical principles, and by contributing to consistency between ethical principles and practice. If students reason through the sorts of difficult situations they are likely to face in business practice, they will be less apt to "cook" their ethical thinking in stressful situations.[27] To the extent that frameworks for ethical deliberation encourage systematic consideration of the more remote consequences of action and their effects on the rights and interests of stakeholders, they are supportive of greater integrity.

## Ethical Conduct

Integrity is ultimately exhibited in conduct that accords with sound ethical judgment. Hypocrisy and cowardice, both reflected in discrepancies between professed beliefs and actual conduct, are the enemies of integrity. Another task of ethics education is to strengthen the capacity for ethical conduct, conduct that reflects our best ethical judgment.

Within the limitations of the classroom, it is impossible to replicate the pressures, temptations, and rationalizations that characteristically lead people to ignore ethical requirements, and even to act against their own ethical judgment. Still, ethics educators can help students better appreciate these pressures and temptations. By examining case studies students can come to recognize and appreciate how the attractions of wealth and status and the very human aversion to criticism and isolation can lead people to overlook important ethical considerations, to betray their own principles, or to compromise their capacity for ethical judgment. Students should have the opportunity not only to consider cases in which people have succumbed to these pressures but also to reflect on cases in which they have overcome them.

Students will have experienced many of the characteristic pressures and temptations to engage in unethical behavior. In all likelihood, however, the stakes will have been lower and the pressures less intense than those they will encounter on the job. One task of ethics education is to expose students to the characteristic ways these pressures and temptations manifest themselves in the business world. Students should be aware, for example, that ethical failures are not just a matter of greed (a popular view in light of recent Wall Street scandals). Frequently, ethical failures occur because people have made an honest mistake and are afraid to reveal it. They fear embarrassment, losing business, losing a promotion, or losing a job. Remedying the mistake may be costly and time consuming and the pressure to meet deadlines and cut costs, great. Students should also be alert to the familiar rationalizations produced in these situations: "I had no choice"; "If I don't do it, somebody else will"; "It won't hurt anyone"; "Everyone else is doing it"; "It's not my responsibility."[28]

Written case studies are a useful vehicle for conveying the types of pressures and temptations found in the workplace. But the usual case falls short in conveying the intensity of the feelings and emotions involved. Novels, plays, well-written biographies, and films are often superior in this respect, and can be a valuable part of an ethics program.

Alerting students to the "red flags" that pose challenges to integrity can contribute to strengthening their resolve and helping them weather the pressures they will encounter. Awareness of likely pitfalls can also help them better manage the ethical climate of the organizations in which they will work. It is important, however, that students be exposed to individuals who have dealt with workplace challenges without compromising their integrity and with organizations that value individuals who have done so.

### Ethical Leadership

The capacity for ethical leadership is associated with the highest levels of integrity. "The superior person," said Confucius, "seeks to perfect the admirable qualities of others and does not seek to perfect their bad qualities. The lesser person does the opposite of this." [29] Most business students will work in organizations in which they will have the power and responsibility not only to exercise their own ethical capacities but to influence the exercise of those capacities in others. They will, consciously and thoughtfully or unconsciously and without reflection, either support or discourage the exercise of ethical capacities among their peers and subordinates. It is impossible to refrain from doing so. As they attain positions of greater managerial responsibility and visibility, their power to influence will grow. Ethical leadership is thus of particular importance for business students who may find themselves held accountable not only for their own integrity but for the integrity of subordinates.

Confucius offered very little guidance about how to elicit the admirable qualities in others beyond exhibiting virtue in one's own conduct. There appears to be some truth to his idea that great virtue can influence others to virtue. Certainly, if we think of great moral figures like Gandhi, we are struck by the incredible power his virtue commanded. Numerous researchers and commentators have attributed critical importance to the ethical example provided by an organization's top officials. [30] It would appear highly unlikely that great integrity would emerge in an organization led by those lacking in basic integrity. Still, examination of ethical failures in organizations suggests that basic integrity of corporate leaders may be a sine qua non for integrity throughout the ranks, but it is only one of many influences.

Another task of ethics education is to strengthen students' capacity for ethical leadership. This can be done, in part, by exposing them to organizational factors likely to affect employees' ethical sensibility, reasoning, and conduct. For example, the potential ethical implications of management by objective or various management incentive plans should be explored. Organizational structures, reporting relationships, and hiring and promotion practices are important, as are formal control systems, explicit standards, and official enforcement procedures. Various informal and undocumented practices can be critical as well: whether matters of ethics are regularly discussed and taken seriously, for instance. All these factors can influence whether a marketing manager, for example, will normally and naturally exercise ethical judgment in deciding on a strategy for learning about the competition.

Features of the external environment can also be influential. Students should be aware of the effects of the broader economic climate, the presence or absence of government regulation, and the nature of industry standards and practices. All of these factors must be taken into account in fashioning an environment in which the exercise of ethical capacities will be encouraged rather than discouraged. Ethical leadership rests on the leader's personal integrity and concern for the integrity of others. But, like personal integrity, it can be enhanced by knowledge and attentive management.

## CONCLUSION

The objective of ethics education should be to enhance students' integrity and the integrity of those they will influence in their business careers. Ethics education, I believe, can contribute to positive character formation by strengthening the capacities I have described. The methods and materials for doing this are varied. Methods range from logical analysis, to the study of history and organizations, to reflection on works of fiction. Tools and analytical frameworks as well as training in the canons of sound reasoning have a role to play. By contributing to better decisions and better conduct, ethical reasoning can contribute to strengthened character in the manner described by Aristotle. But character involves much more than agility in applying analytical tools.

If properly conceived and conducted, ethics education can contribute to positive character development. However, the results of an ethics education program cannot be guaranteed. The educational program I have described is based on a conception of character that admits of change and of degree. It acknowledges human freedom. Ethics education may strengthen students' ethical capacities, but it will not prevent their erosion or inoculate students against ethical failure. Strength of character, I have suggested, depends both on personal qualities and a favorable environment. For many students, maintaining the advances achieved in school will depend on finding a favorable climate in the business world.

## NOTES

1. The 1988 Ruffin Lectures provided the occasion for this paper, but it reflects thoughts stimulated by repeated inquiries about the point of teaching ethics. I once subscribed to a version of the position which I here criticize: the position that ethics courses do not aim to affect students' character. I am grateful to Professor Diane Yeager for pressing me to explain this position, an exercise that led me to see its deficiencies. An earlier version of the part of this paper dealing with ethical capacities was delivered as a lecture at The Mansfield Center's conference "Private Profit and Public Good: Contemporary Issues in Business Ethics," University of Montana, April 1987.

2. Irving Kristol, "Ethics, Anyone? Or Morals?" *Wall Street Journal,* September 15, 1987, p. 32.

3. Lynn Sharp Paine, *Ethics Education in American Business Schools,* a report by The Ethics Resource Center, Inc., Washington, DC, (February 1988).

4. Ibid. According to the report, 51 percent of MBA programs accredited by the AACSB cover this topic in their business ethics programs.

5. See Otto A. Bremer, John E. Logan, and Richard E. Wokutch, "Ethics and Values in Management Thought," in Karen Paul ed., *Business Environment and Business Ethics,* (Cambridge, MA: Ballinger Publishing Col, 1987), pp. 81–82. These authors believe that support for business ethics courses rests on an "unspoken assumption that students who take such courses will act more ethically than those who do not," even though few teachers are willing to make this a stated objective of their efforts.

6. Many of Georgetown University's business school faculty have said they need a framework or model for ethical analysis in order to integrate ethics into their courses successfully.

7. The emphasis on problem solving and dilemma resolution so prevalent among ethical theorists is criticized in Edmund L. Pincoff's, *Quandaries and Virtues* (Lawrence, KS: University of Kansas Press, 1986).

8. Joel Kupperman, "Character and Education," unpublished manuscript (University of Connecticut). See also Kupperman, "Character and Ethical Theory," *Midwest Studies in Philosophy* 13 (Minneapolis: University of Minnesota Press, 1989).

9. Confucius outlines stages of character development: doing what is right comes naturally only when a person has reached full maturity (at age 70). *Confucian Analects,* Bk. II, Ch. IV, in *The Four Books,* James Legge, trans. (Taipei: Wen Yu Shu Tien, 1955). See Kupperman, "Character and Education"; and Kupperman, "Confucius and the Problem of Naturalness," *Philosophy East and West* 18 (1968).

10. Kupperman, "Character and Education." See also R. M. Hare, *Moral Thinking* (New York: Oxford University Press, 1981). Professor Hare has developed an ethical theory that acknowledges the importance of both models and describes the spheres within which they properly apply.

11. I argue that a theory of virtue must occupy a primary position in a moral theory: it cannot be derived from a theory of right action. See my "Utilitarianism and the Goodness of Persons," in Leroy Rouner, ed., *Foundations of Morality* (Notre Dame: Notre Dame Press, 1983), p. 101.

12. See for example, discussion of the virtuous person's power to transform others. Confucius, *The Doctrine of the Mean*, Chs. XXII-XXIII, in *The Four Books*.

13. *Confucian Analects*, Bk. II, Ch. IV, in *The Four Books*.

14. *Nichomachean Ethics*, Bk. II.4, in Jonathan Barnes, ed., *The Complete Works of Aristotle*, Vol. II, rev. Oxford translation (Princeton: Princeton University Press, 1984), pp. 1745–46.

15. George Eliot, *Middlemarch* (Penguin English Library Edition, 1965), p. 178.

16. Ibid.

17. Stanley Milgram, *Obedience to Authority: An Experimental View* (New York: Harper & Row, 1974).

18. Kupperman, in "Character and Education," notes that self-knowledge is useful in monitoring our own conduct and character. Self-assessment is central to integrity in the view of Gabrielle Taylor, author of *Pride, Shame, and Guilt* (Oxford: Clarendon Press, 1985).

19. Compare Ross's prima facie duties (honesty, promise-keeping, justice, non-maleficence, beneficience, gratitude, reparation, self-improvement); Hart's fundamental rules for social life (restrictions on the free use of violence, theft, and deception); Wallace's forms of conscientiousness (honesty, fairness, truthfulness, fidelity to one's word). W. D. Ross, *The Right and the Good* (Oxford: Clarendon Press, 1930), Ch. II; II. L. A. Hart, *The Concept of Law* (Oxford: Clarendon Press, 1961), p. 89; James D. Wallace, *Virtues and Vices* (Ithaca: Cornell University Press, 1978), Ch. IV.

20. The rational egoist, in contrast, must be a hypocrite, one who does not live by the principles she espouses. See Bernard Mayo, "Moral Integrity," in Godfrey Vesey, ed., *Human Values*, Royal Institute of Philosophy Lectures (Atlantic Highlands, NJ: Humanities Press, 1978), p. 27.

21. Gabrielle Taylor emphasizes the association between integrity and acceptance of responsibility for one's self and one's actions. See *Pride, Shame, and Guilt*, pp. 109 ff.

22. Kupperman, in "Character and Education," makes this point.

23. Taylor, *Pride, Shame, and Guilt.*

24. Kupperman, "Character and Education."

25. This is not necessarily so. Some exceptionally strong people manage to maintain their integrity in the most adverse of circumstances. See Bruno Bettelheim's discussion of survival in a concentration camp, quoted in Taylor, *Pride, Shame, and Guilt*, p. 125.

26. One company spokesperson who analyzed his company's hotline calls found a large number of cases had surfaced because no one saw the issue:

the requisite concepts for identifying certain ethical concerns were not part of the mental apparatus of those involved.

27. See R. M. Hare, *Moral Thinking*, p. 38.

28. Some of these rationalizations are discussed in Saul Gellerman's, "Why 'Good' Managers Make Bad Ethical Choices," *Harvard Business Review* (July-August 1986):85.

29. *Confucian Analects*, Book XII, Ch. XVI, in *The Four Books*, trans. by James Legge. Compare the translation by William Edward Soothill: "The man of noble mind seeks to perfect the good in others and not their evil. The little-minded man is the reverse of this." *The Analects of Confucius*, 2d ed., (Shansi, China, 1910), reprinted by Paragon Book Reprint Corp., 1968.

30. See, for example, Report of the National Commission on Fraudulent Financial Reporting (the Treadway Commission Report), Washington, DC (October, 1987), pp. 1–27, 97–98, 154–63.

# II

# CORPORATE LEADERSHIP

Kenneth Goodpaster gives his attention to the challenge that faces both corporate leaders and ethicists. He sees the definition of the "normative core" of ethics as being effected by business persons in their corporations and by ethicists in academia. This "normative core" is what unites the analytical and empirical work of ethicists to a "shared perception" of values held by corporate leaders and their employees.

In Part I of his presentation, Goodpaster analyzes an affliction that has caused a decline in the "moral point-of-view," namely, "teleopathy," an unbalanced pursuit of goals under a limited range of purposes. A type of end-gaming that overlooks the long-run consequences of acts, teleopathy has plagued modern society for some time, finding its way into the professional lives of public servants as well as businesspersons. Careerism, moral schizophrenia, and organizational or functional rationality are terms that amplify this notion of a short-term approach to decision making.

In describing four ways of thinking through ethical dilemmas and arriving at a decision to act, Goodpaster separates out the assumptions inherent in decision-making habits. These assumptions reflect a choice as to what one considers authoritative in moral decision making, whether that is law or conscience, an ideal or a virtue. He argues that actors arrange their rationale around these choices and assumptions.

In Part II of his presentation, Goodpaster proposes a moral agenda for corporate leadership. Such an agenda would serve to orient the company's shared values, to discover what those values are, and to modify those values as needed. A moral agenda for leadership would institutionalize the desired values in order to bring home the primacy of those values to all employees, and it would serve to sustain values through time by passing them along to successive administrations.

The remarks by Daniel R. Gilbert, Jr., on Goodpaster's lecture center on the notion of respect for persons. Gilbert maintains that conventional management theory frustrates "the autonomous pursuit of an ethical life." Whether Goodpaster's recommendations for combatting teleopathy are based on respect for persons is the question Gilbert addresses.

Goodpaster describes three stages of the executives' inculcation of ethical standards in the corporation: (1) modeling the desired behavior; (2) setting up controls to monitor behavior; and, (3) providing incentives for the imitation of the desired behavior. Gilbert maintains that this top-down delivery of standards from management to employees does not reflect a respect for the individual's values because it does not insure an employee the right to express those values. Although Goodpaster's recommendation that the corporation take "soundings" of its employees to see what the company's values are felt to be, the views of employees will not further be taken into consideration in order to set or change policy. Gilbert argues that the prevalent view of corporation sees a company's values as a collective entity rather than a group of individual entities.

Robbin Derry analyzes Goodpaster's account of the institutionalization of ethical motivation, by examining debate over the question: "Why be moral?" She describes the issue as being based on the assumption that human nature is primarily selfish and any attempt to influence to actions of persons must employ the individual's own self-interest in order to be persuasive. Organizations base their incentive and reward schemes upon this belief that self-interest motivates its employees. Derry argues that such an account is based upon an implicit model of the employee as ambitious, competitive, primarily interested in personal gain, and male.

Derry proposes that "dynamic self-interest" be taken as a premiss for the development of a theory of motivation. She defines it as containing two features that distinguish it from simple and enlightened self-interest, namely, that it is based on a broader concept of the self, and that it does not assume that self-interest is the primary motivator of persons. Dynamic self-interest takes into consideration the motive for creating benefits for others as part of human nature.

# 6

# Ethical Imperatives and Corporate Leadership

## Kenneth E. Goodpaster

To improve our understanding of the emerging field of business ethics is no small task, given the explosion of interest in the subject during the past decade. Voices are entering the conversation from virtually every quarter of the academy, the business world, and the media.

This new level of attention is a valuable precondition to positive intellectual and social change and to improved practice. Consider the following developments:

1. Business schools are reaching both outward and inward to address the moral dimensions of their educational mission.
2. Students of business are demonstrating increasing concern about ethical values as they prepare for professional business careers.
3. Corporate leaders and executives are reflecting more than ever before on the ethical aspects of business life.
4. Philosophers and other scholars in the humanities are widening their commitment to constructive social and institutional criticism.
5. The media are expanding the public's understanding of both the conceptual and practical implications of ethical criticism.

This is the good news, as I see it. The not-so-good news is our limited knowledge and our limited focus. With respect to knowledge, we have only begun to appreciate the complexities involved in the application of moral categories to contemporary business life. While the data base has expanded, the knowledge base, in the form of imaginative, coordinated teaching and research programs, has not kept pace. The disciplinary barriers are still strong, making it difficult for academics to communicate with one another, let alone with practitioners.

With respect to focus, there is resistance from those who fear that the new field of business ethics is somehow economically, politically, or educationally subversive. It is variously seen as amateurish, unrealistic, and unteachable. Skeptics damn it when it displays no bottom line, and other critics damn it when it does. This is the state of our art.

In this chapter, I will sketch out some ideas and aspirations about the next act in this unfolding drama. We have developed many of the conceptual tools, and a fair amount of the educational and professional access needed to use them. A period of consolidation is needed, along with cooperative research between disciplines, as business ethics finds its way into professional education and corporate policy. To clarify this suggestion, I offer some reflections on what I take to be the *normative core* of the emerging field of business ethics. If we can connect our analytical and empirical efforts to a shared perception, we will minimize the risk of a Tower of Babel.

In Part I of this presentation, the subject is the common ethical challenge faced by both the business professional (as an individual) *and* the business organization. I will argue that meeting this challenge defines the normative core of business ethics. The task of addressing the challenge in theory lies principally with the academy. The task of addressing it in practice lies principally with corporate leadership.

In Part II I will elicit from the normative core a three-part "moral agenda" for corporate leadership: orienting, institutionalizing, and sustaining shared ethical values. Theoretical and practical reflection on the full implications of this agenda, in my opinion, can provide a touchstone for future teaching and research in business ethics.

## I. THE NORMATIVE CORE

> The claims of morality, as they operate in human life, present on the face of it a very different appearance from the claims of policy or purpose. They come as a recognized obligation to do or not to do, which is often seen to involve the temporary surrender or restriction of a desire in itself innocent, of a perfectly legitimate purpose. All serious moralists have had to recognize this very obvious and familiar contrast.
>
> J. L. STOCKS, 1930

When reflective observers from a striking variety of backgrounds (including psychoanalysis, medicine, law, political and moral philosophy, business administration, and corporate leadership) appear to circle around an idea that has relevance to the field of business ethics, one must take notice and think it through. Let us do just that to introduce and make useful what I am calling the normative core.

### Five Windows on the Core

Fourteen years ago, in an insightful but disturbing book titled *The Gamesman,* psychoanalyst Michael Maccoby described what he called "careerism" as an emotionally self-destructive affliction of many successful executives:

> Obsessed with winning, the gamesman views all of his actions in terms of whether they will help him succeed in his career. The individual's sense of identity, integrity, and self-determination is lost as he treats himself as an object whose worth is determined by its fluctuating market value. Careerism demands [emotional] detachment.[1]

Maccoby's belief was that such emotional detachment corroded integrity—that it led to disintegration of character because it did not allow for a proper balance between what he referred to as traits of the "head" (e.g., initiative, cooperativeness, flexibility, coolness under stress) in contrast to traits of the "heart" (e.g., honesty, friendliness, compassion, generosity, idealism).

The problem, in his view, was that management needed qualities of the heart fully as much as qualities of the head—but modern corporations tended to reinforce careerism instead. Companies (and other institutions) often systematically select against the wholeness needed for managers and leaders, Maccoby argued. Most executives writing to *Fortune* magazine in 1977, after the initial publication of these ideas, confirmed Maccoby's diagnosis. Recent events do not suggest that the problem has disappeared.

Maccoby, drawing on the work of Eric Fromm, identified a central psychological risk of business life. But when we look closely at the traits or virtues to which he paid attention in his study (traits of "head" and "heart"), I think we can see that this psychological view harbors at its core an *ethical* view. For it is the moral integrity as well as the mental health of business professionals that is behind the scenes in Maccoby's study. The question his work posed was whether the moral point of view was systematically "selected against" in the context of modern business life in large organizations.

In a series of *New Yorker* articles that appeared about the same time as Maccoby's work, political theorist and philosopher Hannah Arendt wrote about the "banality of evil," the utter thoughtlessness of wrongdoing, in contrast to our often dramatic preconceptions.

The context of Arendt's remarks was her observation of the mindset of Adolf Eichmann during his trial in Jerusalem in the early sixties:

> The question that imposed itself was, could the activity of thinking as such, the habit of examining whatever happens to come to pass or to attract attention, regardless of the results and the specific content of the activity—could this activity be among the conditions that make men abstain from evildoing, or even actually "condition" them against it? The very word "con-science," at any rate, points in that direction, insofar as it means "to know with and by myself," a kind of knowledge that is actualized in every thinking process.

Ardent's idea—that evil resides in a kind of thoughtlessness—is not only compatible with, but reinforces, Maccoby's reflections on head and heart. Both see integrity as demanding balance and participation by the whole person in decisions and actions.

Arendt and Maccoby each help us to understand the meaning of psychological and moral integrity. It is a kind of wholeness or balance that refuses to truncate or close off both thoughtfulness and the qualities of the heart—that refuses to anesthetize our humanity in the face of what can sometimes be strong temptations to do so, as when people's lives are affected by business decisions in adverse ways. To quote Arendt again:

> Cliches, stock phrases, adherence to conventional, standardized codes of expression and conduct have the socially recognized function of protecting us against reality; that is, against the claim on our thinking attention which all events and facts make by virtue of their existence.[2]

Also in the late seventies, an essay written several years earlier by philosopher John Ladd began to attract the attention of scholars in business ethics. Ladd described corporations (and formal organizations generally) as rationality-driven machines in which

> the interests and needs of the individuals concerned, as individuals, must be considered only insofar as they establish limiting operating conditions. Organizational rationality dictates that these interests and needs must not be considered in their own right or on their own merits. If we think of an organization as a machine, it is easy to see why we cannot reasonably expect it to have any moral obligations to people or for them to have any to it.[3]

Later in the same essay, Ladd described the consequence for the decision maker as "moral schizophrenia." His argument, in my opinion, went too far by grounding substantive moral criticism on logic alone, implying that amorality in business settings was *a matter of necessity* rather than a matter of observation. But the value of Ladd's insight should not be minimized. He was identifying a malaise that had deep linkages to the perspectives of Maccoby and Arendt. He too provided a window on the normative core.[4]

More recently, against the backdrop of these thoughts of the seventies, Saul Gellerman, dean of the University of Dallas Graduate School of Management, wrote a perceptive article in the *Harvard Business Review* entitled "How 'Good' Managers Make Bad Ethical Choices." Gellerman suggested the phenomenon of "rationalization" as a key to understanding the principal source of unethical conduct in business. Focusing on a number of well-publicized cases (Manville, Continental Illinois Bank, and E. F. Hutton), Gellerman wrote:

> In my view, the explanations go back to four rationalizations that people have relied on through the ages to justify questionable conduct: believing that the activity is not "really" illegal or immoral; that it is in the individual's or the corporation's best interest; that it will never be found out; or that because it helps the company, the company will condone it.[5]

Granting that executives have "a right to expect loyalty from employees against competitors and detractors," Gellerman immediately added "but not loyalty against the law, or against common morality, or against society itself."

In 1982, the *Harvard Business Review* established an award "for the best original article written by a corporate manager" that would "inform and expand executives' consideration of ethical problems in business." Our fifth and final window on the normative core comes from the first winner of this award, an essay entitled "The Parable of the Sadhu."

The article was an autobiographical reflection by Bowen H. McCoy, managing director of Morgan Stanley and Company. It describes a mountain-climbing experience in which a group of climbers, intent on reaching the summit, faced a painful decision. At 18,000 feet in the Himalayas, they came upon an Indian holy man, a sadhu, who had somehow gotten lost and was in danger of dying from exposure. The group had to decide whether to take the sadhu to safety or to continue toward the summit. Time and circumstances did not permit both. McCoy described the rationalization and eventual continuation toward the summit and then added:

> I felt and continue to feel guilt about the sadhu. I had literally walked through a classic moral dilemma without fully thinking through the consequences. My excuses for my actions include a high adrenaline flow, a superordinate goal, and a once-in-a-lifetime opportunity—factors in the usual corporate situation, especially when one is under stress.[6]

McCoy applied the parable to individual managers as well as to corporations. He saw in his mountain-climbing experience a symptom and a symbol of an ethical problem in contemporary business life:

> Organizations that do not have a heritage of mutually accepted, shared values tend to become unhinged during stress, with each individual bailing out for himself. In the great takeover battles we have witnessed during past years, companies that had strong cultures drew the wagons around them and fought it out, while other companies saw executives supported by their golden parachutes, bail out of the struggles. . . . Because corporations and their members are interdependent, for the corporation to be strong the members need to share a preconceived notion of what is correct behavior, a "business ethic," and think of it as a positive force, not a constraint.

The phenomena that Maccoby, Arendt, Ladd, Gellerman, and McCoy are attending to (detachment, thoughtlessness, moral schizophrenia, rationalization, singleness of group purpose) display a recurrent pattern. It is striking enough to be given a label and to serve as a paradigm, not only in our thinking about individuals in a *corporate* environment but also about corporations in *their* environment.

### Teleopathy

We can see through these five "windows" an all-too-frequent modern malaise. It is not a sickness that appears in medical or psychiatric texts. Nor does it appear in the manuals of twentieth century moral philosophy, preoccupied as these have been with conceptual analysis in contrast to normative ethics. Nor again is it part of most discussions in the literature of management studies or business administration.

I shall refer to the malaise or problem at the normative core as *teleopathy,* combining Greek roots for "goal or purpose" and "disease or sickness." If there were manuals for character disorders in ethics as there are for physical and emotional disorders in medicine, I submit that teleopathy would be a candidate as central in its manual as heart disease and depression are, respectively, in theirs.

For philosophers, teleopathy can be understood as a habit of character that values limited purposes as supremely action-guiding, to the relative exclusion not only of larger ends, but also moral considerations about means, obligations, and duties. It is the unbalanced pursuit of goals or purposes by an individual or group.

Teleopathy in its most abstract form is a suspension of "on-line" moral judgment as a practical force in the life of an individual or group. It substitutes for the call of conscience the call of decision criteria from other sources: winning the game, achieving the goal, following the rules laid down by some framework external to ethical reflection. These other sources generally have to do with self-interest, peer acceptance, group loyalty, and institutional objectives that themselves may have broad social justification.

Teleopathy is not so much a theory as it is a *condition*. And while we might be inclined to assume that it is a rare condition, I suggest that it is not only common, but even encouraged by the professional climate and culture of modern life. In the business environment, it is evidently widespread. Indeed, it is hard to look at the record of the past decade, including as it does insider trading, industrial espionage, falsifying labor figures on government contracts, ignoring plant safety, deceptive marketing, and insensitivity to employee rights, without a growing recognition that the "bracketing" of moral reflection, both at the level of the individual and at the level of the organized group, is a key part of the explanation.

This is not to say that teleopathy always takes the form of unethical business behavior. But in the vicinity of most unethical business behavior (individual or corporate), we are likely to find teleopathy in one or another of its forms.[7]

Whatever may be the philosophical outcome of the debate over "the moral status of corporations," if we can agree that the normative core of business ethics is similar whether the unit of analysis is the individual in the corporate context or the corporation in the wider social context, we are taking a step forward. I am suggesting that an appreciation of the phenomenon of teleopathy—overemphasis on limited purposes by individuals and corporations—illuminates a fundamental unity in the multileveled and complex field of business ethics.[8]

Moreover, if I am right, this account of the normative core helps to explain why the problems of business ethics *in practice* are so persistent. For, as with their virtues, the pathologies of individuals are both transmitted *to* organizations and reinforced *by* them through the self-perpetuating dynamics of career progression, leadership, management discipline, and corporate culture.

If we add to this organizational dynamic the competitive pressures on the integrity of firms, it is not hard to see how the prospect of reducing teleopathy in the business system can seem overwhelming.

### In Search of Type 3 Management

In order to clarify further the meaning of teleopathy, let me briefly describe four ways of thinking about ethics in business that may prove useful.[9]

*Type 1 thinking: Ethics as a guide to self-interest.* We can imagine an individual holding that his basic value is to look out for himself in a rational way, and that one way of doing so is to be respectful of other persons most of the time. I will refer to this as type 1 thinking. Organizations might exhibit a similar mindset. The belief would be that respecting others, like honesty, is usually "the best policy."

Type 1 thinking is present wherever ethical values are managed solely with an eye to rational self-interest as the overarching value. It is important to emphasize, however, that this need not mean *ignoring* others in the ordinary sense of that phrase. Some interpretations of "issues management" and "public relations," for example, seem to fit the type 1 pattern because of the purely self-interested principles behind them, even though they appear on the surface to involve independent concern for others.

*Type 2 thinking: Ethics as a systemic constraint.* This type of thinking incorporates ethical norms not through the logic of self-interest but through systemic constraints on the choice of business goals. There are two distinct subtypes. The first looks primarily to market forces as surrogates for morality; the second to political and legal forces.[10]

*The invisible hand pattern (type 2a).* Some accord importance to ethical norms in business decision making but quickly add that they are already built into the competitive system. This makes special management attention to ethics redundant. It is what we shall call, remembering Adam Smith, the invisible hand pattern. Nobel laureate Milton Friedman often seems to endorse this way of thinking. The suggestion is that whatever ethical values the business system needs are already programmed in, making supplementary efforts foolish, even morally suspect.

*The hand-of-the-law pattern (type 2b).* This type of thinking relies on non-economic forces outside the organization to secure the value of, say, environmental protection without direct managerial involvement (a more "visible" than "invisible" hand). Externalizing moral judgment in this way does not mean simply subordinating ethics (as a means) to self-interest. But it does mean placing responsibility for moral judgment outside the manager's principal (economic) concerns. We might say that type 2b leaders acknowledge authority, but not accountability, when it comes to ethical values.

*Type 3: Ethics as an authoritative guide.* According to this type of thinking, securing respect for others by the invisible hand—and even by more visible hands external to the marketplace, such as government, labor, and the media—is insufficient. Corporate self-interest is not ignored, and neither are competition and the law, but respect for the rights and concerns of affected parties is given independent force in the leader's operating consciousness. Type 3 thinking not only refuses to see ethics as merely a means, it also rejects surrogates for conscience in the form of systemic constraints. Managerial accountability for ethics goes hand in hand with a recognition of its authority.

If we reflect upon the typology just presented, we can see that only type 3 thinking captures the full meaning of both individual and corporate conscience. For while it is true that the other types espouse ethical values in one way or another, only type 3 embraces moral obligations *directly.* The others do so *conditionally:* in the case of type 1, subject to self-interest; and in the case of types 2a and 2b, subject to institutional structures or systems (the market and the law), which themselves require ethical vigilance both in principle and in operation.

It is with type 3 thinking that the *balanced* pursuit of purpose gets a normative foothold through what scholars in ethics have called the moral point of view.[11] The full discipline implied by the moral point of view is not part of the definition of type 3 thinking, but a basic principle of respect for the freedom and welfare of human beings is certainly at the center.

Worries about ethical relativism in connection with type 3 thinking are natural, of course, and deserve patient attention from both philosophers and managers, especially in the context of multinational business operations. In this paper, however, I will simply state baldly that these concerns are not insuperable. The moral point of view is not a monolith, but it is a practical perspective that takes all human beings seriously. It seems reasonable to expect that the balance implicit in avoiding teleopathy is also a balance that can tell good judgment from intolerance and dogmatism. In the words of philosopher Mary Midgley:

> Moral judgment is not a luxury, not a perverse indulgence of the self-righteous. It is a necessity. . . . Morally as well as physically, there is only one world, and we all have to live in it.[12]

In summary, there are four principal ways in which ethical values are acknowledged in the business mindset. Each can *espouse* values like honesty, concern for others, and fidelity to contracts. But each connects these values to business decision making using a different logic. Figure 6–1 shows the typology in the form of a matrix. Type 1, like type 3, is an internal or actor-centered action guide, while types 2a and 2b are external or system-centered action-guides.

To embrace, consciously or not, either type 1 or type 2 thinking

```
                                E
                                X
                                T
        Type 2a:                E                Type 2b:
                                R
       Market Ethic             N                Law Ethic
                                A
                                L

     C O M P E T I T I V E              C O O P E R A T I V E

                                I
        Type 1:                 N                 Type 3:
                                T
    Self-interested             E                Ethic of
     Rationality                R                Respect
                                N
                                A
                                L
```

**Figure 6–1.** Depiction of the typology in a $2 \times 2$ matrix

as against type 3, I believe, sets the stage for either individual or corporate teleopathy. For it suspends the balancing role of direct moral reflection in management in favor of constrained or unconstrained purposes.

In each of Gellerman's explanations of recent corporate scandals, we can see either type 1 or type 2 thinking. Teleopathy is at the core of each rationalization, along with echoes of Maccoby's notion of careerism, Arendt's talk about thoughtlessness, Ladd's remarks about organizational rationality, and McCoy's concern about the sadhu left behind on the mountain.

It is also important to observe that *all four* of the patterns in the typology can recognize the conventional notion of stakeholders or "constituencies" in the business environment: government, consumers, suppliers, shareholders, employees, etc. The difference lies in the *kind* of attention that each gives to them. Type 1 thinking can see attention to stakeholders as attention to factors that might affect self-interest. Type 2a thinking can regard stakeholders as so many markets within which companies must operate for profit. Concern for each is seen as built into the market system. Type 2b thinking can regard stakeholders as non-market checks on market reasoning: sociopolitical limits on the exercise of economic rationality. Only type 3 thinking views stakeholders apart from their instrumental, economic, or political clout. It refuses to see them merely as what Ladd called "limiting operating conditions" on management attention.

One must conclude, I think, that the notion of a "stakeholder" (originally a play on the word "stockholder") is not, by itself, at the normative core of business ethics—at least not if we accept an interpretation of that core in terms of personal and organizational teleopathy. An examination of the four types of thinking suggests that, while all four can accommodate the stakeholder idea, only one type (type 3) embraces the moral point of view as an authoritative guide.

If the perspective I have outlined (Part I) is on track, then what are some of the challenges it presents to the field of business ethics? I believe we can discern several, under two broad headings:

A. Gaining a philosophical understanding of type 3 leadership
   • Can we reach a reasonable consensus on a set of moral virtues and prima facie obligations that represent the minimal output of type 3 thinking?
   • Can we interpret the fiduciary and other role-related obligations of corporate leadership (e.g., to employees and consumers) in terms of the balance of purpose required by type 3 thinking?
B. Gaining an administrative understanding of type 3 leadership
   • Can we offer practical suggestions and techniques for making this vision part of the corporate leadership agenda?
   • Can we relate type 3 virtues and obligations to the conventional functional areas of business administration (marketing, finance, accounting, production, human resource management, strategic planning, etc.)?

Part II of this paper will focus on the second pair of questions, out of a conviction that unless our philosophical conception of a "normative ethic" is tied to the administrative point of view, it is profoundly incomplete.[13] But I will touch on the first pair of questions before concluding Part II, as some paradoxes emerge. It is through the dynamics of leadership that persons influence organizations and organizations affect society. In the heart and mind of the corporate leader, principle touches practice.

If there is a new openness among both business leaders and the general public to the idea of independent moral judgment guiding business conduct (and there is evidence for this in courts, boardrooms, academic studies, and public opinion research), then we need to improve our understanding of the full implications of making type 3 thinking part of the very definition of leadership.

## II. THREE IMPERATIVES FOR CORPORATE LEADERSHIP

Why were we so reluctant to try the lower path, the ambiguous trail? Perhaps because we did not have a leader who could reveal the greater purpose of the trip to us. For each of us the sadhu

lives. What is the nature of our responsibility if we consider ourselves to be ethical persons? Perhaps it is to change the values of
the group so that it can, with all its resources, take the other
road.

BOWEN MCCOY

A fundamental goal of the study of business ethics is to interpret the
leadership implications of balancing the pursuit of purpose—what
we have called type 3 thinking. The more conventional value of organizational rationality often profoundly narrows the vision of corporate leaders. Adding respect to rationality can be seen from the
leader's point of view as introducing *conscience* into the corporate
mindset, inasmuch as conscience balances a person's pursuit of purpose with a recognition of moral obligations to those who are affected.

We can organize the leader's moral agenda under three broad imperatives—orienting, institutionalizing, and sustaining corporate values. The first two have to do with placing moral considerations in a
position of authority alongside considerations of profitability and
competitive strategy in the corporate mindset. The third imperative
(sustenance) has to do with passing on the spirit of this effort in two
directions: to future leaders of the organization and to the wider
network of organizations and institutions that make up the social
system as a whole. In the sections that follow, I will try to clarify
each of the imperatives and then identify some of the ways in which
they invite deeper reflection and research from students and practitioners of business ethics.

### Orienting

Leaders must first identify and then, where needed, attempt to modify their organization's shared values. Such a prescription cannot be
followed without first performing a kind of moral inventory. What
is needed is a sounding process sophisticated enough to get behind
the natural cautions, defenses, and espoused values of subordinates.
The leader must listen to and understand his or her organization in
ways that reach its character strengths and defects. Such a process is
relatively easy in a small organization because behavior is observable
daily and communication is direct. But in a large divisionalized and
diversified corporation, the task is much more complex, almost different in kind.

The objective is to discern the dominant ethical values of the company. Survey and questionnaire instruments may provide an initial
scan. Such scans are only a first pass, however, More qualitative, clin-
ical methods are needed to identify moral victories, defeats, and di-

lemmas that operating managers experience as they do their work and pursue their careers in the organization. In what circumstances are they willing to follow conscience, even when it might be economically costly? In what circumstances is there a tendency toward teleopathy, toward putting results ahead of ethical concerns when conflicts occur? Are there company policies or practices that have unintended negative ethical implications?[14]

In a divisionalized or diversified firm, are there some business units that tend to have more problems than others? Can we tell why—and whether shared experiences and processes might help? Are there problems relating to international business operations that are more (or less) difficult than in domestic operations? Selective sounding out of outside parties is also important: suppliers, customers, regulators, neighbors, creditors, shareholders. Exit interviews with departing employees can also provide helpful insight into company values.

The result of such sounding efforts will be an inventory of attributions, issues, responses, and concerns that can serve as a preliminary map for leadership initiatives.[15] Is this a type 3 organization? If not, how and where could policies and practices be changed to improve ethical awareness? What can and should be done (and where) in terms of management development? Can the company create its own set of case studies for management education that emerges from the ethical sounding? If a corporate code or credo would be helpful, what should it contain in order to make contact with the strengths and weaknesses that the sounding has uncovered?

In one large manufacturing company that I studied, the sounding was minimal and the resulting ethical communications to employees from senior management were regarded as Sunday School sermons. Little contact was made with the organizational mindset in its operational reality. The leader wanted to orient corporate conscience, but never really located it to begin with. "Getting there from here" is wishful thinking when "here" is a mystery.

In another company, a multinational service firm, the commitment to a sounding was much more in evidence. In an initial workshop session with office managers from around the world, strengths were identified in certain client relationships; policies were identified that enabled managers to avoid conflicts of interest; practices were highlighted that insured great attention to the accuracy of company reports. Weaknesses were acknowledged in specific personnel practices that seemed unfair and discriminatory.

The CEO did not stop there, however. Plans have been laid to focus the sounding at lower levels and horizontally by type of service rather than just geographical location. The Board of Directors then intends to articulate a statement of values and to take steps—as yet undetermined—toward institutionalizing and sustaining the strengths and eliminating or reducing the weaknesses that are meaningful to managers and staff throughout the company.

When orienting values is approached in this way, the sounding can be a device, not only for gathering information, but for raising awareness and tracking future ethical problems and issues. It can actually become part of the institutionalization process.

### Institutionalizing

Once corporate leadership has identified characteristic values and value conflicts—and has clarified the direction it wants to take in whole or in part—the process of institutionalization becomes paramount. How can these values be made part of the operating consciousness of the company? How can they gain the attention and the allegiance of middle management and other employees? The answers lie in three areas: decisive *actions,* a statement of *standards* with regular *audits,* and appropriate *incentives.*

*Actions.* Since "actions speak louder than words," a major factor in the process of institutionalizing corporate values is leadership activity that has both wide visibility and clear ethical content. Such actions serve as large-scale demonstrations to the rank and file of the seriousness and importance that senior management attaches to ethical values.

It is hard to overstate, for example, the significance of James Burke's decisiveness in his handling of the Tylenol poisonings. It sent a powerful message to employees and customers alike regarding the operating values of Johnson and Johnson.

Another example comes from a case study of the Duke Power Company. In 1974, when Bill Lee was faced with a layoff involving 1,500 construction workers, he had to decide between inverse seniority as a criterion and some mechanism that would permit the retention of many recently employed minorities. The company's affirmative action gains were at stake at a point in its history when past injustices could not be ignored. Lee's conviction led him to protect minorities with less seniority and to face criticisms of reverse discrimination.

In 1980, there was another contraction of the company's work force. Because of Lee's courage in 1974, affirmative action gains were not at stake. Lee shared the following reflections on the importance of his original decision for institutionalizing the core value of racial justice:

Having bit the bullet in 1974, and being careful in subsequent restaffing, in 1980 we were able to lay off in inverse seniority without affecting minority percentage employment. The 1974 experience gave a positive signal throughout all departments of the Company that we really care about affirmative action. I believe this helped set the stage of acceptance of upward mobility for minorities and females as one of our published corporate performance goals. Achievement of these goals would result in some financial reward to all employees at every level. It receives wide publicity and monthly progress reports to all employees.[16]

The institutionalization of ethical values depends first and foremost on leadership conviction expressed in action. But there is more to the story than this. For while highly visible examples of values in action give energy to the process, employees need to learn how less visible, but equally important, ethical decisions fall within their own spans of control.

*Standards and audits.* Every company will, because of its special history, industry, and culture, address ethical values somewhat differently. Nevertheless, certain elements will be common to the process of institutionalization in any firm. A statement of standards along with a monitoring process is one of these common elements.

In 1976, Jack Judington, CEO of Dow Corning Corporation, asked four senior corporate managers to serve as a Business Conduct Committee (BCC), reporting to the Audit and Social Responsibility Committee of the Board of Directors. The BCC was charged with developing guidelines that would help to communicate ethical standards to company sites around the world and a workable process for monitoring, reporting, and improving business practices. Once a corporate code was drafted, "it was sent to area managers with instructions that they develop their own codes, paying particular attention to their unique concerns. The only constraint was that area codes not conflict with the corporate code."

Ludington thus did an informal scan or "sounding" of top managers and key outside sources as he identified corporate values. He even involved line management further by asking for area-specific codes consistent with the (more general) corporate code. But he did not stop there.

The code of business conduct was reviewed every two or three years, with an eye to improving its coverage of issues that either corporate or area management thought important. The principal vehicle for this process was a series of regular "Business Conduct Audits" that senior corporate managers undertook on a rotating basis at company offices worldwide.

Area managers were asked to prepare for the audits by using a set of "work sheets" that encouraged concreteness and detail regarding each of the topics raised by the code of conduct. In effect, "cases" were being reported in real time for review by the BCC. Particularly serious issues that emerged from these sessions—issues like questionable payments and abuse of proprietary information—were presented for discussion by the BCC annually to the Audit and Social Responsibility Committee of the Board.

In this way, corporate leadership informed both itself and the relevant employees of the specific nature and extent of the company's ethical concerns. Regularly those concerns involved what I have called teleopathy: How will we let competitive pressure lead us in this kind of situation? What about our "technically legal" practices in that situation? Two-way communication made the implications of the code of business conduct quite concrete. There was, in other words, an attempt at a thoughtful balancing of purpose.[17]

*Incentives.* Are actions at the top and audits throughout the organization enough? No, they are not. Kenneth Andrews emphasizes the impotence of even the strongest convictions when they are not tied to structural and cultural incentives:

> It is quite possible . . . and indeed quite usual, for a highly moral and humane chief executive to preside over an "amoral organization"—one made so by processes developed before the liberalization of traditional corporate economic objectives. The internal force which stubbornly resists efforts to make the corporation compassionate (and exacting) toward its own people and responsible (as well as economically efficient) in its external relationships is the incentive system forcing attention to short-term quantifiable results.[18]

Without a willingness to reward performance based on contributions to the "quality" as much as the quantity of profits, the audit process will accomplish very little. It will not do to encourage ethical behavior simply by denying promotions or bonuses to those who cut moral corners. Removing disincentives to ethical behavior may be as important as, if not more important than, instituting positive rewards and punishments.

I have characterized the ethical challenge to corporate leadership as involving three imperatives—orienting, institutionalizing, and sustaining shared ethical values. Since the efforts of even the best leaders to act on the first two of these imperatives are subject to a kind of winding down, we must say a word about sustaining corporate values over time.

### Sustaining

To sustain type 3 values is to communicate them to the next generation of managers as well as to the wider social system. The objective is what Chester Barnard referred to as "fit"—between the mindset of the organization and the mindsets of both its future leaders ("microfits") and its various communities ("macrofits"). Without some degree of ethical fit or congruence, the corporate mindset simply cannot survive or replicate itself.

Microfits involve such issues as management selection and development, executive succession, and even (in the case of large corporations) acquisition and divestiture of business units. Macrofits involve public communication, government relations, and international business activities.

*Microfits.* I am aware of one chief executive of a *Fortune* "100" company who approaches the challenge of sustaining corporate values with great care and self-awareness. Not only does he monitor personally and regularly the progress of 75 key managers in his corporation, he does so with explicit attention to the congruence between their beliefs and attitudes and the overall corporate values system. In one case, an otherwise very strong executive who was considered in line to be CEO was asked to resign for reasons related directly to his cynicism about the company's stated philosophy of human values. It should be added that this decision was made with the full understanding, counsel, and support of the board of directors.

Another chief executive officer has worked with his board of directors in developing a set of criteria for appraising the character traits and qualifications of candidates for leadership roles in the corporation. The criteria include not only experience, intelligence, and economic performance but also integrity, maturity, balance, and community service.

*Macrofits.* Stabilizing a corporate mindset pattern also requires a reasonable fit in the direction of the larger network of organizations and institutions that we refer to collectively as "society." Corporate values within the social system, like individual values within the organization, can have influence. But when they do not, and the company becomes part of the problem rather than the solution, there may be no alternative to withdrawal.

Corporate signatories to the Sullivan Principles in South Africa sought to resolve the dilemma of disinvesting entirely or contributing to social injustice. Some companies decided that they could not or would not seek such influence. IBM, however, refused for many years to close down its operations in South Africa, reaffirming a policy of working for social change from within, both independently and through its commitment to the Sullivan Principles. In 1986, IBM sold its subsidiary, but continued to sell products through the newly independent South African company. Other companies have pulled out entirely, believing that their continued business activity there only served to reinforce the status quo. In any case, some considered decision is necessary.

### Three Paradoxes: Research Needed

In the moral domain the leader guides the decision-making patterns of the corporation as a whole in the direction of *Type 3* thinking. Beyond this, the leader must influence persons within the organization as well as the social system outside it toward accommodation or fit with that mindset. In Chester Barnard's words, "the distinguishing mark of executive responsibility" is "not merely conformance to a complex code of morals but also the creation of moral codes for others."[19]

This agenda, however, carries with it a number of serious challenges. Business ethics research is needed, both philosophical and empirical, on each of these fronts. For each of the three imperatives (orienting, institutionalizing, and sustaining ethical values) harbors a kind of paradox. And coming to terms with these paradoxes is what gives substance to the moral agenda of corporate leadership. They can be formulated as follows:

1. *The Paradox of Legitimacy.* It seems essential, yet somehow illegitimate, to *orient* corporate strategy by values that go beyond not only pure self-interest, but also conventional economic and legal frameworks.

Leaders must face the fact that the market and the law seem paradoxically definitive and insufficient for corporate responsibility. How far can the responsible leader go beyond the norms defining legitimacy? Can a solid baseline of reasonable ethical principles be identified for public use, even in our pluralistic society? Can a clear understanding of fiduciary obligations to shareholders be given that relates to them?

2. *The Paradox of Motivation.* It seems essential, yet curiously inappropriate, to seek to *institutionalize* ethical motivation in a company by the use of appeals to simple self-interest.

Commonly used management techniques for strategy implementation—various incentives, rewards, and punishments—may appear somewhat incongruous when ethics is the goal. Most of us wonder about, if we do not recoil from, the idea of a bonus for being good. The leader who is mindful of this will want to approach the task of policy implementation in ethics with a special kind of circumspection. Incentives will be important, but just as important will be example, role modeling, open dialogue, and appeals to deeper motives. Like the first paradox, this challenges our conventional understanding of the role of management.

3. *The Paradox of Paternalism.* It seems essential for *sustaining* a group conscience, yet coercive, to seek to influence the value orientation of others, whether inside the corporation or outside.

Ethical values must be communicated in a way that secures maximum adherence among both management (internally) and society (externally). Yet such a demand may seem dogmatic, contrary to the very spirit of the values it seeks to sustain. Imposing morality on employees and society appears to be both intolerant and inescapable. Resolving this paradox in practice may be one of the chief tests of responsible leadership.

If we reflect on these paradoxes, we can begin to appreciate that the three leadership imperatives will be addressed differently if the shared values of an organization involve type 3 thinking, rather than type 1 or type 2. The process by which leadership orients, institutionalizes, and sustains ethical values must be consistent with the content of those values. The moral point of view must play as central a role in the leadership actions that aim to make ethics a reality, as in the clarification of the reality to be aimed at. The implications of this demand for consistency between moral content and moral process are very important and deserve patient study.[20]

These challenges are real. They account for much of the reluctance of top executives to pursue business ethics beyond rhetoric and rulebooks. They call into question deeply entrenched beliefs about corporate governance, human resource management, and the appropriate use of economic power. But unless leaders can learn to manage them, our business institutions will become increasingly mired in a reactive, externally driven approach to ethical responsibility, or worse.

What is striking about these challenges, in my opinion, is that they call for a variety of skills in their resolution. Clearly each paradox has philosophical dimensions. But just as clearly there are dimensions that call for the methods of psychology, sociology, corporate law, and management studies. They provide a formidable agenda not only to corporate leaders but to those of us who would seek to advance the emerging field of business ethics.

## SUMMARY AND CONCLUSION

In Part I of this paper, I described and defended what I take to be the normative core of business ethics: the avoidance of teleopathy at both the level of the individual and the level of the organization as a whole. More positively, this was interpreted as encouraging type 3 thinking in business settings, emphasizing the difference between this and popular versions of the stakeholder idea.

Then, because the leader was seen to be the key to aligning the values of the individual and the organization, in Part II I suggested three broad imperatives as the moral agenda of corporate leadership. Reflecting on the implications of these imperatives, three corresponding paradoxes were revealed, paradoxes that call for the philosophical and empirical attention of the academy as well as the managerial attention of corporate leaders.

I have not, in this paper, tried to relate either the normative core or the leadership agenda to the subject of professional education. To do so would require much more than a few paragraphs. Suffice it to say here by way of conclusion that the implications are profound. Value-neutral education is a myth and always has been, despite its twentieth century dominance as an espoused theory. Education-in-action inevitably conveys ethical content, by omission or commission. Emory University President James T. Laney put it nicely:

> In many academic disciplines there has been a retreat from the attempt to relate values and wisdom to what is being taught. Not long ago, Bernard Williams, the noted British philosopher, observed that philosophers have been trying all this century to get rid of the dreadful idea that philosophy ought to be edifying. Philosophers are not the only ones to appreciate the force of that statement. . . . How can society survive if education does not attend to those qualities which it requires for its very perpetuation?[21]

As the field of business ethics develops, it is my hope not only that philosophical and empirical research will be aimed more toward the leadership agenda but that the business school agenda will serve as a bridge. For if ethics is not integrated into business education (and I am talking about more than simply the addition of a *course*), the academy runs the risk of encouraging (rather than discouraging) teleopathy in its hidden curriculum. The next generation of leadership, after all, is always in school at any given moment.

## NOTES

1. Michael Maccoby, "The Corporate Climber Has to Find His Heart," *Fortune* (December 1976): 101.

2. Hannah Arendt, "Thinking," *New Yorker,* (November 21, 1977): 65–140; (November 28, 1977):135–216; (December 5, 1977):135–216.

3. John Ladd, "Morality and the Ideal of Rationality in Formal Organizations," *The Monist* (October 1970):507. Ladd's observations are similar to those of Scottish philosopher R. S. Downie, who talked of "the 'pathology' of role-governed action—where the personal and the role elements are in various respects in disunity." See *Roles and Values* (London: Methuen, 1971), p. 145.

4. Richard DeGeorge (1987) points out that Ladd sparked a central line of inquiry in business ethics. See DeGeorge, "The Status of Business Ethics: Past and Future," *Journal of Business Ethics* 6, no. 3 (April 1987):206. Ladd's 1970 essay is reprinted with a 1977 critique by this writer in Donaldson and Werhane, *Ethical Issues in Business* (Englewood Cliffs, NJ: Prentice-Hall, 1983), pp. 125–45. The issue was rejoined in Ladd, "Corporate Mythology and Individual Responsibility" and Goodpaster, "Testing Morality in Organizations," *International Journal of Applied Philosophy* 2, no. 1 (1984).

5. Saul Gellerman, "Why 'Good' Managers Make Bad Ethical Choices," *Harvard Business Review* (July-August 1986): 85–90.

6. Bowen McCoy, "The Parable of the Sadhu," *Harvard Business Review* (September-October 1983): 103–8.

7. We might do well to reflect on the implications of these thoughts in connection with the teaching of business ethics by philosophers. If teleopathy is at the normative core, it should be less surprising (and disorienting) to philosophers that carefully honed distinctions *within* the framework of the moral point of view (e.g., between alternative normative ethical theories) often seem beside the point. It is not that philosophy is irrelevant, but that the relevance is to be found more frequently at the normative core rather than at the normative periphery. See my "Business Ethics, Ideology, and the Naturalistic Fallacy," *Journal of Business Ethics* 4, no. 4 (August 1985).

8. It is this conviction, more than any other, that lies behind what I have called the "Principle of Moral Projection." See Goodpaster and Matthews, "Can a Corporation Have a Conscience?" *Harvard Business Review* (January-February 1982); Goodpaster, "The Concept of Corporate Responsibility," *Journal of Business Ethics* 2, no. 1 (1983) and "The Principle of Moral Projection: A Reply to Professor Ranken," *Journal of Business Ethics* 6, no. 4 (1987).

9. A more detailed account of the typology can be found in Goodpaster, "The Moral Agenda of Corporation Leadership: Concepts and Research Techniques (Proceedings of the MacNaughton Symposium, Syracuse University, 1986), pp. 97–129.

10. For critiques of what I am calling type 2 thinking, see Christopher Stone's *Where the Law Ends: The Social Control of Corporate Behavior* (New York: Harper & Row, 1975) and Thomas Donaldson's *Corporations and Morality* (Englewood Cliffs, NJ: Prentice-Hall, 1982).

11. In the history of moral philosophy, the major systematic attempts to ground the moral point of view (e.g., harmony, the golden mean, natural law, the will of God, universalizability, impartiality, consistency, the ideal observer, and the social contract) can be seen as ways of introducing "balance" (both personal and interpersonal) into the pursuit of human pur-

poses. For an overview of systematic thinking in ethics, see Beauchamp and
Bowie, *Ethical Theory and Business* (Englewood Cliffs, NJ: Prentice-Hall, 1983),
Chapters 1 and 9; also Matthews, Goodpaster, and Nash, *Policies and Persons*
(New York: McGraw-Hill, 1985), Appendix B.

12. Mary Midgley, *Heart and Mind* (New York: St. Martin's Press, 1981),
pp. 72, 75.

13. We must begin to take on what Ed Epstein calls a basic question faced
by corporate management: "How can the leadership of a large complex
business organization best incorporate into their firm's decision-making processes the difficult but essential task of defining (and redefining), evaluating,
and institutionalizing the values which underlie its policies and practices as
well as determine its unique culture?" See Edwin M. Epstein, "The Corporate Social Policy Process," *California Management Review* 29, no. 3 (Spring
1987): 99–114.

14. For a case series that illustrates in detail what such an inventory could
have disclosed (had it been undertaken), see "H. J. Heinz Company: The
Administration of Policy," in Goodpaster, *Ethics in Management* (Harvard
Business School, 1984).

15. More needs to be said here about the structure of the sounding, especially certain standard bases to be touched such as human resource management, marketing practices, financial reporting, control systems, production, management incentives, and strategic planning. Some parts of this
structure will be company- or industry-specific, although a generic map would
seem to be a possible focus of cooperative research in business ethics at this
stage.

16. Letter to author from Bill Lee, September 7, 1983.

17. See "Dow Corning Corporation: Business Conduct and Global Values," *HBS Case Services*, 9-385-018 and 019.

18. Kenneth Andrews, "Can the Best Corporations be Made Moral?"
*Harvard Business Review* (May-June 1973): 57–64.

19. Chester Barnard, *The Functions of the Executive* (Cambridge: Harvard
University Press, 1938), p. 279.

20. See Goodpaster, "The Challenge of Sustaining Corporate Conscience," *Notre Dame Journal of Law, Ethics and Public Policy* 2, no. 4 (1987):
825–48.

21. James T. Laney, "The Education of the Heart," *Harvard Magazine*
(September-October 1985): 23–24.

# 7

# Respect for Persons, Management Theory, and Business Ethics

## Daniel R. Gilbert, Jr.

> And what must it be like, he asked, to work at a place like that?
> TRACY KIDDER, *The Soul of a New Machine*
> New York: Avon, p. 26, 1981.

What do we gain if our understanding of the modern corporation is infused with a sense of *respect for persons?* In "Ethical Imperatives and Corporate Leadership" (hereafter, his presentation), Kenneth Goodpaster provides an answer to this enduring question in the form of a proposition: if respect for persons is placed at the core of our sense of corporate community, then the spread of teleopathy—i.e., a widespread moral disorder—can be checked both within and around the modern corporation.[1]

This proposition is certainly heroic in scope. Such scope reflects, in turn, just how faithfully Goodpaster has crafted a story from some basic premises of management theory. My thesis is that for precisely these reasons the proposition turns on a fundamental contradiction. In particular, I will show that a *disdain for persons* as autonomous agents—i.e., capable of directing and restraining their own actions—marks the "normative core" of Goodpaster's story.[2] Moreover this disdain is a direct consequence of the premises on which Goodpaster depends. Hence, we should not be surprised that his presentation reflects a contradiction: in order to internalize "respect for persons" in our conception of the modern corporation, we must treat persons generally as moral neophytes.[3]

I make this argument in the context of a larger concern. Goodpaster presents a faithful rendition of the kind of story that contem-

111

porary management theory supports. And that is the problem. If the logic behind his presentation marks the state of the art, then the prospects for business ethics research and practice are quite constrained.[4] Thus, my analysis is an invitation to consider more skeptically than is currently fashionable the moral status of conventional management theory. In short, I interpret his presentation as a case example of a larger problem.

I develop my critique in three parts. First, I trace the heritage of Goodpaster's "corporate moral agenda" to certain well-known assumptions from management theory. Second, I ask: what meaning of "respect for persons" is implied by that agenda? Focusing on the three leadership processes that Goodpaster emphasizes, I show how his framework relies on three assumptions that reflect a basic skepticism about persons' capabilities to act as moral agents. As a result, "respect for persons" is effectively reduced to not much more than a slogan. I conclude with an observation that his presentation marks an important crossroad for those interested in the developing business ethics as a useful commentary. We can choose a future limited by the idiosyncracies in conventional management theory, or we can make a serious effort at placing persons at the "normative core" of our stories about the modern corporation.

## TYPE 3 THINKING AND CORPORATE LEADERSHIP PROCESSES

Goodpaster presents a straightforward formula for implanting respect for persons, rather than teleopathy, as the guiding norm for activities at the modern corporation. He urges "corporate leadership"—presumably a small cadre of top-level executives—to adopt a disposition that he calls type 3 thinking, by which:

> Corporate self-interest is not ignored, and neither are competition and the law, but respect for rights and concerns of affected parties is given independent force in the leader's operating consciousness.[5]

Teleopathy can be counteracted, he argues, if these executives embed type 3 thinking in the consciences of all other persons associated with the corporation. To that end, Goodpaster proposes that executives implement three managerial processes; that is, "three ethical imperatives for corporate leadership."[6] This formula—leader's vision enacted through managerial processes—is a classic application of management theory to the problems of business ethics. I will show

how this is true in three respects, as a prelude to considering the ironic consequences.

### The Formula for Counteracting Teleopathy

Goodpaster searches first for the strongest basis by which executives can convince persons to take account of the moral consequences of corporate activities. This search leads to type 3 thinking, which Goodpaster distinguishes from other possible moral dispositions in terms of the standards of self-restraint implicit in each.[7] He claims that respect for persons—the hallmark of type 3—outdistances egoism (type 1), adherence to the "rules" of the competitive marketplace (type 2a), and faithfulness to the law (type 2b) as a basis for a sense of community grounded in "the *balanced* pursuit of purpose."[8]

Goodpaster searches next for the means by which to infuse a corporate context with type 3 reasoning. He urges executives to take a "moral inventory" of the dominant moral disposition at the corporation.[9] In the course of this investigation, termed "orienting," executives talk with employees and other stakeholders to determine how far the corporation's moral climate deviates from the type 3 ideal.[10] Once this measure of corporate climate has been taken, the executive moves to recast the (likely) deficient sense of community into the model of type 3. These efforts mark the "institutionalizing" phase, where executives seeks answers to such questions as:[11] "How can these values be made part of the operating consciousness of the company? How can they gain the attention and allegiance of middle management and other employees?" Once type 3 has been institutionalized, Goodpaster's executives enter the "sustaining" phase. There they act as missionaries who seek "to communicate [type 3 values] to the next generation of managers as well as to the wider social system."[12] In this way, the executives build defenses that solidify the gains against teleopathy in a larger social context.

### The Links to Conventional Management Theory

The footprints of conventional management theory are prominent throughout Goodpaster's presentation, insofar as questions about values are concerned.[13] I am concerned here with three such traces, which I interpret as assumptions central to his formula.

First, Goodpaster assumes that the corporation is both an extension of those persons who have ascended to the executive suite and a reflection of their values. This interpretation is a faithful application of the Harvard Policy Framework developed over time at the Harvard Business School.[14] According to that view, the sense of community that evolves at the firm is a direct consequence of the preferences that executives articulate and model. This is why the orientation phase is so crucial in Goodpaster's framework. For a type 3 corporation to emerge, the executives whose values are to displace teleopathic norms must understand the scope of their challenge. In the classic Harvard tradition, when it comes to values, all eyes are trained on the top-level executives.[15]

Second, his presentation reflects the premise that in order for values such as type 3 to be adopted persons whose values miss the mark must be subjected to external stimuli. According to the canon commonly linked to Herbert Simon and his contemporaries, those stimuli are applied in the form of organizational process.[16] Goodpaster clearly argues in that tradition. It is no accident that the triad of orienting, institutionalizing, and sustaining processes constitute the centerpiece of his corporate leadership framework.[17] He pays homage to this assumption most prominently with his account of the institutionalization phase. Note that the variables in that phase are all applied from "outside" the recalcitrant persons through a set of routines: executives model proper behavior; executives set up control mechanisms; and executives provide others with incentives designed to induce proper behavior.[18] By this tenet of management faith, then, values can be changed on a large scale if executives adhere to the process. All this makes possible, in turn, the crusade against teleopathy that Goodpaster commissions for top-level executives.

Third, his presentation reflects the assumption that values are meaningful as collective phenomena and, hence, attributes of the corporation. It is this premise that elevates the corporate moral agenda to a heroic, corporation-wide scale that requires carefully orchestrated leadership process. To the orthodox management theorist, it is meaningful—indeed essential—to interpret the corporation as an entity separate from autonomous persons.[19] The appeal to this premise is quite evident when Goodpaster claims that without executive attention to the "sustaining" phase "the corporate mindset simply cannot survive or replicate itself."[20] Against as pervasive a force as teleopathy, it is only natural that an appeal to "corporate mindset" is deemed necessary.

### Segue

The framework that Goodpaster presents is clear enough as an application of management theory, particularly the Harvard genre, to business ethics. But, it is not at all clear how the framework either contributes to, or relies on, an ordinary understanding of "respect for persons." In the following analysis, I show that it cannot logically do so.

## LEADERSHIP PROCESSES AND
## A DISDAIN FOR PERSONS

What sense of respect for persons is implied by Goodpaster's framework and, hence, the supporting assumptions from management theory? On the basis of an ordinary understanding of "respect for persons," the answers are not encouraging. Each of the three assumptions noted earlier, along with Goodpaster's adaptation, reflects a distinct disdain for persons as autonomous, reasoning entities. One way to arrive at this ironic conclusion about respect for persons is to examine what is missing from each assumption.

First, the overwhelming emphasis on top-level executives and their understanding of values excludes any "non-executive" persons from active roles in the story.[21] We are left to conclude then that these other persons are either incapable of making decisions on matters of values or are not interested in doing so.[22] Either way, the implication about persons is disparaging. Apparently, top-level executives show respect for persons by excluding them from decisions regarding the values that can affect them. This denies, it seems, an elementary notion of respect for persons: due process where a person's projects are significantly affected.[23] Certainly, executives have values. But so too does everyone else at the corporation. Respect through exclusion is a contradiction that Goodpaster makes no effort to defend.[24]

Second, there is no provision for lasting and constructive dialogue about values in Goodpaster's leadership agenda. Goodpaster wants us to assume that values can change only through externally applied processes. We are left to conclude that no non-executive at the corporation can, or is willing to, enter into debate with other persons about the values by which they interact. Once again, the framework turns on an apparent disdain for persons as moral agents.

On this last point, we must take care not to be fooled by the apparent dialogue in the executives' orientation activities. The sole purpose of those discussions is for the executives to take the measure of the dominant values at the corporation. Non-executives are involved, to be sure, but only as respondents about those dominant values.[25] Once orientation is completed, such exchanges cease.

The absence of dialogue and, hence, debate about values suggests further that the diversity of values that non-executives might bring to the discussion is threatening. Since an ordinary understanding of respect for persons arguably includes a disposition to accept and work through differences in values, the paper clearly implies that "respect for persons" denotes an aversion to these likely differences. This contradiction goes to the core of Goodpaster's leadership agenda. If non-executives entertain values from the outset that are consonant with top-level executives' values, this is coincidental and not the result of discussions leading to agreements among autonomous persons. If, on the other hand, they entertain errant values, they become the grist for the processes. Either way, we have another ironic result: respect for these persons entails ignoring the diverse perspectives that they might bring to the corporation.[26]

Third, there is no room for individual introspection by non-executives. Since the values that count in the framework are corporate values, the possibility is excluded that non-executives ask questions like, "How are these values meaningful for me?" The legitimacy of corporate values, it seems, must be independent of the interests of non-executives affected by those values. So, respect for persons must entail the irrelevance of any one person's values.

The reason for this omission, and a resulting contradiction, follows from the overriding emphasis on *corporate* values. Goodpaster gives top-level executives their marching orders couched in terms of reining teleopathy. Nothing in those orders addresses values at a level less global than the corporation. (Remember that the top-level executives have already imparted their values to the corporation.) At best, Goodpaster implies that this epic struggle between "respect for persons" and teleopathy will produce, through some invisible mechanism, eventual benefits for non-executives.[27] But, this matter is unimportant to the paper, since the legitimacy of corporate values is a function of their clout against teleopathy.

The upshot is that Goodpaster's interpretation of "corporate values" impedes his development of a meaningful sense of "respect for persons." If an ordinary understanding of respect for persons includes a concern about each person's benefit from involvement at the corporation, then the emphasis on corporate values implies a third contradiction: respect for persons turns on the irrelevance of a person's pursuits as a standard of legitimacy for corporate values. Put differently, "respect for persons" is a mere slogan in the war against teleopathy.

## Segue

It is difficult to see where *respect for persons,* as we might commonly understand the term, has any meaningful place in Goodpaster's presentation. The general absence of persons as decision makers, the absence of debate as a means for exploring diverse—and perhaps more worthy—values, and the irrelevance of persons' pursuits as a standard of corporate legitimacy all suggest a profound disrespect for persons as capable, self-directing, and self-critical entities. For these leadership processes to work, persons generally must be treated as moral beginners who need to be coerced into treating others with respect. And, all this is done in the name of "respect for persons."

For the argument to work, "respect for persons" must be an oxy-moron.

## TAKING PERSONS SERIOUSLY
## AT THE MODERN CORPORATION

The problem that Goodpaster sets out to solve is a crucial one: how to enrich our conceptions of the modern corporation through ethical analysis. As William Frederick reminds us, the popular forays into this problem—namely, the popular models of corporate social responsibility—push matters of respect and responsibility to the fringe of the modern corporation.[28] Goodpaster acknowledges this short-coming and, in the spirit of Frederick's call for the inclusion of ethics in corporate responsibility, sets out to bring threads of management theory and ethical theory to bear on the modern corporation as a thoroughly moral phenomenon. Yet, he chooses to saddle his interpretation with the heavy baggage of conventional management theory. What results is a convoluted interpretation of so basic a notion as "respect for persons."

Still, it is important to understand, the contradictions notwithstanding, how Goodpaster calls our attention to one crossroad that we have reached in the study of business ethics. It is here, perhaps inadvertently, that Goodpaster makes a contribution. On one hand, we can follow his lead by tinkering with conventional management theory in hopes of finding a moral thread in a genre that is designed largely to frustrate autonomous pursuit of an ethical life.

Alternatively, we can scrap that endeavor. Instead, we can choose to interpret the modern corporation as an arena in which autonomous persons shape their interdependence through (1) individual searches for meaning and (2) bargaining processes by which those persons tailor their relationships to their respective values.[29] To pursue such an alternative route can be costly, however. We must be willing to discard some time-honored articles of faith about management and the corporation. We must accept the optionality of such tenets as the three assumptions that I have ascribed to Goodpaster's line of argument. Most prominently, we must be willing to toss aside the notion that the modern corporation is anything more than a mere means for individual human accomplishment. Only then can we begin to write stories where "respect for persons" squares with our considered understandings of the concept.

## NOTES

1. Kenneth Goodpaster writes about "respects for the rights and concerns of affected parties" and "respect for others," but not "respect for persons"

per se. I refer to the latter for convenience of expression and argument. See K. Goodpaster, "Ethical Imperatives and Corporate Leadership", in R. Edward Freeman, ed., *Business Ethics: State of the Art* (New York: Oxford University Press, 1991).

2. "Normative core" is Goodpaster's term. See Goodpaster, "Ethical Imperatives," pp. 121–133.

3. For one discussion of the neophyte theme, see R. E. Freeman, "What the Surveys Don't Tell Us," *Ethics Digest*, 6, no. 1 (Charlottesville, VA: Olsson Center for Applied Ethics, 1988) pp. 3–4.

4. This is one of the concerns expressed by Professor Richard DeGeorge during the Ruffin Lectures discussions. His point was that business schools, hardly bastions of critical analysis, have come to "love business ethics too much," to the point of treating business ethics as simply another social science.

5. See Goodpaster, "Ethical Imperatives," p. 129.

6. Ibid., pp. 134–142.

7. In fact, this matter of standards of self-restraint might prove to be a better means for distinguishing types 1, 2a, 2b, and 3 than Goodpaster employs. He claims that type 3 is a more "direct" kind of reasoning (p. 130). Yet, type 1 thinking is certainly direct, albeit focused on a standard of self-interest. He also suggests that types 1, 2a, and 2b, as harbingers of teleopathy, reflect the "suspension of 'on-line' moral judgment" (p. 126). Yet, he later describes these three dispositions as rational choices to deny, in some fashion, one's obligations to another (pp. 126–129). So, the distance between type 3 and the others is not as clear as it could be.

8. See Goodpaster "Ethical Imperatives," p. 130. The basis for "balance" remains a mystery. All four dispositions involve a balance. It is simply the case that the scales can be tipped in four different directions, a fact that Goodpaster acknowledges (p. 131).

9. Ibid., pp. 135–137.

10. Note the trivial sense in which the stakeholder concept is used in the argument: stakeholders are meaningful only as indicators of some collective phenomenon. This theme pervades his presentation, and most references to "stakeholder" in the management literature more generally.

11. Ibid., pp. 137–141.

12. Ibid., p. 141.

13. By "conventional management theory," I refer primarily to organizational behavior, strategic management, organization theory, and social issues in management where researchers have discovered the usefulness of values in their interpretations of corporations. For example, the fascination with "managing corporate culture" and "managing values" runs across these research communities.

14. See D. Gilbert, E. Hartman, J. Mauriel, and R. E. Freeman, *A Logic for Strategy* (Cambridge, MA: Ballinger, 1988) pp. 39–54.

15. John Marquand captures this theme strikingly when his character, Charles Gray, drinks a toast to bank president Tony Burton:

> I should like to drink a toast not to our president but to everyone who tries to look like him. When I walk, I always walk like Tony, because Tony knows just how to walk; and when I talk, I always talk like Tony, because Tony knows just how to

talk. . . . But no matter how I try, I cannot be like Tony. I can never make myself sufficiently astute.

See J. Marquand, *Point of No Return* (Chicago: Academy Chicago Publishers, 1985 ed.) p. 81.

16. See R. E. Freeman and D. Gilbert, *Corporate Strategy and the Search for Ethics* (Englewood Cliffs, NJ: Prentice-Hall, 1988) pp. 132–156.

17. Note that the key concepts in Goodpaster's framework are three verbs. There are no nouns, in the form of distinct persons, connected to those verbs. It should not be surprising then that the connection between type 3 thinking and the three processes defies ready comprehension. Lynn Sharp Paine and others raised this point in the Ruffin Lectures discussions. Goodpaster made reference to this issue in the revised version of his presentation (p. 144). But, his comment simply restates the question raised by Paine. Discussions with R. Edward Freeman, Jeffrey Barach, and William Evan have helped me sharpen the verb-noun point.

18. This interpretation takes issue with Goodpaster's suggestion that we must develop a better understanding of three apparent paradoxes in his corporate moral leadership agenda. See Goodpaster "Ethical Imperatives," pp. 143–145. My point is that these "paradoxes" are *necessary* consequences of his argument that cannot logically be denied. Put differently, he presents a model for coercion.

19. Ibid., p. 126–128. It is ironic to find an appeal to "corporate good" in his presentation, since Goodpaster seeks to override such appeals to "systemic" versions of self-restraint.

20. Ibid., p. 141. Goodpaster never addresses the question about why "corporate mindset" is a useful way of talking about the modern corporation, only that it is possible to do so. See K. Goodpaster and J. Matthews, "Can a Corporation Have a Conscience?" *Harvard Business Review* (January–February 1982):131–2.

21. See R. E. Freeman, D. Gilbert, and E. Hartman, "Values and the Foundations of Strategic Management," *Journal of Business Ethics* (1989), 7, 821–834.

22. In fact, the story line would collapse if these other persons were permitted to participate.

23. I am simply following the conception of a person as a pursuer of projects of importance to her. See L. Lomasky, *Persons, Rights, and the Moral Community* (New York: Oxford University Press, 1987).

24. Goodpaster leaves room for correcting this with the caveat: "The full discipline implied by the moral point of view is not part of the definition of type 3 thinking . . ."

See Goodpaster, "Ethical Imperatives," p. 130. Still, the first returns leave one to wonder what such "full discipline" will bring.

25. This, once again, is a trivial reference to stakeholders.

26. Consider the fact that there is no room in Goodpaster's model for asking questions about whether the executives "have their values straight." Such self-criticism could be aided by the very dialogue that is omitted from the story.

27. Again, we have the ironic result that "respect for persons" will accrue through indirect processes that look much like type 2a and 2b reasoning.

Hence, we might redesignate type 3 thinking as type 2bb thinking on the basis of this indirect concern for persons.

28. See W. Frederick, "Theories of Corporate Social Performance," in S. Sethi and C. Falbe, eds., *Business and Society: Dimensions of Conflict and Cooperation* (Lexington, MA: Lexington Books, 1987), pp. 142–61.

29. Edward McClennen observed during the Ruffin Lectures that from a contractarian perspective on the modern corporation there is nothing necessarily inconsistent between Goodpaster's type 1 and 3. My point is not to be taken that managerial processes are irrelevant per se, but rather that it is the meaning of those processes that we cannot ignore. Discussions with George Brenkert, Norman Bowie, and Gregory Dees have helped me clarify this interpretation.

# 8

# Institutionalizing Ethical Motivation: Reflections on Goodpaster's Agenda

Robbin Derry

Kenneth Goodpaster has offered a moral agenda for corporate leaders. He argues that they must face the three-part challenge of orienting corporate strategy to ethical values and goals, institutionalizing ethical motivation among employees, and sustaining the desired ethical standards over successive generations of managers, customers, and suppliers. Goodpaster's proposed agenda is a worthwhile one, encompassing three critical areas that have indeed baffled and constrained leaders in their attempts to integrate ethics in the workplace. I would like to address the second issue on the agenda: institutionalizing ethical motivation.

The institutionalization of motivation has challenged organizational managers and theorists for decades. It has raised controversy over what rewards are appropriate and effective. Ongoing debates focus on the varieties of motivation and how leaders can tap into them for the good of the organization. In some respects the question of ethical motivation overlaps with this larger question of motivation in general. What is it that drives people and why do they do what they do? How can they be encouraged and rewarded to do more or better work? The question of ethical motivation similarly asks how an organization can best support and encourage ethical behavior.

However, ethical motivation also raises the unique question, "Why should I, as an individual, or we, the organization, be moral?" Work organizations encourage and reward self-interested behavior on the part of individuals and departments. Of course management needs the commitment of the individuals to the good of the whole, but they buy this commitment primarily by rewarding the individuals' self-interest when they contribute to the profit of the larger organization. A dilemma then arises in instituting ethical motivation. When self-interest is the premiss for action, it is necessary to ask, "Why is it in my self-interest to be ethical?"

Although ethical theorists have a variety of useful answers to the question of how to be ethical, they have many fewer answers to the question, "Why be moral?" If we are to motivate people in organizations to be ethical and make sound ethical decisions, we must not only be able to talk about what morality is (i.e., what it is we want employees to do when we tell them to be ethical), and how to be ethical (clarity about how to enact ethical decisions and choices), but we must also have an answer to the question, "Why should I be moral?" Certainly the question is a critical one for both organizations (the corporate we) and individuals. There are many times when it is not in one's self-interest to be moral. Why should either the corporation or the individual choose the ethical rather than the unethical action?

"Why be moral?" can be answered from many perspectives. I will address the question of individual motivation as it might be addressed by leaders as they plan the integration of ethical standards and behaviors into their organizational culture. The first item on Goodpaster's moral agenda for leaders is the orientation of corporate strategy by shared ethical values. I delegate to this first step the defining of ethical goals and behaviors. It is at this initial stage that the questions of "What are the ethical standards?" and "What is ethical behavior on the part of the employees?" should be addressed. At the stage of institutionalization of motivation we face the question, "Why should I be moral?" How do self-interest and ethical behavior fit together?

In resolving the dilemma of ethical motivation in organizations there are two important questions to be answered. These are (1) Why should I be moral? and (2) How can an organization support and encourage ethical behavior?

I will argue here that in order to answer the first question we need a better understanding of human nature. To answer the second question we need a two-part approach that removes the disincentives to ethical behavior and introduces rewards and systemic support for ethical behavior. These steps work together to help corporate leaders recognize the current constraints on ethical action and ways in which they may support and encourage ethical decision making in their organizations.

## WHY SHOULD I BE MORAL?

The question, "Why is it in my interest to be ethical in my business dealings?" is built on the assumption that people are motivated by self-interest. Organizational theorists and economists frequently assume that people are self-interested by nature and that this characteristic is the motivating force in nearly all actions. If we accept the concept of people as primarily motivated by some form of self-interest, then we design organizational reward and incentive systems grounded in self-interest.

If we change the assumptions, we are free to redesign the incentives. Theories of motivation that are based primarily on self-interest are built on a narrow view of human nature. We need a broader view of human nature and of motivation. I suggest that a concept of the self as intrinsically collaborative is (1) required to institutionalize ethical motivation and (2) made possible by recognizing human characteristics beyond "man as driven by self-interest," a prominent feature of the rational economic model.

When we expand our conception of self to recognize the collaborative self, we are motivated toward different goals and respond to different rewards. Both organizations and individuals may make use of this expanded understanding of self to incorporate ethical considerations into daily decision making. Before exploring the collaborative self, it is useful to differentiate simple and enlightened self-interest. These assumptions about motivation are found in current organizational thinking. The limitations of these models lead us to the collaborative self.

### Simple Self-Interest

Simple self-interest suggests that people will select the course of action that benefits themselves the most. The benefit to be achieved may be money, power, education, vacation time, status, or any other tangible or intangible good. The good directly accrues to the benefit of the individual. Many motivational strategies build on the assumption that people will work the hardest if they see a direct contribution to their own good, be it money, power, promotion, or recognition.

A major breakthrough in behavioral theories of motivation occurred in the 1950s [1,2] when it was recognized that some people are motivated by intrinsic goods such as self-worth, self-esteem, and sense of achievement, whereas others are motivated by extrinsic goods such as money, cars, vacation time, and stock bonuses. Several motivational theories variated on this theme of intrinsic and extrinsic factors,[3–6] but all of these were clearly grounded in simple self-interest.

For these theorists it was a matter of deciding which goods were most desirable for what people, under what circumstances. Once that was determined, employees could be goaded and rewarded with the good that best fit their individual interests.

Current reward systems in most organizations are still based on this assumption of simple self-interest. Sales bonuses, innovation rewards, plaques, titles, and corner offices are all allotted on the premiss that people work harder for the organization if they receive a tangible personal reward. It appears essential to appeal to simple self-interest only because organizations are structured on the assumption and reinforcement of man as a self-interested being. How can organizations encourage members to act beyond self-interest when all the incentive systems are tied to self-interest?

### Enlightened Self-Interest

Enlightened self-interest argues that when people recognize what is good for other people often benefits themselves in the long term, they will accordingly choose actions that extend the immediate good beyond themselves. It is "enlightened" because it reflects the realization that we are in a society or organization in which the health and wealth of the individual are dependent on the health and wealth of the whole. For an individual to be promoted and to accrue bonuses, the organization as a whole must be successful, profitable, and reputable. This view also reflects an understanding of the social contract at work within most organizations; mutual sacrifices and exchanges are made because they are understood to be for the good of the whole and the ultimate good of the individual.

Many worthwhile contributions to the field of professional ethics have been premissed on enlightened self-interest. Solomon and Hanson argue that ethical self-regulation will save corporations from intrusive governmental regulation of business activities.[7] Mathews highlights the effects of unethical corporate actions on the attitude of the employees:

> Perhaps the least noted but the most important element in the morale of individuals in an organization is the way in which their corporation is regarded by other corporations and the general public. . . . [A] reputation for being unethical . . . is likely to adversely affect the morale of those within the corporation.[8]

These views rightly suggest that the self-interest of the firm is strongly linked to the ethical behavior of individual members and that the self-interest of individuals is equally linked to the ethical standards and reputation of the organization as a whole. The underlying concepts of enlightened self-interest have also been used to encourage ethical decisions by organizations for their effects on society as a whole.[9,10]

Enlightened self-interest functions well to provide a motivation for ethical action. While enlightened self-interest and simple self-interest share the assumption of human beings as primarily self-interested, enlightened self-interest is able to answer the question, "Why should I be moral?" with specifics. It is sometimes in the individual's interest to be ethical and it is sometimes in the organization's interest to be ethical. The direct benefits may include increased trust and therefore increased ability to conduct business, a cleaner community in which to raise children, or a reputation for quality products and therefore increased consumer loyalty. If the benefits are not obvious and direct, often they can be seen to be indirect. As society or the organization benefits, there will be benefits to the individual as a member of these groups.

Simple self-interest, the basis for most of the current corporate incentive systems, is less useful as a motivator for ethical action because such action is by nature about strengthening relationships and commitment to mutual trust. This demands going beyond one's own narrow interests, as Solomon and Hanson explain:

> Business is ultimately about relationships between people—our compliance with the rules we all form together, our contributions to the well-being of others as well as our own, the consequences of our activities, for good or otherwise. There is nothing amoral or unethical about it.[11]

Simple self-interest is an outmoded view of motivation and is dysfunctional in organizations for the purpose of promoting ethical behavior. Enlightened self-interest is useful in those situations in which ethical behavior clearly contributes to the good of the organization or the individual. However, there are numerous situations in which the self-interest of the individual or the organization is at odds with ethical behavior. In these cases, enlightened self-interest loses its justification on behalf of the ethical choice. At the same time, the use of enlightened self-interest has perpetuated the fundamental assumption of self-interest as the driving motivator of man and in doing so has continued the rationales and rewards for such behavior.

## The Collaborative Self

I propose an alternative to enlightened self-interest, which may be called the collaborative self. The collaborative self has two prominent features: (1) It is based on a broader concept of self. For organizations this means broader boundaries of "us" and "our." (2) It does not assume that self-interest in the standard sense is the primary motivator of women and men. Rather it draws on the motivations to encourage mutual growth, to combine efforts toward shared goals, to help others achieve their potential, to build relationships for the sake of relationships, to respond to the needs of others. All these are integral to human nature and critical to the success of free enterprise.

For the collaborative self the role of personal benefit as a motivator is substantially reduced, although not entirely ignored. It is unarguable that we have certain survival instincts that guide us to be self-interested to the extent of meeting our basic human needs. But it is not necessary to relate all motivation to such instincts. We are motivated to accomplish significantly more complex tasks than merely to survive physically. Other aspects of our motivational make-up can be supported, encouraged, and rewarded.

The model of "man, the worker," as primarily self-interested represents the traditional stereotyped image of "man, the toiling factory worker," or "man, the hardworking executive," both of whom labor to support their families, to provide better opportunities for their children, and to generally improve their lot in life. Early industrial organizations as well as the modern corporation have been structured to compensate and promote these men in exchange for their contributions to the corporate goals.

As the work force has become more diverse the needs of the individual workers and managers have changed, but the stereotypes and the bureaucratic structures have lagged behind. An underlying component of the collaborative self is an understanding of self as something other than the stereotypes of workers and managers. The concept of the collaborative self builds on the strengths of women and men of many backgrounds and colors. Women have long been an integral part of the work force, although their contributions and potential are only beginning to be recognized.

Our understanding of motivation must be reconstructed to encompass the diversity of people who comprise the many levels of employees and managers. A critical question is, Who are the "selves" that have been sampled and analyzed in the development of the economic theory of man as primarily self-interested? My interpretation of past research is that the sample has been (1) men or (2) men and women in organizations that are structured to reward and therefore promote self-interest and in which the route to achievement is through self-interested behavior. In such organizations the learned behavior will likely match the rewarded behavior.

Nearly all corporations have been structured in the image of man, not in the image of woman. Motivational systems have been designed to support and reward self-interested behavior and team behavior, neither of which represent the traditional strengths or motivations of women. My earlier research indicates successful women have had to learn the necessary behaviors as well as men in order to succeed in these organizational roles.[12] However, the models are not accurate representations of what motivates all people if the sample is seriously skewed. Further, the models have deleterious effects on organizations by promoting self-interested behaviors that are harmful to the organization as well as to society. Such behavior is detrimental to the institutionalization of ethical values.

The contribution of feminist theory to business ethics is a perspective of self in relation to others. Organizations that have been designed in the image of men now need to incorporate some of those features that represent women's ways of thinking and relating. What are these features? They include listening, responding on the basis of others' needs rather than on the basis of one's own needs, building strong relationships, decisions on the basis of responsibility to others, giving feedback, nurturing, building cooperation rather than confrontation.

Recognizing the distance between feminism and business ethics, in fact feminism and anything else, on the mental maps of many scholars today, I would like to offer a few general comments about feminist theory.

### General Comments on Feminist Theory

Feminism is not a description of "the way women are" as opposed to "the way men are." Feminism, in part, is the understanding that thought patterns, behaviors, logic, and realms of action that have traditionally been attributed to women must be incorporated into the dominant patterns, behaviors, and realms of action in order for society to grow in freedom, equality, and achievement. It can be fairly said that feminism represents qualities that have been attributed to women, but certainly many men embrace those qualities, and many women embrace the "dominant male" qualities of their environment. Neither is predominantly genetic or biological, in my understanding. Both orientations are the result of strong socialization about the roles of boys and girls, men and women in society.

Men and women need to recognize the strengths available in each other's ways of thinking and relating to the world. In reading feminist theory, it should be kept in mind that "men" does not mean all men, rather it means the characteristics that have been traditionally and primarily associated with men. Correspondingly, "women" does not literally mean all women, rather it refers to the characteristics that have been traditionally associated with women.

### The Role of Feminist Theory
### in the Collaborative Self

Feminist theory provides us with an important opportunity to redefine our concept of human beings as motivated primarily by simple or enlightened self-interest. By taking into account women's lives and experiences we arrive at a different view of the goals of life. If these goals are incorporated into our understanding of human activity and motivation, rather than relegated off to the side as "the study of women" while the study of men defines the norms and models, we gain a much broader definition of "self," inclusive of men and women. The driving purpose of that self is quite different.

> If we look at what women have been doing in life, we see that a large part of it can be called "active participation in the development of others." . . . One way of describing what women do is to say that women try to interact with others in ways which will foster the other person's development in many psychological dimensions, that is, emotionally, intellectually, and so on. . . . Another way to describe this activity is to say that women try to use their powers, that is, their intellectual and emotional abilities, to empower others, to build other people's strength, resources, effectiveness, and well-being.[13]

These observations remind us that much of our motivation as men and women in families, communities, and work organizations is to build mutually supportive systems, whether those take the form of old boy networks, unions, women's and men's support groups, Alcoholics Anonymous, or fraternal and civic organizations. Innumerable activities highlight our widespread commitment to mutual growth and development. If we are willing to recognize this, we must adopt a revised view of what motivates women and men. With this revised view, we will be able to create new organizational reward systems.

A further excerpt explains why this view of motivation, inclusive of men and women, has been largely overlooked in the past.

> It is clear that the large element of human activity that involves doing for others has been separated off and assigned to women. When this is combined with the fact that what women do is generally not recognized, we end up with some strange theories about the nature of human nature. These strange theories are, in fact, the prevailing theories in our culture. One of these is that "mankind" is basically self-seeking, competitive, aggressive, and destructive. Such a theory overlooks the fact that millions of people (most of them women) have spent millions of hours for hundreds of years giving their utmost to millions of others. While this fact has important consequences for women, in an ultimate sense it has equally serious implications for men and for the dominant culture's theories about

the nature of human beings. Since man is the measure of all things—and man literally, rather than human beings—we have all tended to measure ourselves by men. Men's interpretation of the world defines and directs us all, tells us what is the nature of human nature.[14]

The collaborative self encompasses the view that women and men are motivated to create benefits for others, not merely because it is in their own long-term interest as enlightened self-interest suggests, but because part of our nature as humans is to work with others, to be interested in their development as well as our own, and to strive for accomplishments that will benefit many people.

Simple and enlightened self-interest assume that we act in ways to benefit our individual or organizational selves. We may act to benefit others if we perceive that it is in our personal interest to do so. As our concept of self is expanded to include those beyond the boundaries of our skin, or in the case of organizations, the boundaries of our payroll, to include those whom we are interested in supporting and developing, ethical behavior becomes not only possible but requisite. If we see ourselves as connected to others in such a way that our responsibilities to them are as great as, and in some instances greater than, those to ourselves, then we act ethically toward them, not because it may benefit us personally to do so, but because we care about the welfare of the others.

This concept of the collaborative self is perhaps most easily understood in families. Parents' self-concern is extended to their children in a natural way. Their desire to help their children is often stronger than the desire for personal benefits. They have expanded their sense of self to include their immediate family. On some issues people extend their sense of self to include their large families, or their community or nation. As loyalty and commitment are developed, individuals take actions that may be difficult for them and may require great personal sacrifices, but those actions benefit the community with which the individual identifies. The collaborative self is concerned with the process of mutual growth and development. Therefore, the individual is looking to benefit those to whom she or he is committed.

This is familiar enough in families and nations. Sometimes it is healthy behavior, sometimes not, as when an individual acts out of blind loyalty to a group without stopping to question the broader implications of action. The collaborative self may be seen by some as simply a larger format for simple or enlightened self-interest. It may be misinterpreted as a broader focus for the familiar "us versus them" mentality. The "us" has merely become a larger group. This does not express an accurate understanding of the collaborative self. The collaborative self reflects the human inclination to act in ways that

balance the interests and needs of many people. It reflects the satisfaction of contributing to the accomplishment of greater goods beyond one's own needs. The collaborative self gives us a vehicle for
understanding motivation from the view that people are motivated
to help others as well as help themselves. They are not only interested in assisting others if it also benefits themselves; they are interested in benefiting others for the sake of benefiting others.

### Reprise: Why Be Moral?

How does the collaborative self respond to the question, "Why should
I be moral?" It doesn't. "Why be moral?" is not an important question for the collaborative self because simple self-interest is no longer
an underlying assumption of motivation. Only if we believe that
everything needs to be justified from the perspective of how the individual profits is "Why be moral?" an important question. As we
change our view of human nature to include that aspect of motivation that strives to create benefits for many people and organizations, to nurture and develop strengths in others as well as ourselves,
we face the challenge of "a single cooperative game, whose goal is
the enrichment of everyone."[15]

If we change our model of motivation for women and men in
organizations, we need no longer stumble over the question of "Why
is it in anyone's interest to be moral?" Integrating ethical motivation
into organizations becomes consistent with normal attitudes and behavior.

### HOW CAN AN ORGANIZATION SUPPORT
### AND ENCOURAGE ETHICAL BEHAVIOR?

What can an organization do to institutionalize ethical motivation?
Top management has already decided what its ethical standards are,
what policies are to be followed, and how its ethical culture will fit
with the overall corporate strategy. How then to persuade employees
that the organization really does want them to be making ethical
choices and actively upholding ethical policies? In today's corporations two major and complex steps must be taken. The first is to
remove the disincentives, the second is to provide positive incentives
and rewards.

"Aha!" someone will say, "you do believe in self-interest after all!
Why else would you provide incentives and rewards?"

Not entirely. I believe that people learn to behave in certain ways
in certain environments. Motivation is learned, but that doesn't mean
it is entirely self-interested. We each have many complex motives.

An organization can choose to reward and therefore support different aspects of our motivational systems. Rewards are not necessarily personal goods. A reward may be a visible change in a system as a result of an individual pointing out inherent problems. A reward may be a manager listening and pursuing an employee's idea. It may be as simple as being able to communicate dissatisfaction with the way things are done, without negative repercussions. Self-interest is currently overrewarded and ethical action is currently underrewarded. In fact, ethical action is not only underrewarded, it is downright punished. In order to encourage greater ethical action, an organization must let its members know that it supports and encourages such behavior.

The steps outlined in the sections that follow are preliminary suggestions. Each is based on field research on the moral conflicts experienced by managers in their work life.[16] The disincentives have been mentioned repeatedly in research interviews with managers at many levels of corporate life. Both the disincentives and the support systems proposed here require further investigation and research as to the methods of implementation. I offer them as a way of opening the discussion of specific steps to be taken.

In my view the suggestions that follow are the most obvious and necessary steps. They will be difficult to implement in many cases because they contradict longstanding traditions of authority and power. The most difficult will be organizations in which asking questions and challenging existing rationales is not tolerated. The type of organization in which the boss gives an order and "by god you salute" even if it contradicts commonsense views of morality will not eagerly adopt suggestions to create an ombuds committee that allows people to step outside the hierarchy to discuss ethical conflicts. Public praise for internal whistleblowing is unthinkable when managerial pride and self-importance surpass the desire for an ethically managed company. Nonetheless, these are, to me, the most urgent steps. If we back away from challenging the way things are done simply out of fear of resistance, we will never institutionalize ethical motivation.

## Remove Disincentives

Nearly anyone who has worked in a large bureaucratic organization can readily list activities and patterns that inhibit the fulfillment of articulated ethical guidelines. These include:

1. *Rewards for quantity over quality.* In many positions the responsibility for quality and quantity rest with the same person. If the financial and recognition rewards are all based on quantity, quality

will be sacrificed. This system is a disincentive to maintain quality. Both the structure and the rewards must be changed.

2. *Bottom line pressure: profits at any cost.* As in the E. F. Hutton check-kiting case, the operating policy is frequently communicated as "bring in profits, regardless of means and legalities." As long as that pressure and communication are dominant, no employee will believe that ethical actions are truly desired by top management.

3. *Open-door policies, closed-door practices.* Too many executives have official open-door policies that are never used to their potential benefit because the employees know full well that they will only gain the reputation for whining if they attempt to discuss a problem in the organization. By announcing an open-door policy and not adhering to it, management undercuts the trust of workers in its commitment to working with employees to resolve conflicts and problems. Management also loses credibility in honesty and follow-through.

4. *Punishment for reporting policy violations.* Several managers have reported internal policy violations to their bosses only to receive the response, "Don't make trouble, I don't want to hear about it. If this gets out it will just make our department look bad." So employees learn not to enforce ethical standards and learn that such standards are not very important to their managers. Negative responses are clearly disincentives to adhere to ethical actions. Not only do lower level employees need support for such actions, but also middle managers who uphold ethical policies must be rewarded rather than punished further up the line.

5. *Uncertainty about the ethical standards.*

> One major problem for members of the organization faced with unethical/illegal requests is the lack of guidelines. Frequently written guidelines are just not available to assist the concerned individual.[17]

Not knowing the ethical policy is certainly a disincentive to upholding it. Ignorance of morality is never accepted as a legitimate defense, but management should not leave the achievement of ethical behavior to the guesswork of the employees. As with all goals and objectives in organizational life, these must be clearly articulated and communicated.

6. *Promotion of those known to be less than ethical.* As mentioned before, if the rewards contradict the words about ethical management, the workers at all levels will learn from the rewards. Hold all managers accountable for the practice and integration of ethical actions. Do not promote those who are good at everything but ethical decisions. Such a message reaches to all ends of the corporation.

7. *Patterns of deception throughout management.* Only honest treatment

of employees and managers will convey the commitment to ethical practices in all aspects of the organization's operations. Dishonesty and deception in internal relationships will set negative role models and encourage such deception with other stakeholders in the organization.

Removing the disincentives to ethical behavior is more important than all kinds of hoopla announcing ethical codes of conduct. People in work organizations will only begin to incorporate ethical considerations into their decisions when they do not suffer ostracism and job loss for doing so.

## Build Systems and Positive Rewards to Support Ethical Action

Earlier we considered features of women's ways of thinking and relating as we reconstructed the model of motivation for the collaborative self. What are those features and how do they offer guidance in restructuring reward systems? They include listening, responding on the basis of others' needs rather than on the basis of one's own needs, building strong relationships, decisions on the basis of responsibility to others, giving feedback, nurturing, building cooperation rather than confrontation. The following proposals attempt to express these characteristics in action.

*Formulate and articulate ethical standards.* This first step properly occurs under the first item on Goodpaster's moral agenda, orienting corporate strategy. These articulated standards may take the form of a policy statement or an ethical code of conduct. As Mathews has shown so clearly, such codes hold the potential for setting ethical standards in corporations, but ethical codes without further commitment or action are worse than completely useless. Goodpaster suggests a process of active listening to the shared values of organizational members, taking "soundings" of the organization.[18] The articulation of shared values is not to be a dictatorial process. The corporate ethical policy should be understood by those to whom it applies to be an expression of mutual purpose. As such, its development must incorporate input from all levels of the organization.

*Communicate ethical policies, repeatedly.* Ethical codes of conduct are famous for gathering dust on shelves. The communication of ethical standards must happen often and more frequently through actions than through employee mail. I have tried to use consistently such words as support and encourage ethical action, rather than terms like enforce. Ethical goals and policies should not be seen as edicts but as means for accomplishing the shared ethical goals of the organizational members. Recalling the concept of the collaborative self, one should think about the organizational members in the broadest possible sense of all related stakeholders. All of these have stakes in the formulation and communication of high ethical standards that will protect their mutual interests.

*Establish channels of communication.* There will be repeated needs to clarify uncertainties about ethical policies. Initial communication of standards is not only necessary, it also provides a known channel (other than the immediate supervisor) for more information. Some corporations maintain ethics hotlines for this purpose. Anonymity may be a critical feature in such channels. This step is a way of communicating to employees a commitment to ethical practices by making the information readily available and by creating a "user friendly" means of thinking about ethical issues in the corporate setting. If information on ethics in the organization is hard to find and requires asking a great many people, this will act as a disincentive. The purpose is to be helpful and nurturing as people learn to think more clearly about ethical issues, not to make the process of getting information more challenging than the ethical issues themselves.

*Ethical ombuds committee.* There must be a way of discussing ethical conflicts outside the hierarchy of power and authority. Ethical conflicts of employees must be listened to. It is important that employees have a resource to help resolve conflicts with superiors, peers, subordinates, organizational practices. There are currently too many negative repercussions associated with raising problems or reporting ethical violations to expect this to happen within the corporate hierarchy of power. Employees and managers at all levels fear loss of promotability if they are seen as less than committed team players. Unfortunately, being a team player is often equated with going along with the system, regardless of its ethical value. An employee may have the good of the organization at heart in protesting unethical practices, but he or she is likely to be treated as a disloyal member. An ombuds committee is significantly more effective than an ombudsperson who may become ineffectual or ignored if perceived to be a token gadfly.[19] A committee has the potential of incorporating different levels and perspectives of employees and management. An additional benefit of this committee is as a vehicle for monitoring the kinds of conflicts persisting within the organization, which is critical information for monitoring progress on the ethical policies.

*Follow through.* Monitoring progress on ethical goals is as important as monitoring progress on financial goals or personnel goals. In order to know if the goals are being achieved there must be regular assessment of accomplishments and failures, of strengths and weaknesses. The executive who establishes ethical policies and goals and then neglects to monitor them is inviting neglect throughout the entire corporate system. As with all corporate goals and strategies, monitoring makes use of feedback to redefine and reshape policies. Ethical goals are not absolute. They must be honed and corrected by experience to provide appropriate guidance.

*Reward and support ethical behavior.* Designing rewards behavior will require creativity, but only because managers are not accustomed to using rewards for ethical actions. The rewards themselves are all familiar ones: praise, recognition, action on suggestions, responsiveness, setting examples, making positive examples of people for desired ethical actions. Change in behavior, especially behavior that may contradict previous corporate traditions and culture, requires ongoing and enthusiastic encouragement. There should be nothing stoical about ethical achievements and cooperation.

The goal of institutionalizing ethical motivation in the corporate world holds great challenges as well as great potential rewards. If we are able to broaden our views of our own motivation and to act on goals of cooperation and mutual benefit, we may find that we are able to effect changes far beyond our expectations. Jean Baker Miller expresses her vision in global terms:

> Practically everyone now bemoans Western man's sense of alienation, lack of community, and inability to find ways of organizing society for human ends. We have reached the end of the road that is built on the set of traits held out for male identity—advance at any cost, pay any price, drive out all competitors, and kill them if necessary. . . . It now seems clear we have arrived at a point from which we must seek a basis of faith in connection—and not only faith but recognition that it is a requirement for the existence of human beings. The basis for what seem the absolutely essential next steps in Western history if we are to survive is already available.[20]

That basis is an understanding of our interrelatedness, and our ability to respond to each other's needs institutionally as well as individually. Business is about finding and responding to unmet needs. Institutionalizing ethics in business maintains that purpose of professional service.

## NOTES

1. Douglas M. McGregor, "The Human Side of Enterprise," *Management Review* (November 1957).

2. Frederick Herzberg, "One More Time: How Do You Motivate Employees?" *Harvard Business Review* (January-February 1968).

3. David C. McClelland, *The Achieving Society* (Princeton: Van Nostrand, 1961).

4. Edward E. Lawler III and Lyman W. Porter, "The Effect of Performance on Job Satisfaction," *Industrial Relations* 7 (October 1967): 20–28.

5. Edward E. Lawler III, *Pay and Organizational Effectiveness* (New York: McGraw-Hill, 1971).

6. Gary P. Latham and Sydney B. Kinne, "Improving Job Performance Through Training in Goal Setting," *Journal of Applied Psychology* 59 (1974): 187–91.

7. Robert C. Solomon and Kristine R. Hanson, *It's Good Business* (New York: Harper & Row, 1985).

8. M. Cash Mathews, *Strategic Intervention in Organizations* (Newbury Park, CA: Sage Publications, 1988).

9. Thomas Donaldson, *Corporations and Morality* (Englewood Cliffs, NJ: Prentice-Hall, 1982).

10. William C. Frederick, "Toward CSR-3: Why Ethical Analysis is Indispensable and Unavoidable in Corporate Affairs," *California Management Review* 28, no. 2 (1986): 126–41.

11. Solomon and Hanson, *Good Business,* p. 90.

12. Robbin Derry, *Moral Reasoning in Organizations: A Study of Men and Women Managers* (Ann Arbor: University Microfilms International, 1987).

13. Jean Baker Miller, *Toward A New Psychology of Women,* 2nd ed. (Boston: Beacon Press, 1986).

14. Ibid., p. 70.

15. Solomon and Hanson, *Good Business,* p. 90.

16. Derry, *Moral Reasoning.*

17. Mathews, *Strategic Intervention,* p. 24.

18. Kenneth E. Goodpaster, "Ethical Imperatives and Corporate Leadership," in R. Edward Freeman, ed., *Business Ethics: The State of the Art* (New York: Oxford University Press, 1991).

19. Richard T. DeGeorge, *Business Ethics,* 2nd ed. (New York: Macmillan, 1986).

20. Miller, *A New Psychology,* p. 88.

# III

# MULTINATIONAL CORPORATE RESPONSIBILITY

In considering the questions of the moral obligations of multinational corporations, Thomas Donaldson asks whether there exist internationally valid rights that multinationals can be expected to honor wherever they operate. By looking at documents such as the "Universal Declaration of Human Rights" and the "International Covenant on Social, Economic and Cultural Rights," Donaldson shows the direction that these documents take in defining minimal human rights.

In his book, *Basic Rights,* Henry Shue uses a guideline for the notion of a basic right; the guideline says that the deprivation of a basic right poses a threat to rights in general. Shue's list of basic, or welfare, rights links the provision of basic rights, such as the right to food, to the preservation of non-basic rights, such as the right to freedom.

Donaldson raises the question of honoring non-basic rights and basic rights with respect to their importance and to their inviolability in differing situations. He then shifts the focus to examine "the grounding of rights in general." By using a list of ten basic rights, Donaldson examines the correlative duties imposed on corporations that observe those rights.

In examining three conditions imposed on "fundamental, international rights," Donaldson considers whether a list of given rights can be identified as having fundamental importance. Donaldson next considers the correlative duties that attach to basic rights and that multinationals would be in a position to observe or not. Beyond fulfilling their duties in honoring rights, multinationals can be seen to possess an ability to avoid depriving others of their rights, to protect others from such deprivation, and to aid the deprived in the realization of their rights. Whether each of these classes of duties is fulfilled by a corporation is considered with a view to the minimal/maximal distinction between duties and the "affordability-fairness" condition.

In his development of Donaldson's framework, Edwin Hartman adds the duty to avoid helping to deprive others of their rights. Hartman maintains that Donaldson's multinational corporation, finding itself in a situation as messy as South Africa's policy of apartheid, is able to avoid helping to deprive by leaving the country. A company that departs from South Africa can satisfy itself that it has stopped helping to deprive persons of their rights (through participation in an immoral economy and social system), but it has failed in one of Donaldson's other three duties: by leaving the moral fray, the firm is no longer able to protect people from the deprivation wrought by others.

Hartman comments that Donaldson's distinctions between actions that are unrelated to business decisions and those that are related to business decisions is not valid inasmuch as the organization's influence on society is so prevalent that its actions cannot easily be divorced from its moral context, its "zone of obligations." "Business decisions that the corporation's managers make in the normal course of corporate activity have moral consequences that cannot be detached from them."

Hartman reflects on the views of the corporation as a moral actor, a persona ficta, a citizen in much the same sense as an individual is a moral citizen, and concludes that it is a mistake to consider the corporation as "the individual writ large."

# 9

# Rights in
# the Global Market

## Thomas J. Donaldson

Rights we take for granted are sometimes trampled abroad. Child labor plagues Central America, and dozens of interviews with workers in Central America conducted in the fall of 1987 reveal that most respondents started working between the ages of 12 and 14.[1] In other countries the rights to minimal education, free speech, basic nutrition, and freedom from torture are little more than dreams. What obligations do multinational corporations have in such contexts? Are they obliged not only to honor but to encourage the protection of such rights? Consider the claim that persons everywhere have a right to adequate food. What are we to say when a multinational corporation, working in a country where malnutrition is rampant, buys a parcel of land and converts it from the production of a staple food source to one for cash export? If the land is purchased from a wealthy landowner and converted from growing black beans to coffee, has the company indirectly violated a right to adequate food if it turns out that the purchase lowers the food supply?

These questions exist in a class of questions concerned with establishing minimal conditions upon the behavior of multinational corporations. They are ones that have been largely neglected by academic researchers. Business academics have contributed significantly to understanding the problems of international business; they have offered a bounty of empirical analysis relevant to multinational corporations, and have conducted detailed inquiries into the structure of global markets and the strategies of multinational corporations.[2] Yet few of their efforts highlight the moral element. The notable exceptions are academics working out of the so-called social issues and business environment perspectives,[3] yet even here only a fraction of such normative work from academic business researchers has found application to multinational corporations, and when it has, the context has tended to be issue-specific, for example, Bhopal, or South African divestment.[4]

This paper will attempt to develop a list of fundamental human rights serviceable for international business. Ten specific rights are advanced to establish bottom-line moral considerations for multinational corporations. The paper concludes that corporations, individuals, and governments must respect these 10 rights, although it argues that the correlative duties that corporations must shoulder in honoring those rights are different from those of nation states and individuals. Much of the analysis is drawn from a more extensive treatment offered in my recent book, *The Ethics of International Business.*[5]

## RIGHTS ESTABLISH MINIMAL CORPORATE RESPONSIBILITIES

We should first distinguish those corporate responsibilities that hold as minimal conditions from those that exceed the minimum. "Minimal" duties for multinational corporations are similar to Kant's "perfect" duties; that is, they are mandatory and allow no discretion as to when or how they are performed. A "maximal" duty, on the other hand, is one whose fulfillment would be praiseworthy but not absolutely mandatory. Our concern, in turn, is with "minimal," rather than "maximal" duties. Our aim is to inquire, for example, whether a foreign corporation's minimal duties include refusing to hire children in a Honduran assembly plant, even if doing so harms the company's competitive position. It is not to establish guidelines for exemplary or "model" multinational behavior.

Our strategy will be to assume that most if not all minimal responsibilities can be framed through the language of rights, a language recognized for establishing minimal moral obligations. Rights may be seen to lie at the rock bottom of modern moral deliberation. Maurice Cranston writes that the litmus test for whether or not something is a right is whether it protects something of "paramount importance."[6] If I have a right not to be tortured, then in violating that right you threaten something of paramount value to me. It would be splendid if you did even more—if, for example, you treated me with love and charity; but *at a minimum* you must respect my rights.

The flip side of a right typically is a duty,[7] a fact that gives aptness to Joel Feinberg's well-known definition of a right as a "justified entitlement *to* something *from* someone."[8] It is the "from someone" part of the definition that reflects the assumption of a duty, for without a correlative duty that attaches to some moral agent or group of agents, a right is weakened—if not beyond the status of a right entirely, then significantly. If we cannot say that a multinational corporation has a duty to keep the levels of arsenic low in the workplace, then the worker's right not to be poisoned means little.

Often, duties fall upon more than one class of moral agent. Consider, for example, the furor over the dumping of toxic waste in West Africa by multinational corporations. During 1988, virtually every country from Morocco to Zaire on Africa's west coast received offers from companies seeking cheap sites for dumping waste.[9] In the years prior, toxic waste dumping had become enormously expensive in the United States and Europe, in large part because of the costly safety measures mandated by U.S. and European governments. In February 1988 officials in Guinea Bissau, one of the world's poorest nations, agreed to bury 15 million tons of toxic wastes from European tanneries and pharmaceutical companies. The companies agreed to pay about $120 million, which is only slightly less than the country's entire gross national product. And in Nigeria, in 1987, five European ships unload toxic waste containing dangerous poisons such as polychlorinated biphenyls, or PCBs. Workers wearing thongs and shorts unloaded the barrels for $2.50 a day, and placed them in a dirt lot in a residential area in the town of Kiko.[10] They were not told about the contents of the barrels.[11] Who bears responsibility for protecting the workers' and inhabitants' rights to safety in such instances? It would be wrong to place it entirely upon a single group of agents such as the governments of West African nations. As it happens, the toxic waste dumped in Nigeria entered under an import permit for "non-explosive, non-radioactive and non–self-combusting chemicals." But the permit turned out to be a loophole; Nigeria had not meant to accept the waste and demanded its removal once word about its presence filtered into official channels. The example reveals the difficulty many developing countries have in generating the sophisticated language and regulatory procedures necessary to control high-technology hazards. It seems reasonable in such instances, then, to place the responsibility not upon a single class of agents but upon a broad collection of them, including governments, corporate executives, host country companies and officials, and international organizations. The responsibility for not violating the rights of people living in West Africa from the dangers of toxic waste then potentially falls upon every agent whose actions might harm, or contribute to harming, West African inhabitants. Nor is one agent's responsibility always mitigated when another "accepts" responsibility. To take a specific instance, corporate responsibility may not be eliminated if a West African government explicitly agrees to accept toxic waste. There is always the possibility—said to be a reality by some critics—that corrupt government officials will agree to accept and handle waste that threatens safety in order to fatten their own Swiss bank accounts.

Rights with international relevance should be viewed as occupying an intermediary zone between abstract moral principles such as liberty or fairness on the one hand, and national specifications of rights on the other.[12] International rights must be more specific than abstract principles if they are to facilitate practical implication, but be less specific than the entries on lists of rights whose duties fall on national governments if they are to preserve cosmopolitan relevance. One nation's particular social capacities or social traditions may favor the recognition of certain rights that are inappropriate to other nations. Citizens of a rich, technologically advanced nation, for example, but not of a poor, developing one, may be viewed as possessing a right to a certain technological level of health care. You, as a citizen of the United States, may have the right to kidney dialysis; but a citizen of Bangladesh may not.

As a first approximation, then, let us interpret a multinational's obligations by asking which *international rights* it should respect, where we understand international rights to be sort of moral precepts that lie in a zone between abstract moral principles and national rights specifications. Multinationals, we shall assume, should respect the international rights of those whom they affect, especially when those rights are of the most fundamental sort.

But whose list of international rights shall we choose? Libertarians tend to endorse well-pruned lists of liberty-centered rights, ones that look like the first 10 amendments to the U.S. Constitution (the Bill of Rights) without the subsequent constitutional amendments, while welfare liberals frequently endorse lush, well-tangled structures that include entitlements as well as freedoms. Who is to say that a given person's list, or a given country's list, for that matter, is preferable to another's?

One list receiving significant international attention, a list bearing the signatures of most of the world's nations, is the "Universal Declaration of Human Rights."[13] However, it and the subsequent "International Covenant on Social, Economic and Cultural Rights," have spawned controversy despite the fact that the Universal Declaration was endorsed by virtually all of the important post–World War II nations in 1948 as part of the affirmation of the U.N. Charter. What distinguishes these lists from their predecessors, and what serves also as the focus of controversy, is their inclusion of rights that have come to be called alternatively "social," "economic," "positive," or "welfare" rights. Nuances separate these four concepts, but they need not detain us; all formulations share the feature of demanding more than forbearance from those upon whom the right's correlative duties fall. All four refer to rights that entail claims by rights holders to specific goods, where such goods must at least sometimes be provided by other persons (although sometimes by unspecified others). The goods at issue are typically such things as food, education, and shelter. For convenience, we shall use the term "welfare rights" to refer to all claims of this kind. Some international rights documents even specify *as* welfare rights claims to goods that are now regarded as standard benefits of the modern welfare state. For example, Articles 22 through 27 of the Universal Declaration assert rights to social security insurance, employment, protection against unemployment, health care, education, and limits on working hours.[14]

Many have balked when confronted with such lists, arguing that no one can have a right to a specific supply of an economic good. Can anyone be said to have a "right," for example, to 128 hours of sleep and leisure each week? And, in the same spirit, some international documents have simply refused to adopt the welfare-affirming blueprint established in the Universal Declaration.[15] The issue is critical for establishing the minimal responsibilities of multinational corporations, for it is only to the extent that, say, the right to adequate food exists, that multinationals can be chided for violating it.

Henry Shue advances a compelling notion of welfare rights—one with special relevance to our task—in his book, *Basic Rights*.[16] Shue's guiding concept of a "basic right" entails the existence of welfare rights. The essence of a basic right, says Shue, is "something the deprivation of which is one standard threat to rights generally."[17] Basic rights include the right to subsistence, or "minimal economic security," to freedom of physical movement, security, and political participation. By way of explanation, the right to *subsistence* entails a claim to, e.g., "unpolluted air, unpolluted water, adequate food, adequate clothing, adequate shelter, and minimal preventative public health care."[18] The right to *freedom of physical movement* is a right to not have "arbitrary constraints upon parts of one's body, such as ropes, chains, . . . and the absence of arbitrary constraints upon the movement from place to place of one's whole body, such as . . . pass laws (as in South Africa)."[19] The right to *security* is a right not to be subjected to "murder, torture, mayhem, rape, or assault"; and the right to *political participation* is the right to have "genuine influence upon the fundamental choices among the societal institutions and the societal policies that control security and subsistence and, where the person is directly affected, genuine influence upon the operation of institutions and the implementation of policy."[20] The key to understanding a basic right for Shue is recognizing that it is a prerequisite for the enjoyment of other rights. Thus being secure from beatings is a prerequisite for the enjoyment of, e.g., the right to freedom of assembly, since one's freedom to hold political meetings is dependent upon one's freedom from the fear of beatings in the event one chooses to assemble. Shue insists correctly that benevolent despotism cannot ensure basic rights. One's rights are not protected even by the most enlightened despot in the absence of social institutions that guarantee that basic rights will be preserved in the event such benevolence turns to malevolence.[21] Illusions, as the saying goes, are not liberties.

Shue's analysis, moreover, provides a formidable argument on behalf of such rights. The argument is successful because it unpacks the sense in which it is contradictory to support any list of rights without at the same time supporting those specific rights upon whose preservation the list can be shown to depend. It is a strategy with direct application to the controversy between defenders and critics of welfare rights, for if Shue is correct, even a list of *non*-welfare rights ultimately depends upon certain basic rights, some of which are welfare rights. His arguments utilizes the following, simple propositions:

1. Everyone has a right to something.
2. Some other things are necessary for enjoying the first thing as a right, whatever the first right is.
3. Therefore, everyone also has rights to the other things that are necessary for enjoying the first thing as a right.[22]

We shall grasp Shue's point even better by considering, on the one hand, a standard objection to welfare rights, and on the other, a response afforded by Shue's theory. Now many who criticize welfare rights utilize a traditional philosophical distinction between so-called negative and positive rights. A "positive" right is said to be one that requires persons to act positively to *do* something, and a "negative" right requires only that people not deprive directly. Hence, the right to liberty is said to be a negative right, whereas the right to enough food is said to be a positive one. With this distinction in hand, it is common to conclude that no one can be bound to improve the welfare of another (unless, say, that person has entered into an agreement to do so); rather, at most they can be bound to *refrain* from damaging the welfare of another.

Shue's argument, however, reveals the implausibility of the very distinction between negative and positive rights. Perhaps the most celebrated and best accepted example of a negative right is the right to freedom. Yet the meaningful preservation of freedom requires a variety of positive actions: for example, on the part of the government it requires the establishment and maintenance of a police force, courts, and the military, and on the part of the citizenry it requires ongoing cooperation and diligent (not merely passive) forbearance.

And the protection of another so-called negative right, the right to physical security, necessitates "police forces; criminal rights; penitentiaries; schools for training police, lawyers, and guards; and taxes to support an enormous system for the prevention, detention, and punishment of violations of personal security."[23]

This is compelling. The maintenance and preservation of many non-welfare rights (where, again, such maintenance and preservation is the key to a right's status as "basic") requires the support of certain basic welfare rights. For example, certain liberties depend upon the enjoyment of subsistence, just as subsistence sometimes depends upon the enjoyment of some liberties. One's freedom to speak freely is meaningless if one is weakened by hunger to the point of silence.

## THE PROBLEM WITH "BASIC" RIGHTS

But while establishing the legitimacy of some welfare rights, Shue's argument is nonetheless flawed. To begin with, from the standpoint of moral logic, his methodology appears to justify the more important in terms of the less important. That is to say, insofar as a basic right is defined as one whose preservation is necessary for the preservation of all rights generally, the determination of what counts as "basic" will occur by a process that takes as fundamental all rights, including non-basic ones, and then asks which among those rights are rights such that their absence would constitute a threat to the others. Not only does this fail to say anything about the moral grounding of rights in general, it also hinges the status of the basic rights on their ability to support all rights, including non-basic rights, and this appears to place the hierarchical cart before the horse.[24] This problem enlarges when we notice that many of the so-called non-basic rights such as freedom of speech appear to be of equal importance to some so-called basic rights. One wonders why a few of the world's most important rights, such as the rights to property, free speech, religious freedom, and education, are regarded as nonbasic. One can see why, given Shue's concept of a basic right, they are non-basic, but then one wonders whether they might be basic in an even more important sense.

Shue himself acknowledges that status as a basic right does not guarantee that the right in question is more important. At one point, while contrasting a non-basic right, such as the right to education, to a basic right, such as the right to security, he states, "I do not mean by this to deny that the enjoyment of the right to education is much greater and richer—more distinctively human, perhaps—than merely going through life without ever being assaulted." But he next asserts the practical priority of basic rights by saying, "I mean only that, if the choice must be made, the prevention of assault ought to supersede the provision of education."[25] So while denying that basic rights are necessarily more important than non-basic ones in all respects, he grants that they are more important in the sense that probably matters most: they are give priority in decisions where a choice must be made between defending one right and defending another. He concludes, "therefore, if a right is basic, other, non-basic rights may be sacrificed, if necessary, in order to secure the basic right."[26]

But what Shue leaves obscure is the matter of which rights *other* than basic rights are deserving of emphasis. For Shue, every right must occupy one of two positions on the rights hierarchy: it is either basic or not. But if so, then how are individuals, governments, and corporations to know which rights should be honored in a crunch? Shue clearly believes that individuals, governments, and corporations must honor *basic* rights, but how are the remaining non-basic rights to be treated? What of the right to freedom of speech, to property, or to a minimal education? Are these rights *always* to be given second-class status? And if they are to be given priority in some instances, then why? Then too, surely, Shue will agree that all *nation states* must honor the right to freedom of speech, but is the same true of all individuals and corporations? Does it follow that corporations must tolerate all speech affecting the workplace and never penalize offending workers, even when the speech is maliciously motivated and severely damages profitability? Similarly, are all states responsible for defending *all* other non-basic rights?

## FUNDAMENTAL INTERNATIONAL RIGHTS

Let us adopt another method of approach. Let us attempt to determine which rights are most fundamental directly, i.e., by using criteria that ground fundamental rights. In other words, instead of employing an analytic argument that takes for granted a body of rights and then analyzes the logic of their interdependence (as Shue does), let us employ a normative argument that looks to the grounding of rights in general. Let us stipulate three conditions that will be independently necessary and jointly sufficient for considering a given prospective as (a) a right and (b) a right of fundamental importance. Such a right we shall label a "fundamental international right." These three conditions are that (1) the right protects something of extreme importance, that (2) it is subject to significant, recurring threats, and that (3) the obligations or burdens it imposes are economically affordable and fair with respect to the distribution of burdens generally. These three conditions resemble, although they are not identical to, three of the four conditions advanced by James Nickel, in his book, *Making Sense of Human Rights*,[27] for identifying rights imposing claims on nation-states. In the present context, however, they are advanced as having application to all three of the major classes of international actors, i.e., nation-states, individuals, and multinational corporations.

Consider each condition. The first recognizes that if claims are made to things that have little or only moderate importance, then even if those claims happen to be valid, they cannot aspire to the status of "rights." We are reminded of Maurice Cranston's "paramount importance" test cited earlier for bona fide rights. The second notes that rights also must be subject to what Shue calls "standard" threats or what Nickel has alternatively dubbed "recurrent" threats. A right must be subject to significant, recurring threats for the simple reason that the list of claims centering on interests of fundamental importance would otherwise expand indefinitely. And finally, as Nickel has shown convincingly, any right must satisfy what could be called an "affordability-fairness" criterion in that it must impose obligations or other burdens that are in Nickel's words "affordable in relation to resources, other obligations, and fairness in the distribution of burdens." Part of the justification for this condition is as simple as the time-honored dictum in moral philosophy that "ought implies can," or, in other words, that no person or entity can be held responsible for doing something if it is not in their power to do it. We need only add the reasonable proviso that sometimes a duty may be of a kind that is discouraged for moral reasons, i.e., either because it conflicts with another bona fide obligation or because it constitutes an unfairness in the distribution of burdens.

Next, consider the following list of fundamental international rights:

1. The right to freedom of physical movement
2. The right to ownership of property
3. The right to freedom from torture
4. The right to a fair trial
5. The right to non-discriminatory treatment (i.e., freedom from discrimination on the basis of such characteristics as race or sex)
6. The right to physical security
7. The right to freedom of speech and association
8. The right to minimal education
9. The right to political participation
10. The right to subsistence

This seems a minimal list. Some will wish to add entries such as the right to employment, to social security, or to a certain standard of living (say, as might be prescribed by Rawls's well-known "difference" principle). Disputes also may arise about the wording or over-

lapping features of some rights: for example, is not the right to freedom from torture included in the right to physical security, at least
when the latter is properly interpreted? We shall not attempt to resolve such controversies here. Rather, the list as presented aims to
suggest, albeit incompletely, a description of a *minimal* set of rights
and to serve as a point of beginning and consensus for evaluating
international conduct. If I am correct, many would wish to add entries, but few would wish to subtract them.

The list has been generated by application of the three conditions
and the compatibility proviso. Readers may satisfy for themselves
whether the ten entries fulfill these conditions; in doing so, however,
they should remember that in constructing the list one looks for *only*
those rights that can be honored in some form by *all* international
agents, including nation-states, corporations, and individuals. Hence,
to consider only the issue of affordability, each candidate for a right
must be tested for "affordability" by way of the lowest common de-
nominator—by way, for example, of the poorest nation-state. If, even
after receiving its fair share of charitable aid from wealthier nations,
that state cannot "afford" dialysis for all citizens who need it, then
the right to receive dialysis from one's nation state will not be a fundamental international right, although dialysis may contribute a bona
fide right for those living within a specific nation-state, such as Japan.

Although the hope for a definitive interpretation of the list of rights
is an illusion, we can add specificity by clarifying the correlative duties entailed for different kinds of international actors. Because by
definition the list contains items that all three major classes of international actors must respect, the next task is to spell out the correlative duties that fall upon our targeted group of international actors,
namely, multinational corporations.

Doing so requires putting the third condition from Nickel's revised list to a second, and different, use. This "affordability-fairness"
condition—which, again, concerns the affordability of respecting a
right from the perspective of an agent's resources, other obligations,
and overall fairness in the distribution of burdens—was used first as
one of the criteria for generating the original list of fundamental
rights. There it demanded satisfaction of an affordability-fairness
threshold for each potential respecter of a right. For example, were
the burdens imposed by a given right not fair (in relation to other
bona fide obligations and burdens) or affordable for nation-states,
individuals, and corporations, then presumably the prospective right
would not qualify as a fundamental international right. In its second
use, to which it is about to be put, the condition goes beyond the
judgment *that* a certain affordability-fairness threshold has been
crossed to the determination of *what* the proper duties are for mul-

tinational corporations in relation to a given right. In its second use, in other words, the condition's notions of fairness and affordability are invoked to help determine *which* obligations properly fall upon corporations, in contrast to individuals and nation-states. We shall use the condition to help determine the correlative duties that attach to multinational corporations in their honoring of fundamental international rights.

As we look over the list, it is noteworthy that except for a few isolated instances multinational corporations have probably succeeded in fulfilling their duty not to *actively deprive* persons of their enjoyment of the rights at issue. But correlative duties involve more than failing to actively deprive people of the enjoyment of their rights. Shue, for example, notes that three types of correlative duties are possible for any right, namely, duties to (1) avoid depriving, (2) help protect from deprivation, and (3) aid the deprived.[28]

While it is obvious that the honoring of rights clearly imposes duties of the first kind, i.e., to avoid depriving directly, it is less obvious, but frequently true, that honoring them involves acts or omissions that help prevent the deprivation of rights. If I receive a threat from Murder, Inc., and it looks like they mean business, my right to security is clearly at risk. If a third party has relevant information that if revealed to the police would help protect my right, it is no excuse for the third party to say that it is Murder, Inc., and not they (the third party), who wishes to kill me. Hence, honoring rights sometimes involves not only duties to *avoid depriving*, but to *help protect from deprivation* as well, and it is interesting that many critics of multinationals, have faulted them not for the failure to avoid depriving but for failing to take reasonable protective steps.

Similarly, the duties associated with rights can often include duties from the third category, i.e., that of *aiding the deprived,* as when a government is bound to honor the right of its citizens to adequate nutrition by distributing food in the wake of a famine or natural disaster, or when the same government in the defense of political liberty is required to demand that an employer reinstate or compensate an employee fired for voting for a particular candidate in a government election.

Nonetheless, the honoring by multinational corporations of at least *some* of the ten fundamental rights requires the adoption of only the first class of correlative duties, i.e., the duty to avoid depriving. Correlative duties do not extend either to protecting from deprivation or aiding the deprived, because of the relevance of the "fairness-affordability" condition discussed before. This condition requires, again, that the obligations or burdens imposed by a right must be affordable in relation to resources, other obligations, and fairness in the distribution of burdens. (Certain puzzles affecting the affordability-fairness condition are discussed later in the context of the "drug lord" problem.)

Corporations cannot be held to the same standards of charity and love as individuals. Nor can corporations be held to the same standards to which we hold civil governments for enhancing social welfare—since frequently governments are dedicated to enhancing the welfare of, and actively preserving the liberties of, their citizens. The profit-making corporation, in contrast, is designed to achieve an economic mission and as a moral actor possesses an exceedingly narrow personality. It is an undemocratic institution, furthermore, which is ill-suited to the broader task of distributing society's goods in accordance with a conception of general welfare. The corporation is an economic animal; although one may deny that its sole responsibility is to make a profit for its investors, one will surely wish to define its responsibilities differently than for civil governments.

Let us employ a "minimal/maximal" distinction to draw the inference that duties of the third class, i.e., to aid the deprived, do not fall upon for-profit multinational corporations, except, of course, in instances where the corporations themselves have done the depriving. For example, although it would be strikingly generous for multinationals to sacrifice some of their profits to buy milk, grain, and shelter for persons in poor countries, assisting the poor is not one of the corporations' minimal moral requirements; such minimal obligations belong more properly to the peoples' respective governments or, perhaps, to better-off individuals. If corporations possess duties to aid those deprived of the benefits of rights (except, again, in instances where they have done the depriving), then they possess them as "maximal" not "minimal" duties, which means that a given corporation's failure to observe them does not deprive that corporation of its moral right to exist. Furthermore, since rights impose minimal, not maximal duties, it follows that whereas a corporation might have a maximal duty to aid the deprived in a given instance, their failure to honor that duty could not be claimed necessarily as a violation of someone's *rights*.

The same, however, is not true of the second class of duties, i.e., to protect from deprivation. These duties, like those in the third class, are also usually the province of government, but it sometimes happens that the rights to which they correlate are ones whose protection is a direct outcome of ordinary corporate activities. For example, the duties associated with protecting a worker from the physical threats of other workers may fall not only upon the local police but also to some extent upon the employer. These duties, in turn, are properly viewed as correlative duties of a person's right—in this instance, the worker's right—to personal security. This will become clearer in a moment when we discuss the correlative duties of specific rights.

Table 9–1 of correlative duties reflects the application of the "affordability-fairness" condition to the earlier list of fundamental international rights, and indicates which rights do, and which do not, impose correlative duties upon multinational corporations of the three various kinds. A word of caution should be issued for interpreting the list: the first type of correlative obligation, i.e., of not depriving directly, is broader than might be supposed at first. It includes *cooperative* as well as exclusively individual actions. Thus, if a company has personnel policies that inhibit freedom of movement, or if a multinational corporation operating in South Africa cooperates with the government's restrictions on pass laws, then those companies actively deprive persons of their right to freedom of movement, despite the fact that actions of other agents (in particular, of the South African government) may be essential in effecting the deprivation. Similarly, in an instance where a corporation cooperates with political groups in fighting land reforms designed to take land from a tiny aristocratic minority (a minority that, say, owns virtually all of a country's usable land) for redistribution to peasants, those corporations may well—at least under certain circumstances—violate the right to private property.

Still, the list asserts that at least six of the ten fundamental rights impose correlative duties of the second kind upon corporations, that is, to protect from deprivation.[29] What follows is a brief set of com-

**Table 9–1.** Minimal Correlative Duties of Multinational Corporations

| Fundamental Rights | To Avoid Depriving | To Help Protect from Deprivation | To Aid the Deprived |
|---|---|---|---|
| Freedom of physical movement | X | | |
| Ownership of property | X | | |
| Freedom from torture | X | | |
| Fair trial | X | | |
| Non-discriminatory treatment | X | X | |
| Physical security | X | X | |
| Freedom of speech and association | X | X | |
| Minimal education | X | X | |
| Political participation | X | X | |
| Subsistence | X | X | |

mentaries discussing sample applications of each of those six rights from the perspective of such correlative duties.

## SAMPLE APPLICATIONS

### Discrimination

The obligation to protect from deprivation a person's freedom from discrimination properly falls upon corporations as well as governments insofar as everyday corporate activities directly affect compliance with the right. Because employees and prospective employees possess the moral right not to be discriminated against on the basis of race, sex, caste, class, or family affiliation, it follows that multinational corporations have an obligation not only to refrain from discrimination but in some instances to protect the right to non-discriminatory treatment by establishing appropriate procedures. This may require, for example, offering notice to prospective employees of the company's policy of non-discriminatory hiring, or educating lower level managers about the need to reward or penalize on the basis of performance rather than irrelevant criteria.

### Physical Security

The right to physical security similarly entails duties of protection: if a Japanese multinational corporation operating in Nigeria hires shop workers to run metal lathes in an assembly factory but fails to provide them with protective goggles, then the corporation has failed to honor the workers' moral right to physical security (no matter what the local law might decree). Injuries from such a failure would be the moral responsibility of the Japanese multinational despite the fact that the company could not be said to have inflicted the injuries directly.

### Free Speech and Association

In the same vein, the duty to protect the right of free speech and association from deprivation finds application in the ongoing corporate obligation not to bar the emergence of labor unions. Corporations are not obliged on the basis of human rights to encourage or welcome labor unions, but neither are they morally permitted to destroy them or prevent their emergence through coercive tactics; to do so would violate the workers' international right to association. Their duty to protect the right to association from deprivation, in turn, includes refraining from lobbying host governments for restrictions that would violate the right in question, and perhaps even to protesting host government measures that do violate it.[30]

## Minimal Education

The correlative duty to protect the right of education may be illustrated through the very example used to open this paper: namely, the prevalence of child labor in developing countries. A multinational in Central America is not entitled to hire a 10-year-old child for full-time work because, among other reasons, doing so blocks the child's ability to receive a minimally sufficient education. While what counts as a "minimally sufficient" education may be debated, and while it seems likely, moreover, that the specification of the right to a certain level of education will depend, at least in part, upon the level of economic resources available in a given country, it is reasonable to assume that any action by a corporation that has the effect of blocking the development of a child's ability to read or write will be proscribed on the basis of rights.

## Political Participation

In some instances corporations have failed to honor the correlative duty of protecting the right to political participation from deprivation. The most blatant examples of direct deprivation are fortunately becoming so rare as to be non-existent, namely, cases in which companies directly aid in overthrowing democratic regimes, as when United Fruit helped overthrow a democratically elected regime in Honduras during the 1950s. But a few corporations have continued indirectly to threaten this right by failing to protect it from deprivation. A few have persisted, for example, in supporting military dictatorships in countries with growing democratic sentiment, and others have blatantly bribed publicly elected officials with large sums of money. Perhaps the most celebrated example of the latter occurred when the prime minister of Japan was bribed with $7 million by the Lockheed Corporation to secure a lucrative Tri-Star Jet contract. Here, the complaint from the perspective of this right is not against bribes or "sensitive payments" in general, but to bribes in contexts where they serve to undermine a democratic system in which publicly elected officials are in a position of public trust.

Even the buying and owning of major segments of a foreign country's land and industry has been criticized in this regard. As Brian Barry has remarked, "the paranoia created in Britain and the United States by land purchases by foreigners (especially Arabs, it seems) should serve to make it understandable that the citizenry of a country might be unhappy with a state of affairs in which the most im-

portant natural resources are in foreign ownership."[31] At what point
would Americans regard their democratic control threatened by foreign ownership of U.S. industry and resources? At 20 percent ownership? At 40 percent? At 60 percent? At 80 percent? The answer is
debatable, yet there seems to be some point beyond which the right
to national self-determination, and in turn national democratic control, is violated by foreign ownership of property.[32]

### Subsistence

Corporations also have duties to protect the right to subsistence from
deprivation. Consider the following scenario: a number of square
miles of land in an underdeveloped country has been used for years
to grow black beans. Further, the bulk of the land is owned, as it has
been for centuries, by two wealthy landowners. Poorer members of
the community work the land and receive a portion of the crop, a
portion barely sufficient to satisfy nutritional needs. Next, imagine
that a multinational corporation offers the two wealthy owners a
handsome sum for the land, and does so because it plans to grow
coffee for export. Now *if*—and this, admittedly, is a crucial "if"—the
corporation has reason to *know* that a significant number of people
in the community will suffer malnutrition as a result; that is, if the
company has convincing reasons to believe that those persons will
not be hired by the company, or that if forced to migrate to the city
they will earn less than subsistence wages, i.e., inadequate to provide
proper food and shelter, then the multinational may be said to have
failed in its correlative duty to protect persons from the deprivation
of the right to subsistence. This despite the fact that the corporation
would never have stopped to take food from workers' mouths, and
despite the fact that the malnourished will, in Coleridge's words, "die
so slowly that none call it murder."

### Disagreements: The Relevance of Facts and Culture

The commentaries above are obviously not intended to complete the
project of specifying the correlative duties associated with fundamental international rights; only to begin it. Furthermore, here—as
in the matter of specifying specific correlative duties generally—dis-
agreements are inevitable. Take the land acquisition case above. One
may claim that multinationals are never capable of knowing the consequences of land purchases with sufficient certainty to predict malnutrition or starvation. The issue obviously requires debate. Furthermore, one may wish to argue for the moral relevance of predictions
about the actions of other agents. If the corporation in question re-
frains from buying land, won't another corporation rush in with the

same negative consequences? And might not such a prediction miti-
gate the former corporation's responsibility in buying land in the
first place? Here both facts and meta-moral principles must be debated.

The same point arises in the context of an even more controversial
issue, one related also to the right of persons to subsistence. Critics
have asserted that by promoting high technology agriculture in developing countries where wealthier farmers are preferred risks for
loans to buy imported seeds and fertilizer, multinationals encourage
the syndrome of land concentration and dependence upon imported
food and fertilizer, leading to the situation where proceeds from cash
crops buy luxuries for the rich and where poor farmers are forced
to sell their small plots of land and move to the city. Whether such
practices do violate rights will obviously be a subject of controversy.
But what is central to the resolution of such a controversy is the
*empirical* question of whether such practices *do* lead to starvation and
malnourishment. That is to say, the problem may be positioned for
solution, but it is certainly not solved, by establishing the right to
subsistence and its correlative duties: facts remain crucial.

More generally, the solution to most difficult international problems requires a detailed understanding not only of moral precepts
but of particular facts. The answer does not appear, as if by magic,
simply by referencing the relevant rights and correlative duties, any
more than the issue of whether welfare recipients in the United States
should be required to work disappears by appealing to the state's
correlative duty to aid the disadvantaged. Elsewhere I propose an
"ethical algorithm" to aid multinational managers in making difficult
trade-offs between home and host country values,[33] but while that
algorithm augments the appeal to fundamental international rights
established in this paper, neither it nor any other theory can draw
moral conclusions when key facts are in dispute. Put simply, when
facts are in irreconcilable dispute, so too will be the moral outcome.[34]

It may be that some of the above rights would not be embraced,
or at least not embraced as formulated here, by cultures far different from ours. Would, for example, the Fulanis, a nomadic cattle
culture in Nigeria, subscribe to this list with the same eagerness as
the citizens of Brooklyn, New York? What list would they draw up
if given the chance? And could we, or should we, try to convince
them that our list is preferable? Would such a dialogue even make
sense?[35]

I want to acknowledge that rights may vary in priority and style of
expression from one culture to another. Yet in line with the conclusions of the earlier discussion of cultural relativism, I maintain that
the list itself is applicable to all people even if they would fail to

compose an identical list. Clearly the Fulanis do not have to *accept* the list of ten rights in question for it to constitute a valid means of judging the Fulani culture. If the Fulanis treat women unfairly and unequally, then at least one fundamental international right remains unfulfilled in their culture, and our discussion implies that their culture is poorer for that practice. Three of the rights are especially prone to varying cultural interpretation. These include that of non-discriminatory treatment (with special reference to women), to political participation, and to the ownership of property. The latter two raise tendentious political issues for cultures with traditions of communal property and non-democratic institutions. The list has no pretensions to solve these age-old political problems. While I may (as, in fact, I do) subscribe to a modified Lockean notion of property in which certain political systems incorporating social ownership violate individual rights, the right to property advanced in our list need not be so narrowly interpreted as to rule out any instance of public ownership. For example, even primitive societies with communal property practices might be said to recognize a modified version of the right to property if those practices entail mutually agreed-upon, and fairly applied, rules of use, benefit, and liability. I am not prepared to say that each and every such instance violates the right to own property.

Even so, there will be a point beyond which the public ownership of property violates individual rights. State ownership of all land and movable property violates the individual's right to own property. Is the point passed when a country nationalizes its phone systems? Its oil industry? Is it passed when a primitive culture refuses to subordinate family to individual property? Although it is clear that such questions are of decisive significance, it is equally clear that establishing such a point is a task that cannot be undertaken satisfactorily here.

The same holds true for interpreting the right to political participation. I affirm the merits of a democratic electoral system in which representatives are chosen on the basis of one-person-one-vote; yet the list should not be interpreted to demand a photocopy of U.S. or English style democracy. For example, it is possible to imagine a small, primitive culture utilizing other fair means for reflecting participation in the political process—other than a representative electoral system—and thereby satisfying the right to political participation.

### The Drug Lord Problem

One of the most difficult aspects of the rights list proposed concerns the affordability-fairness condition. We can see it more clearly by reflecting on what might be called the "drug lord" problem.[36] Imagine that an unfortunate country has a weak government and is run by various drug lords (not, it appears, a hypothetical case). These drug lords threaten the physical security of various citizens and torture others. The government—the country—cannot afford to mount the required police or military actions that would bring these drug lords into moral line. Or, perhaps, this could be done but only by imposing terrible burdens on certain segments of the society that would be unfair to others. Does it follow that members of that society do not have the fundamental international right not to be tortured and to physical security? Surely they do, even if the country cannot afford to guarantee them. But if that is the case, what about the affordability-fairness criterion?

Let us begin by noting that the "affordability" part of the affordability-fairness condition does imply some upper limit for the use of resources in the securing of a fundamental international right (such that, for example, dialysis cannot be a fundamental international right). With this established, the crucial question becomes *how* to draw the upper limit. The preceding argument commits us to draw that limit through at least two criteria: first, compatibility with other, already recognized, international rights, and second, the level of importance of the interest (moral or otherwise) being protected by the right (the first of the three conditions). As for the former, we remember that the affordability-fairness principle already entails a "moral compatibility" condition requiring that the duties imposed be compatible with other moral duties. Hence, a prima facie limit may be drawn on the certification of a prospective right corresponding to the point at which other bona fide international rights are violated. As for the latter, trade-offs among members of a class of prospective rights will be made by reference to the relative importance of the interest being protected by the right. The right not to be tortured protects a more fundamental interest than the right to an aesthetically pleasing environment.

This provides a two-tiered solution for the drug lord problem. At the first tier, we note that the right of people not to be tortured by the drug lords (despite the unaffordability of properly policing the drug lords) implies that people, and especially the drug lords, have a duty not to torture. Here the solution is simple. The argument of this chapter establishes a fundamental international right not to be tortured, and it is a right that binds all parties to the duty of forbearance in torturing others. For on the first pass of applying the affordability-fairness condition, that is, when we are considering simply the issue of which fundamental international rights exist, we are only concerned about affordability in relation to *any* of the three classes of correlative duties. That is, we look to determine only whether duties of *any* of the three classes of duties are fair and affordable.

And with respect to the issue of affordability, clearly the drug lords along with every other moral agent can "afford" to refrain from actively depriving persons of their right not to be tortured. That is, they can afford to refrain from torturing. It follows that people clearly have the fundamental international right not to be tortured, which imposes at least one class of duties upon all international actors, namely, those of forbearance.

At the second tier, on the other hand, we are concerned with the issue of whether the right not to be tortured includes a duty of the government to mount an effective prevention system against torture. Here the affordability-fairness criterion is used in a second pass, one that helps establish the specific kinds of correlative duties associated with the right not to be tortured. Here surely all nation states can "afford" to shoulder duties of the second and third categories, i.e., of helping prevent deprivation, and of aiding the deprived, although the specific extent of those duties may be further affected by considerations of fairness and affordability. For example, given an instance like the country described in the drug-lord problem, it clearly seems questionable that all countries could "afford" to *succeed* completely in preventing torture, and hence the duty to help prevent torture presupposed by a fundamental international right to freedom from torture probably cannot be construed to demand complete success. Nonetheless, a fairly high level of success in preventing torture is probably demanded by virtue of international rights, because, as I have argued elsewhere,[37] the ordinary protection of civil and political rights, such as the right not to be tortured, carries a negative rather than positive economic cost. That is, the economic cost of allowing the erosion of rights to physical security and fair trial—as an empirical matter of fact—tends to exceed the cost of maintaining the rights.

## CONCLUSION

What the list of rights and corollary corporate duties establishes is that multinational corporations frequently do have obligations derived from rights where such obligations extend beyond abstaining from depriving directly, to protecting from deprivation. It implies, in other words, that the relevant factors for analyzing a difficult issue like that of hunger and high technology agriculture include not only the degree of factual correlation existing between multinational policy and hunger but also the recognition of the existence of a right to subsistence along with a specification of the corporate correlative duties entailed.

Hence the paper has argued that the ten rights identified earlier constitute minimal and bedrock moral considerations for multinational corporations operating abroad. While the list may be incomplete, the human claims it honors, and the interests those claims represent, are globally relevant. They are, in turn, immune from the Hobbesian or relativistically inspired challenges offered by skeptics. The existence of fundamental international rights implies that no corporation can wholly neglect considerations of racism, hunger, political oppression, or freedom through appeal to its "commercial" mission. These rights are, rather, moral considerations for every international moral agent, although, as we have seen, different moral agents possess different correlative obligations. The specification of the precise correlative duties associated with such rights for corporations is an ongoing task that the paper has left incomplete. Yet the existence of the rights themselves, including the imposition of duties upon corporations to protect—as well as to refrain from directly violating—such rights, seems beyond reasonable doubt.

## NOTES

Portions of this essay are contained in Thomas Donaldson, *The Ethics of International Business* (New York: Oxford University Press 1990), and are reprinted here with permission.

1. James LeMoyne, "In Central America, the Workers Suffer Most," *New York Times,* October 26, 1987, p. 1.
2. Some work explores the issue of political risk (for example, Thomas Poynter, *Multinational Enterprises and Government Intervention* (New York: St. Martin's Press, 1985); Thomas Moran, ed., *Multinational Corporations; The Political Economy of Foreign Direct Investment* (Lexington, MA: Lexington Books, 1985); and J. N. Behrman, *Decision Criteria for Foreign Direct Investment in Latin America* (New York: Council of the Americas, 1974); while other work explores the nature of international corporate strategy (See W. J. Keegan, "Multinational Scanning: A Study of Information Sources Utilized by Headquarters Executives in Multinational Companies," *Administrative Science Quarterly* (1974): 411–21; and D. Cray, "Control and Coordination in Multinational Corporations," *Journal of International Business Studies* 15, no. 2 (1984): 85–98); and still other work explores multinational public policy issues (See Lee Preston, "The Evolution of Multinational Public Policy Toward Business: Codes of Conduct," in Lee Preston, ed., *Research in Corporate Social Performance and Policy,* Vol. 10, Greenwich, CT: JAI Press, 1988).
3. This group has produced what is probably the best developed ethical literature from business schools. Their efforts evolve from the tradition of "business and society" research with roots in the sixties and early seventies. Contributors such as Buchholz, Cochran, Epstein, Frederick, Freeman, and Sethi have made significant advances, not only in developing descriptive studies with moral relevance, but in advancing normative hypotheses. See, for ex-

ample, Rogene A. Buchholz, *Business Environment and Public Policy* (Englewood Cliffs, NJ: Prentice-Hall, 1982); Stephen L. Wartick and Philip L. Cochran, "The Evolution of the Corporate Social Performance Model," *Academy of Management Review* 10 (1985): 758–69; Edwin Epstein, "The Corporate Social Policy Process: Beyond Business Ethics, Corporate Social Responsibility, and Corporate Social Responsiveness," *California Management Review* 29 (Spring 1987); William C. Frederick, "Toward CSR3: Why Ethical Analysis is Indispensable and Unavoidable in Corporate Affairs," *California Management Review* 28 (1986): 126–41; R. Edward Freeman, *Strategic Management: A Stakeholder Approach* (Boston: Pitman Press, 1984), and *Corporate Strategy and the Search for Ethics* (Englewood Cliffs, NJ: Prentice-Hall, 1988); and S. Prakash Sethi, "Corporate Law Violations and Executive Liability," in Lee Preston, ed., *Corporate Social Performance and Policy, Vol. 3* (Greenwich, CT: JAI Press, 1981), pp. 72–73, and S. Prakash Sethi et al., *Corporate Governance: Public Policy Social Responsibility Committee of Corporate Board* (Richardson, TX.: Center for Research in Business and Social Policy, 1979).

4. An exception is Duane Windsor's, "Defining the Ethical Obligations of the Multinational Enterprise," in W. M. Hoffman et al., eds., *Ethics and the Multinational Corporation* (Washington, DC: University Press of America, 1986).

5. Thomas Donaldson, *The Ethics of International Business* (New York: Oxford University Press, 1990). See especially Chapter 6.

6. Maurice Cranston, *What Are Human Rights?* (New York: Tamlinger, 1973), p. 67.

7. H. J. McCloskey, for example, understands a right as a positive entitlement that need not specify who bears the responsibility for satisfying that entitlement. H. J. McCloskey, "Rights—Some Conceptual Issues," *Australasian Journal of Philosophy* 54 (1976): 99.

8. Joel Feinberg, "Duties, Rights, and Claims," *American Philosophical Quarterly* 3 (1966): 137–44. See also Feinberg, "The Nature and Value of Rights," *Journal of Value Inquiry* 4 (1970): 243–57.

9. James Brooke, "Waste Dumpers Turning to West Africa," *New York Times*, July 17, 1988, p. 1.

10. Ibid.

11. Nigeria and other countries have struck back, often by imposing strict rules against the acceptance of toxic waste. For example, in Nigeria officials now warn that anyone caught importing toxic waste will face the firing squad. Brooke, "Waste Dumpers Turning to West Africa," p. 7.

12. James W. Nickel, *Making Sense of Human Rights: Philosophical Reflections on the Universal Declaration of Human Rights* (Berkeley: University of California Press, 1987), pp. 107–8.

13. See Ian Brownlie, *Basic Documents on Human Rights* (Oxford: Oxford University Press, 1975).

14. For a contemporary analysis of the Universal Declaration of Human Rights and companion international documents, see James W. Nickel, *Making Sense of Human Rights: Philosophical Reflections on the Universal Declaration of Human Rights* (Berkeley: University of California Press, 1987).

15. For example, the "European Convention of Human Rights" omits mention of welfare rights, preferring instead to create an auxiliary docu-

ment ("The European Social Charter of 1961") which references many of what earlier had been treated as rights as "goals."

16. Henry Shue, *Basic Rights* (Princeton, NJ: Princeton University Press, 1982).

17. Ibid., p. 34.

18. Ibid., p. 20–23.

19. Ibid., p. 78.

20. Ibid., p. 71.

21. Ibid., p. 76.

22. Ibid., p. 31.

23. Ibid., pp. 37–38.

24. I am indebted to Alan Gewirth who made this point in a conversation about Shue's theory of basic rights.

25. Shue, *Basic Rights*, p. 20.

26. Ibid., p. 19.

27. James Nickel, *Making Sense of Human Rights*, (Berkeley: University of California Press, 1987), pp. 108–19. The phrasing of the third condition is derived almost directly from Nickel's condition that "the obligations or burdens imposed by the right must be affordable in relation to resources, other obligations, and fairness in the distribution of burdens."

28. Shue, *Basic Rights*, p. 57.

29. It is possible to understand even the remaining four rights as imposing correlative duties to protect from deprivation by imagining unusual or hypothetical scenarios. For example, if it happened that the secret police of a host country dictatorship regularly used corporate personnel files in their efforts to kidnap and torture suspected political opponents, then the corporation would be morally obligated to object to the practice, and to refuse to make their files available any longer. Here the corporation would have a correlative duty to protect from deprivation the right not to be tortured. The list of rights identified as imposing correlative duties of protection was limited to six, however, on the basis of the fact that their protection is directly related to activities frequently undertaken by corporations in the real world.

30. The twin phenomena of commercial concentration and the globalization of business, both associated with the rise of the multinational, have tended to weaken the bargaining power of organized labor. It is doubtful that labor is sharing as fully as it once did in the cyclical gains of industrial productivity. This gives special significance to the right in question.

31. Brian Barry, "The Case for a New International Economic Order," in J. Roland Pennock and John W. Chapman, eds., *Ethics, Economics, and the Law: Nomos Vol. XXIV* (New York: New York University Press, 1982).

32. Companies are also charged with undermining local governments, and hence infringing on basic rights, by sophisticated tax evasion schemes. Especially when companies buy from their own subsidiaries, they can establish prices that have little connection to existing market values. This, in turn, means that profits can be shifted from high-tax to low-tax countries with the result that poor nations can be deprived of their rightful share.

33. See Donaldson, *The Ethics of International Business*, Chapter 5.

34. It is important to remember that it is "key" or "crucial" facts that are being discussed here. The 10 fundamental international rights are not to be eroded in every instance by the old argument that "we don't have enough facts." Such a defense clearly has its limits, and these limits are overstepped by the demand that evidence be definitive in every sense. An excellent example of excess in this vein is that of cigarette companies denying that their products are dangerous because we do not yet understand the causal mechanism whereby cigarette smoking is correlated with cancer.

35. Both for raising these questions, and in helping me formulate answers, I am indebted to William Frederick.

36. I am indebted to George Brenkert for suggesting and formulating the "drug lord" problem.

37. Thomas Donaldson, "Trading Justice for Bread: A Reply to James W. Nickel," in Kenneth Kipnis and Diana T. Meyers, eds., *Economic Justice: Private Rights and Public Responsibilities* (Totowa, NJ: Rowman and Allenheld, 1985), pp. 226–29.

# 10

# Donaldson on Rights and Corporate Obligations

## Edwin M. Hartman

### DONALDSON ON RIGHTS AND CORRELATIVE DUTIES

Thomas Donaldson[1] spells out the corporate duties that he claims are correlative to the fundamental rights of employees and others. Some, but not all, of these rights generate duties for corporations. To assist in determining the correlative duties, Donaldson brings to bear an affordability-fairness condition, first used in chiseling out the ten fundamental commandments: rights generate no obligations from those who cannot afford to fulfill them or from those who cannot fairly be expected to accept responsibility for them.

Donaldson follows Shue[2] in dividing correlative duties into three categories:

1. The duty to avoid depriving people of their rights
2. The duty to help protect people from such deprivation
3. The duty to aid those who are deprived

The first obligation corporations clearly have: they are not permitted to violate human rights. The third, aiding the deprived, they do not: it entails an active response that is not minimal, perhaps supererogatory, possibly inappropriate. The second is the most interesting case; for, according to Donaldson, corporations may have obligations of this kind correlative to six of the ten fundamental rights, since "the rights to which they correlate are ones whose protection is a direct outcome of ordinary corporate activities."

Donaldson's account of corporate obligations makes essential reference to human rights, but with due regard for the scope of the corporation's legitimate activity. Business decisions that the corporation's managers make in the normal course of corporate activity have moral consequences that cannot be detached from them. Managers cannot escape moral decisions, cannot remain neutral on moral issues where not to decide is to decide by default, rightly or wrongly.

For example, given that the organization must hire people, it must decide the basis for hiring, and that can be done well or badly, but not with moral neutrality. So it is with decisions about workplace safety, about unions, and about rules and practices that incorporate some level of employee rights. So with strategic decisions that make the manager consider actions that would damage certain stakeholders. The manager cannot say, that's none of our business. Such obligations are generated for the organization by just six of the 10 rights Donaldson identifies. In these cases the corporation has the resources to respond to stakeholders' rights and, in view of what its normal activities are, may fairly be expected to do so.

But certain situations, for example, that of property ownership, are outside the company's business scope. In the course of carrying out business operations the company is not faced with deciding whether any employee can own property, or be tried fairly, or be protected from torture in the local police station.

The Sullivan Principles call on American companies in South Africa to uphold employee rights that Donaldson identifies as coming up in the normal course of business. Neither Donaldson nor Leon Sullivan claims that American companies have an obligation to take a hand in South African politics to the extent of attacking the roots of apartheid in the state, for these companies' normal business practices do not cause them to make decisions that implement apartheid. Here it becomes pertinent that Donaldson rejects the argument that the corporation ought to use its awesome power to set at liberty those who are oppressed or alleviate their suffering, though it must avoid using its power to deprive employees and others of their fundamental rights—all of Donaldson's ten. Affordability is a necessary but not sufficient condition of the application of a duty.

Donaldson's account of helping protect refers to one's duty to inform an intended victim of the possibility of a hit by Murder, Inc. But the example is a somewhat surprising one, for his claim of obligation seems to rest in this instance not on an issue of legitimate scope, but rather on one's being able to prevent a heinous crime without any cost to oneself. It appears the affordability criterion is crucial here. The point then is that a corporation has an obligation to prevent a terrible wrong if in the ordinary course of corporate events an opportunity arises to ward off undeserved harm to someone without significant expenditure of corporate resources. That is affordable; and it is fair too, presumably because the corporation does not have to go out of its way to do the right thing. (Affordability and fairness seem to overlap somewhat.) Because it does not, not to act morally is to act immorally.

To explicate this kind of duty Donaldson invokes the notion of contributing to protection from deprivation, as well as the notion of a legitimate sphere of influence within which the corporation cannot fairly choose to remain neutral. The relative importance of these criteria is revealed by Donaldson's occasional omission of the words "help to." Part of the point of talking about merely helping seems to be to emphasize the restriction of the corporation's duty to the scope of its usual activity, and so to distinguish this duty from the third kind, which the corporation does not have, to aid the deprived.

## A FOURTH CATEGORY OF DUTY

I claim there is a fourth significant kind of duty, which in some ways lies between the first and the second. It is more active than just avoiding depriving, but less than helping to protect from depriving. We can call it avoiding helping to deprive. It is indirect, and it is partial or merely contributory, in some ways I shall make clear. To fulfill this duty the company need not contribute to protecting anybody from privation; it need only make sure that nothing it does helps the depriver get the job done. The notion of legitimate scope applies here as well, but in some unexpected ways.

In the case of the threat from Murder, Inc., the distinction I am drawing is between the third party's failure to warn the victim and the third party's informing some employee of Murdco that the intended victim's office is in the philosophy department at Loyola University and that his office hours are from two to three on Mondays and Wednesdays. If I know that Murdco is after the victim because he has made unfavorable reference to the corporation in a Ruffin Lecture, then in giving that employee this information I am doing something worse than avoiding protecting the victim. On the other hand, I am not myself depriving the victim of a fundamental right, or even participating in that deprivation. I may steadfastly refuse to do the job myself, or even to hold the victim while the Murdco people shoot him, despite being offered a handsome fee. In that sense I am avoiding depriving, but I am helping deprive. I could argue that, after all, I merely gave the Murdco people publicly available information; but in the circumstances that was morally significant, and my defense would be morally inadequate.

The additional kind of duty, the duty not to help deprive, rests on a distinction between being an agent of deprivation and only cooperating passively with its agent. On the other side, it depends on distinguishing between cooperating with the agent and doing nothing—failing to intervene when it would have been affordable to do so and fair to be expected to do so.

In identifying this fourth kind of duty I accept Donaldson's view that the corporation's duties are restricted by its legitimate scope and its generally accepted purpose. But I hold that to invoke the scope and purpose of the organization takes us beyond the obligations that arise from the day-to-day decision making of senior managers. I do not refer to obligations that arise from the mere ability of the corporation to do good; Donaldson dismisses these, I think rightly. I refer instead to the obligations a corporation assumes just by virtue of being in a society, existing on its sufferance, contributing to and profiting from its economy, hence to some degree supporting its political life. These obligations do not depend on the specific activities of the corporation.

One could find a great many small distinctions among kinds of correlative duty; some may be easier to make out than this one. As elsewhere, particularly in discussions of morality, one's attitude toward this taxonomy will reflect one's commitments about what is important. I put this way of categorizing duties forth for consideration because it captures a kind of moral shortcoming that should be of particular interest to those who discuss international issues.

Donaldson's second category of duties as applied to South Africa suggests that adherence to something like the Sullivan Principles justifies an American company's operations there. Now a standard criticism of companies that maintain well-behaved subsidiaries in South Africa is that, while they themselves adhere to the Sullivan Principles and in other ways help protect the rights of their employees and other nearby stakeholders, they also help to deprive black South Africans of their rights by contributing to the support of the oppressive government. The criticism is not (or not only) that the companies stand idly by instead of helping protect the oppressed within the limits set by the affordability-fairness condition in a way that violates Donaldson's second class of duties: they are not guilty of violating the rights "whose protection is a direct outcome of ordinary corporate activities." Still less do they themselves deprive people of their rights. Even many of the corporations' critics concede that the corporations scrupulously avoid oppressing black people within the workplace, and instead make a policy of treating the workers as they are not treated elsewhere. The problem is rather that corporations contribute to the oppression in that the oppressive system as a whole might in some respects function less effectively without their help and that of other well-meaning international companies.

It is not clear that Donaldson can address the difficulties in this sort of passive acquiescence and tacit support by extending his first kind of correlative obligation to cover cooperative actions. The sort of duty I am suggesting demands more than refraining from making common cause with the government in particular oppressive acts. To cooperate with the government in that way (which Sullivan signatories characteristically manage to avoid doing) is worse than providing general support to South Africa's economic and social system (which Sullivan signatories plainly do not avoid doing). The fourth category of duty condemns even the latter, at least prima facie.

Some well-intentioned companies in South Africa go so far as to aid the deprived beyond the usual scope of corporate decision. For example, Ford has told its employees that the corporation will give them legal and financial assistance if they are civilly disobedient. Ford is not thereby responding to an obligation that Donaldson considers minimal, for it is not a response to the sort of moral question forced on the corporation in the ordinary course of its business. Ford is going out of its way.

The obligation to avoid helping deprive is the basis of a company's decision to take its operations out of South Africa. Its presence there does not actually deprive black South Africans of their rights—on the contrary, if it is a Sullivan signatory, the company grants blacks rights within its decision-making sphere. Nor is the departure based on fulfilling obligations thrust on the company in the course of day-to-day decision making. Nor is the business taking the supererogatory step of aiding oppression's victims. The reason for departure is that the company by its presence is indirectly supporting apartheid, and in that way and in that sense helping deprive black citizens of their rights.

Johnson and Johnson is not depriving black South Africans of their rights; it is helping protect some of them (their employees) from deprivation; but by its presence it is helping to deprive all black South Africans of their rights. If that is correct, then there must be a morally significant distinction between depriving and helping deprive, and a morally significant distinction between helping protect and avoiding helping deprive.

One of the distinctive properties of the obligation not to help deprive—in fact, possibly a factor in its being ignored by Shue and Donaldson—is that in many cases it applies prima facie only, and so can sometimes be overridden by strong utilitarian considerations. To begin with, there is a presumption against the corporation helping to deprive employees and others of all ten minimal rights. For example, insofar as an American company is supporting the South African social and legal system by its presence in that country, it is prima facie doing wrong, because it is helping an immoral government. On the other hand, it is at the very least arguable that the corporation is doing more good than harm by helping protect the rights of its employees and other nearby stakeholders; and if so, then it is arguable that on balance it is not always morally mandatory to avoid helping the immoral government by one's presence and indirect support for the economy and the rest of the society.

This feature of the fourth kind of obligation helps distinguish it from the obligation not to deprive. Utilitarian considerations that work in defending a corporation's indirect and tacit support of apartheid would not ordinarily work in defending a corporation's actual violation of rights, since utilitarian considerations justify violating rights much less easily than they justify certain kinds of contribution to the violation of rights, especially if the violation is likely to happen anyway. Hard-line moralists might not agree, but the case of South Africa shows that some serious people—for example, those who agree with Helen Suzman that American companies ought to stay and try to change or ameliorate the system while to some degree they help support it—have very different intuitions about it. To the extent that these intuitions can be justified, they cleave off depriving from helping deprive. And so they should, since there is a clear moral difference between cooperating with a system that blights people's lives in order to improve other people's lives and actually blighting people's lives in order to improve others' lives.

I am aware that the sentence immediately previous will not seem self-evident to all. It is philosophically respectable to argue that there is no clear moral difference here, and that argument plays an important role in debates about divestment. For that very reason it would be a mistake to foreclose the issue by adopting a taxonomy that makes it more difficult to see whatever moral difference there might be.

Having failed to assimilate avoiding helping deprive to avoiding depriving, one might try to eliminate the new category by assimilating it to helping protect from deprivation. For reasons roughly opposite to those just cited, that will not do either. If you take your well-behaved Sullivan company out of South Africa, you are ceasing to help protect from deprivation. By so doing, you avoid helping deprive while doing nothing at all to help protect from deprivation. But this failure to help protect from deprivation does not constitute a failure to do your duty correlative to Donaldson's second right, for now your "ordinary corporate activities" no longer include any that generate duties to help protect.

Insofar as Donaldson's minimal correlative duties do not cover the case of well-meaning American companies in South Africa, his taxonomy has a significant weakness, for the South African situation typifies the dilemmas of the moral corporation in an immoral society, of which the multinational corporation encounters more than a few. Neither doing the best one can while permitting oneself to be tainted by association with the bad system nor withdrawing to monkish solitude and foregoing opportunities to ameliorate is wholly satisfactory. It is no coincidence that the debate over South Africa continues to divide people of good will. Donaldson's account of fundamental rights and correlative duties is neat and on the whole convincing, but it is convincing in part because it avoids at least one class of difficult issues.

## SOME LESSONS

Among the most difficult and important of the extraordinary range of issues that international business raises for moral philosophers and for businesspeople who take morality seriously is that of cooperating with immorality that is not of one's own making nor eliminable by one's own efforts. As Donaldson notes, American businesspeople operate on foreign shores in bad societies under repressive regimes. In some cases American companies are directly responsible for the repression: Donaldson cites United Fruit in Honduras. In some cases American companies have distorted the economy of the host country to the detriment of its citizens. It is not hard to assess these activities from a moral point of view: the company is a major participant in depriving the populace of some rights.

The issue is one that comes up elsewhere in business ethics. For example, within a company there may be an oppressive culture to which one indirectly contributes by cooperation while behaving oneself better than others but not actually violating the constraints that the culture puts on one, as signatories to the Sullivan Principles do not violate South Africa law. One may decide on utilitarian grounds not to blow the whistle on some dubious corporate practice. The issue relates also to the controversial distinction between committing an evil and letting it happen, or at any rate not interfering; cooperating with the commission of evil is somewhere in between.

We get moral dilemmas when there is something wrong with any course of action we can take. Among the most difficult dilemmas are those that force an agent to decide between doing something that has bad consequences and doing nothing with the result that worse consequences ensue. Doing wrong is worse than letting wrong happen; but where the wrong would be greater, should one prevent it and thus do the lesser? Ever? When? How much, if any, evil forestalled outweighs any evil done in the forestalling? Is it appropriate to talk about "outweighing" here?

Large companies are potentially great forces for good and for evil, and their massive effects are not easily controllable even by the best of managers. It is tempting to say, following Hippocrates, first, do no harm. Donaldson takes a position somewhat along those lines, but he contributes to the discussion by delineating one area in which the

company is not permitted to shrink from doing good with the excuse
that it is none of its business. But this position is not enough. The
influence of the organization is so pervasive, its very presence so
important directly and indirectly and symbolically to the society it is
in, that we cannot so easily rule out of moral consideration these vast
areas of influence as being unrelated to business decisions. Unlike
the duties in Donaldson's help-protect category, these areas of influence are not generated by the implications of ordinary business decisions. Unlike the non-duties in Donaldson's aid-the-deprived category, they are not generated by the corporation's mere ability to
perform praiseworthy actions.

Norman Bowie's Ruffin Lecture[3] contributes to our understanding of what is distinctive about business ethics, which is sometimes
wrongly taken to be ethics with examples from business, hence
teachable by one who knows ethics but not necessarily anything about
business. It is characteristic of business ethics that in discussing a
company we are dealing with a moral agent whose existence and
nature, such as they are, are closely tied to the society in which it
functions, and whose actions reverberate.

Here I must seem to be on dangerous ground, since I am suggesting that a corporation can be a moral agent and ignoring the
plausible view that as a persona it is purely ficta. (If so, I would be
in accord with French's[4] very controversial position.) I do not think
I need to take a position on that question beyond stating that a corporation is a creation of a government, not a legal fiction so much
as a legal creation, like money. (Partisans of J. L. Austin[5] might think
here of his famous discussion of what is real.) The corporation exists
insofar as there is a contract between the government and the corporation, and the purpose of the contract is to benefit both parties.
From a practical as well as legal point of view, it is usually profoundly enmeshed in its society in a hundred familiar ways. This
does not entail, nor is it true, that the corporation has to regard the
welfare of all its stakeholders as essential to its mission, but it does
generate a zone of obligations—not very well defined, to be sure.
(For more on strategy, stakeholders, and obligations, see Freeman
and Gilbert[6].)

Part of our task as business ethicists is to explore the role of the
corporation in the moral fabric of society, and the obligations that
its role implies. Whatever that role is, it is in several important ways
different from the role any individual could have. Nobody seriously
discusses whether Bishop Tutu or Alan Boesak or Helen Suzman
ought to leave South Africa rather than support its oppressive government by their very presence. Individuals are not creatures of
governments, and their rights and obligations must be explored in
full view of their autonomous essence. Corporations, endowed as they

are by their creator with certain eminently alienable rights, get some obligations as part of the package. It is only a small piece of the story to say that these obligations extend beyond those that arise in the day-to-day course of business, that they are affected by the intentions of their incorporators and—one might add, therefore—by the expectations of their stakeholders.

At this point one might object that it is a mistake to consider even individuals and their obligations in abstraction from their surroundings. Numerous and varied are the senses in which the self has been called a social product; each sense raises questions about moral implications. One may think of MacIntyre's[7] account of how figures as different as Sartre and Erving Goffman arrive at the view that there is no self over and above its roles and relationships, and of his question—a difficult one for liberal individualism—whether the cost of liberation from the duties imposed on the individual by society is the loss of any possible justification of one's moral principles.

Moral critics since Plato have gone wrong by taking the collective to be the individual writ large. Perhaps because it is less plausible, we are less misled by taking the individual to be in some ways the collective writ small. In this context, one of the issues worth exploring is the extent to which, by virtue of citizenship in a country or socioeconomic status or employment or professional affiliation, the individual has moral duties. As the basis of legal relations has changed from status to contract (the expression is Maitland's [cf. Williams[8]]), it is tempting to think the basis of our ethics, too, is now no longer a matter of our station in the social world but of our autonomous commitment to one moral principle or another. Noblesse is no longer the sort of thing that obliges. In this we think we differ significantly from the corporation, a social creation. I am warning against overconfidence on this issue.

Whether we do differ so greatly, and how, is a long story and not one to be told here. But that story, like its counterpart story of the basis of the obligations of the corporation, is one whose telling can profit from the participation of business ethicists. The peculiar status of the corporation generates rights and duties not only for the corporation but also for many stakeholders, including the employees who have roles and positions and accountabilities. The story is best told by one who is sensitive to the moral implications of the social (including economic) origins of our corporate natures and of our individual selves as well. Surely business ethicists are particularly well qualified. I claim that our ability to give an account of the category of duties arising from one's legal and social context—the category I have introduced as an obligation not to help deprive—enhances our qualifications.

The un-Kantian view that ethics is in an essential way about not only the good will but also effective action, including in some cases the creation of institutions that support right action, ought to be interesting and attractive to business ethicists. The primary questions in our field have to do with right action in the management of organizations, hence with the characteristics of organizations that are good from a moral point of view. The ethical manager undertakes to create a community that is, if not democratic, at least adequately respectful of employees' rights. But insofar as ethics involves politics, the ethical manager's intentions must extend beyond politics internal to the organization, owing to the corporation's legal and social relationship to the community and its legal institutions. One of the functions of business ethics, then, is to explore the ethical implications of the corporation's peculiar status in the community. My differences with Donaldson are over the importance of certain duties that follow from that status.

## NOTES

1. Thomas Donaldson, "Rights in the Global Market," in R. Edward Freeman, ed., *Business Ethics: The State of the Art* (New York: Oxford University Press, 1990).

2. Henry Shue, *Basic Rights* (Princeton: Princeton University Press, 1982).

3. Norman E. Bowie, "Business Ethics as a Discipline: The Search for Legitimacy," in R. Edward Freeman, ed., *Business Ethics: The State of the Art* (New York: Oxford University Press, 1991).

4. Peter A. French, *Collective and Corporate Responsibility* (New York: Columbia University Press, 1984).

5. J. L. Austin, *Sense and Sensibilia* (New York: Oxford University Press, 1962).

6. R. Edward Freeman and Daniel R. Gilbert, Jr., *Corporate Strategy and the Search for Ethics* (Englewood Cliffs, NJ: Prentice-Hall, 1988).

7. Alasdair MacIntyre, *After Virtue: A Study in Moral Theory* (Notre Dame: University of Notre Dame Press, 1981).

8. Bernard Williams, *Ethics and the Limits of Philosophy* (Cambridge: Harvard University Press, 1985).

# IV

# WIDER RESPONSIBILITIES: BUSINESS AND LITERACY

Ezra Bowen, a senior writer at *Time, Inc.*, gives a practitioner perspective to the leading edge of business ethics. In particular he looks at literacy on three levels, each of which dramatically affects business: primary, functional literacy; cultural and civic literacy, which knits a nation together in a cultural consciousness; and the literacy of purposive language and persuasion.

Changes in industry and business have left behind the illiterate or minimally literate worker. These people are unable to compete for a good job until they can read, and until they can read they are likely to remain on welfare. The predicaments of unemployment, low productivity, and unskilled workers are all affected by illiteracy. Business will be unable to thrive if the problem of illiteracy continues unabated.

Not only must businesspersons ensure themselves of a literate and trainable work force in order to stay competitive, they must also ensure that there will be decently paid consumers for their products. Company-based programs that address the existing illiteracy of employees are essential, but not sufficient. In order to stem the growth of illiteracy, businesses must involve themselves with the community's schools and colleges. In addition to cooperating with community educators, businesses have lobbying power in Congress to elect literacy-supportive representatives who will draft and vote in literacy-furthering legislation.

At the level of cultural and civic literacy, Bowen sees a need for the use of careful thought and clear language instead of bureaucratic smokescreens that serve to distance leaders from their employees and publics. Language used persuasively to influence decisions must be imbued with integrity and not mere professional competence. The misuse of language to dissemble, deceive, and confuse has been part of numerous disasters, on the smaller scale of job references to the grander scale of the *Challenger* tragedy. Although it does not prevent tragedies, language can obscure responsibility for them. Bowen illustrates the point that people have often chosen to hide their purposes behind facile language.

Bowen comments on the so-called gray areas of moral responsibility and argues that these areas have expanded in the public consciousness to a point where confusion concerning responsibility in corporate and public life is considered a valid excuse for unethical actions. He stresses the inescapability of personal ethical responsibility as a precursor of clear communications and, indeed, of freedom itself.

The rift between the business world and the liberal arts—both in academic thinking and in the working world—is exemplified in Ezra Bowen's discussion of the levels of literacy. Robert Solomon selects Bowen's third level of literacy, what Bowen calls "ethical literacy," for his remarks. Concerning this level, which Bowen defines as "the use of language to articulate and achieve high purpose," Solomon asks the question, "Why should an employee read the 'good books'?" It is at this level, Solomon believes, that a variety of notions concerning educational and cultural advantages can intrude upon our ideas of the value of reading excellent fiction and non-fiction.

To discuss the importance of good books is to discuss shared experiences, "education in the classical sense—being brought up to be part of something, not just successful in a career." The kind of literacy that results from reading and discussing good books is what allows a person to share in other lives, to educate his or her feelings, and to choose from a greater range of emotions with which to deal with people.

Solomon takes up the idea of educating the emotions and describes how books function to teach us how to feel and how other people feel. Solomon's point is that business students learn—somewhere—how to treat people on the job, and they learn to be either tough and dispassionate or sensitive and compassionate. It is through exposure to books (as well as the other arts) that opportunities for the development of empathy and compassion are met. These experiences, seemingly vicarious, are only fictive in the details, the emotional experiences are real, and enable us to choose to become the people the world (as well as organizations) needs more of.

Joanne Ciulla asks us to see the problems of literacy in ethics as one of the development of the moral imagination. Rather than lament the "shades of gray" as Ezra Bowen does, Ciulla celebrates the existence of ethical dilemmas because it is these that allow us to exercise the moral imagination to remake the world in line with creative solutions and dissolutions of problems.

Specifically Ciulla recommends the use of fairy tales to cultivate the imagination. Fairy tales are full of instances where disempowered, usually children, use their wits to outsmart the bad guys. By turning to fairy tales, and an even broader notion of literature, as relevant to business, we can redefine what is practical and workable in corporate life. Thus, literacy, in the sense of understanding and using moral language, must be understood broadly in order to develop the critical faculties and creative perspective necessary for life.

# 11

# The Role of Business in Three Levels of Literacy

## Ezra F. Bowen

Today, no single element is more important to business than is literacy—a vital facility that operates (or fails to operate) on three levels:

1. Functional/technological—I put them together because, in many cases today, they are all but inseparable. This is the ability to read and write (and cipher) well enough to function with a decent degree of satisfaction and opportunity in an increasingly complex and demanding world.
2. Cultural or civic literacy—the ability to absorb and transmit ideas and information in one's business with an awareness of the sociopolitical context and obligations of one's life as a citizen.
3. Ethical literacy—the use of language to articulate and achieve high purpose (or not).

Is there any component more important to the health and welfare of business? Without a highly literate work force, even profits can have a sorrowfully short life. In fact, with our declining curve in functional literacy, in the ability to understand and do a job, a great many businesses are experiencing a decline in profits. For example, Metropolitan Life must send back 70 percent of its correspondence for simple grammatic and spelling errors, even with a spell check on the machines. Translate that into lost hours, lost dollars, and try to keep telling your client policyholders that they must continue to accept climbing rates and downsliding dividends because you can't find, hire, and pay well-trained—or trainable—employees.

Lest we hang all this on the insurance business, a steelworker who could not read misordered spare parts from a warehouse, a mistake that cost the company $1 million. And those are just the dollar costs. A feed-lot laborer accidentally killed a herd of cattle when he mis-read a package label and fed them poison. A train motorman being tried for negligence in a fatal accident admitted that he had trouble reading his service manual.

Or, for another rival component to literacy, how about productivity?

Right now, in Michigan alone, 250,000 automobile and other heavy-metal workers are laid off. Two hundred and fifty thousand—count 'em: that's close to four Superbowls full of folks, knocked out of work by the closing of the old Charlie Chaplin assembly lines that have been replaced by robot plants. These new plants, whose equip-ment requires 12 to 14 years of education to operate, employ one-quarter of a million fewer people to produce the cars that a lagging America is still able to sell into its own markets. Those 250,000 peo-ple are just one state's worth, just one industry's worth of America's technological illiteracy—and of sagging productivity. Just one state and just one industry's worth of unemployed—of unemployables.

Most of these people, heads of families, mature Americans, are without opportunity. There is no more severe economic or moral crisis facing the country than this one. Out of work, these citizens carry all the obligations—mortgages, the cost of their children's ed-ucation, and the like—that burdened them when they were taking home $15 to $17 per hour on the assembly line. Now they may be able to find lesser paying jobs and if so, those people, en masse, are making all together $6.5 billion less money per year.

For those who can't find any work pile, on 200,000 or more an-nual welfare checks, for a total of $8.5 billion, just in one area of industry, in one state. This is the price tag on functional/technolog-ical illiteracy, a national blight (and human tragedy) that few busi-nesses and few universities are not doing enough about.


## FUNCTIONAL/ TECHNOLOGICAL LITERACY

Depending on the standard you use to score functional/technological literacy, we have somewhere between 17 million and 60 million illit-erates. And their annual cost to businesses and taxpayers is about $225 billion.

For years the generally accepted standard for defining functional literacy was an eighth to ninth grade education. At that level, for almost a century, you could get a pretty good job, support your fam-ily. You could get by. And that eighth to ninth grade level was very common across America. Alas, it still is: 30 to 35 million people are there. But the trouble is that level can no longer get by.

Hear the words of Jim Cates, of the University of Texas in Austin. No one in the country is better informed on the roots, the facts, the dangers of illiteracy than Dr. Cates, a distinguished scholar in the field who lived the realities of illiteracy as a boy. Cates grew up in rural Texas when a person did not need to read or write to run a straight fence, raise grass-fed cattle, or make a good dollar as an oilfield roustabout or even a wildcat speculator. "Old careers are dying out," he said. "The times have passed those people by."

That observation holds for much of the depressed sectors of America of today. "They spent their lives in the oil patch," Cates says, "or on farms or in smokestack factories and nobody needs those skills anymore. Farmers have sophisticated $120,000 tractors now," he explains, "and there are all kinds of manuals for them—if you aren't educated you could destroy those machines in an hour."

The same holds true for the textile industry. Now it's either gone high-tech or gone altogether. Charles Williams, South Carolina Superintendent of Education, says about the mill-hand. "His educational level didn't drop, but the job demands went off and left him." These laid-off workers grew up in the 1930s and 1940s, when only 20 percent of all Americans graduated from high school (the current figure is about 90 percent), and the average U.S. citizen indeed got no farther than eight grade: far enough then—today not even close. This is what we mean by our declining literacy curve: our abilities are declining, relative to the demands of the market.

Nowhere has this been more dramatic than, as noted, in Detroit—the auto business. During the palmy years of the zero-IQ assembly lines of Chaplin's *Modern Times,* there was only one qualification for work: "Just be there," says a United Auto Workers spokesman. "All you had to do was install something. Somebody would say, 'Hey here's what you have to do.' " And you did not have to read or write very well to do it. Today you surely must. And, as we know, today, more and more automobiles are made abroad in countries such as Japan that have been quicker to go high-tech (and where the literacy rate is about 98 percent), while Detroit's corporations and employees scramble to catch up.

That UAW official says, "Now you've got to learn to program the computer to make it do the things you want it to do. You've also got to be able to diagnose the computer, so if it malfunctions you know what the problems are. Anyone who reads below the twelfth-grade level can be absolutely lost."

At a place like the Ford parts plant in Ypsilanti, the workers are already lost. "We're in a tremendous swing away from manual labor," says Industrial Relations Manager Andrew Jackson, who estimates that between 30 and 35 percent of his work force is functionally illiterate—and very much at risk. Two years ago 250 to 300 employees went into intensive reading, math, and computer classes. Typical is High Wieldon, 49, an Oregon farm boy who dropped out of school in eighth grade and drifted to Michigan where he got a job installing coils at Ford. Retrained and reading at twelfth grade plus level, he now runs a complex push-button welding machine.

Other auto workers who are unable or unwilling to lift themselves up will be (or already have been) cut from the business, with little hope of rehabilitation. The U.S. Department of Labor estimates that because of the dramatic upswing in job requirements and shortage of money for retraining, perhaps 75 percent of today's unemployed cannot qualify for productive jobs or even be trained to handle them.

For business, this is the bottom line on the level 1 literacy balance sheet. At a meeting of the National Governor's Association two years ago, Tennessee's Lamar Alexander, now president of the University of Tennessee, told fellow chief executives that "more than anything else it is the threat to the jobs of the people," and ultimately, to the economy of the whole nation, that makes illiteracy such an urgent concern. Without a literate work force capable of competing with the rest of the world, Alexander reminded his audience, jobs simply will go elsewhere, to nations that are more successful educationally.

That's the good news. The bad news, as we contemplate the future of American business—not to mention the future of America itself— is that every year 700,000 to 1 million high-schoolers drop out. Imagine that the whole Los Angeles or New York City school population vanished, or that 68 bus loads of humans a day plunged into a desperate, festering, impoverished underclass of illiterates. Where are they going to go from there? Eighty-five percent of all adjudicated delinquents are illiterate. Something like 70 percent of unwed teenager mothers are illiterate. Sixty to 80 percent of all adult prison inmates are illiterate (at a cost of $25,000 to $32,000 per year to keep them there, versus $18,000 to $20,000 per year at Harvard).

Add to these dropouts one and one-half million illiterate immigrants, legal and otherwise. And you get a total of 2.3 million in Illiterate U's Class of '90. At this rate, by the year 2000 one-third of the nation will be too miserably educated, too illiterate, to work in your business, and too poor to buy your products. Every year it gets worse.

A study by the Educational Testing Service in 1987 called the "Nation's Report Card: Learning to be Literate in America" affirms, "that minimum levels of literacy are no longer sufficient for people who must live and work in an increasingly complex and technological age." That observation leads back to the question of just what literacy means, and what must be done by business and other institutions so that all Americans can be functionally literate in our society.

We will not chronicle here all the major U.S. programs aimed at fighting base-level illiteracy. For one thing, we have already done so in *Time*. Moreover, this is primarily a conversation about the ethical and pragmatic imperatives for business in confronting illiteracy.

Fortunately, some American corporations have arrived at the realization that business must contribute to the fight against illiteracy, for reasons of both good business and good corporate citizenship— perhaps the highest form of good business. In fact, a few companies have already taken the initiative to correct some of the literacy problems that they face internally, through programs for employees. For example, Aetna, Standard Oil (Indiana), and New York Telephone all have retraining programs for employees who wish to boost their reading skills to the minimal level they need to be effective workers. AT&T alone spends $6 million each year to teach its employees basic writing and math. And we have already talked about one of Ford's programs.

However, such efforts, while both praiseworthy and necessary, are also the business world's last line of defense against illiteracy. For the companies are trying to correct the problem after it is upon them.

Beyond these eleventh-hour retraining programs are efforts to stem the tide of illiteracy before it reaches the company door. The best all-purpose statement of what must be done by business comes from the Research and Policy Committee of the Committee for Economic Development, an independent research and educational organization of 200 business executives and educators. The pertinent part of the statement says:

> Working together, businesses and schools must determine the appropriate goals of business involvement in each community. Each firm will have to make its own choice as to the degree of its involvement, depending on local circumstances. Business dollars and involvement can contribute to education research and curriculum development, and corporate funds can be leveraged with private foundation funds to broaden opportunities for public schools.

> There is little doubt that the influence and power of the business community can be persuasive in arguing the case for increased public financing of the schools. This is an appropriate role for business to play.

The most enlightened executives have launched business-backed programs to promote school-level literacy, not only as a sound investment but as a national necessity in the face of dwindled federal education dollars. "This is no less than a survival issue for America," writes Xerox Corporation's Chairman and CEO, David Kearns.

Over a score of major corporations are helping to upgrade the quality of school education, particularly in public, inner-city schools, and have made strong commitments toward that improvement. Some examples:

- Coca-Cola has slashed the dropout rate among Hispanic teenagers in four cities with a pilot program the company developed in 1984. With a $2 million fund, the company has worked with over 700 students so that in some schools the dropout rate among Hispanics is less than a third that of the general student population.
- American Can Company has joined in a partnership with Martin Luther King, Jr., High School in New York City to strengthen the school, its curriculum, and the future employment opportunities for students.
- In Boston, over 300 firms have formed the Boston Compact, a consortium that began by linking job opportunities to improved school performance. Now, more fundamentally, the consortium is working with the schools to strengthen study programs. Thus what began as a job opportunity experiment has developed into a major commitment by Boston business to education.

That kind of commitment—and more—is absolutely essential if we are to avoid the projected disaster in literacy of the year 2000, when one-third of our nation will be unable to work or earn effectively and unable to buy the goods and services that educated, literate employees produce.

Business must start, or continue, to influence our politicians, to let them know that literacy will be a top priority for the United States for federal, state and local governments.

*Time* has just completed two years of exhaustive, nationwide research, showing that, to avoid illiteracy you must catch a child before third grade. We're not doing that with one-fourth or more of all our children. We must, therefore, generate more funds, more taxes, more cooperation, more commitment. For example, U.S. elementary school teachers now earn about $20,000 to $25,000. How can we do that, tolerate that, when Japan pays its teachers in the top 10 percent of all national incomes—and 98 percent of that nation is literate? And, in America we are allocating only two to four cents of discretionary tax dollars to education, while we hand 55 cents to defense.

It is past time for business to bring the leverage, the power of its influence, its money, and its lobbying pressure to correct such absurd and unethical imbalance in our spending, in our priorities. Beyond such priority pressuring are opportunities to lobby for specific measures such as the proposed Literacy Corps, which would reward a one- or two-year tutoring commitment with major college tuition assistance. And beyond that are opportunities for new cooperative programs between business, schools, and government—like the Boston Compact, and for individual corporate programs such as Coca-Cola's and American Can's.

Let me end this most detailed section of the pragmatic and ethical obligation of business to level 1 literacy by quoting a fine old Philadelphia Quaker named Stuart Rauch, former CEO of the Philadelphia Saving Fund Society (PSFS). Some 20 years ago, during Philadelphia's very impressive downtown renaissance, PSFS, under Rauch, began underwriting very low cost (5¼ percent, as I recall) mortgages for financially "underqualified" minorities, so they could acquire and/or improve their own homes in the tough, rundown Strawberry Hill section.

I asked him why he was doing this. He said—and I have never forgotten his immediate, very direct reply, or its inherent priorities: "We're doing it, initially, because ethically and morally it is the right thing to do. And," he added, "in the long-run I'm sure it is going to be good business." I believe the same can be said for level 1 literacy.

## CULTURAL/CIVIC LITERACY

At the second level, literacy, cultural and civic, it seems to me the primary responsibility for instructive action lies with publishers, TV networks, members of the fourth estate, disseminators of news and information—such as *Time* magazine. And with universities like Virginia. Because if *we* don't do it, who will? Professors have academic freedom to aid and impel. The media have a constitutional amendment. What a unique set of blessings, and what a formidable responsibility.

Speaking to the very heart of civic and cultural literacy, I hope that we include a significant portion of sociology, history, and philosophy (as you are surely including ethics) in your graduate business programs. Here I can think of two people very worth heeding. When Robert Hutchins first took over the Yale Law School, in 1927, a date wonderfully analogous to these present, raider-ridden, crash-prone times, he announced requirements in history, philosophy, and, I believe, literature. This, of course, was greeted by an uproar, which bothered Hutchins not a bit. To the angry chorus of "Whys?" he replied, "Because I am going to produce a generation of educated lawyers, not sophisticated rule-beaters." As a measure of Hutchins's effectiveness, I believe that the Yale Law School put three justices on the Warren Court.

The other person much worth heeding is Jim Laney, president of Emory University. Laney, who deplores the self-centered, acquisitive aims of too many of today's students, and the self-serving collusion of too many universities that "educate" (so-called) for narrow, dollar-driven competence, says this: "We must educate not just for competence, but for the public good." And I would add, for accountability.


## ETHICAL LITERACY

Language can be employed, as an Elliot Abrams uses it, to evade, to deny, to subvert, to contravene, to conceal, to dissemble. Or it can be used as James Madison and Thomas Jefferson did, to elevate the philosophy and function of government, of human affairs, to the highest levels in the history of humankind.

Take just a half dozen words from the entire spectrum of our language, and analyze them for their ethical implications. Begin with "influence." And let's play to our audience a bit. Ethicists may *influence* business students to make ethics a more pervasive consideration in their business careers. Or turn the coin over and try this lead paragraph from a recent *New York Times* article: "A former executive of the Wedtech Corporation testified yesterday that he paid the personal lawyer of Attorney General Edwin Meese about $800,000 for 'his influence with Ed Meese.'" On the one hand, an ennobling word, with high purpose. On the other hand, gutter talk. Same word. Just depends on how you use it.

Or let's try "research." Albert Sabin, for example, performed *research* on viruses, from which came the most effective of the polio vaccines to lift the condition of mankind. Then, quite recently, a professor named Terry Wilson, who runs West Virginia University's Marketing 321 class at the graduate business school, sent students out to do *research* of the coveted "real-world" kind, that takes one's education beyond dry academic theory into the exciting milieu of business.

Professor Wilson's students were assigned to check out inventories, sales volumes, ad expenditures, and potential new-product introductions at various heavy-equipment makers in the area. They were just students on a *research* project—right? Well, turns out Professor Wilson has a consulting contract with Caterpillar, a fact that profoundly depressed the people who had been *researched* at H.O. Penn, Yancey Brothers, et al., when they discovered it through a reporter from the *Wall Street Journal*.

When Wilson was confronted by the matter, he simply shrugged and said, "No harm done." No harm. One of the students, when asked what he had learned from the exercise, said he found it worthwhile. "You learn," he explained, "that the boss [Wilson, who gave out the grades] has the final say in everything, that you get things done, or forget it."

How about the phrase "checking sources"? A friend of mine in New York who is a very heavy headhunter tells me that phrase is the focus of perhaps the most agonizing dilemma in his high-powered and highly confidential business. Some headhunters get fees as high as 40 percent of the first year's salary of a top executive whose head they have successfully hunted. And thus the temptation to ease back on source checks, once the fish is coming close to the boat, can be great indeed. I'm happy to say my friend comes out on the right side of this dilemma. Not long ago he recruited a new college president. The man looked ideal, and held up handsomely through a character check of nine sources. But something nagged my friend. A tenth source had been suggested for a final check. By this time, the man had been sounded out for the job, had accepted it, had been confirmed by the trustees, and the formal public announcement was only days away.

My friend called the tenth source who told him, "You better speak to so and so"—a lawyer. The lawyer informed him that the candidate for president had paid off three women a total of $150,000 in settlements for sexual harassments. The headhunter's diligence prevented the college from making a serious mistake. How many other headhunters have been less dogged, less meticulous, less forthright in checking sources?

"Progress." Now there's a fine word, very upbeat and forward-moving. In fact, for a couple of centuries in America, *progress* was pretty close to a national canon. But the use of the word has changed. Rear Admiral Richard Truly, NASA's associate administrator for space flight, described himself as very pleased with the *progress* being made toward resuming flight after the *Challenger* tragedy. Of course two or three workers had been incinerated in a fuel accident. And in the vehicle then being made ready, there were some worrisome problems with the rocket nozzles, a faulty weld in a pressurized fuel turbo-pump, and some tiny cracks on the aft skirts of the booster rockets. But, said another NASA spokesman, none of these problems would affect the launching schedule.

Finally, let's try that very popular euphemism or rationale, "pressure." More and more people, it turns out, have done odd, or just plain awful, things because of what they describe as *pressure.*

For example, some of those kids in Marketing 321 at West Virginia claim they sensed something wrong with bootlegging so-called academic *research* to a professor who had a conflicting commercial contract. But they felt pressure to please the professor, the boss, to get a good grade.

And the folks at Morton Thiokol and NASA claimed they were under tremendous pressure to hold to launch schedule when they sent up a seriously flawed *Challenger.* Those flaws were known, battled over, were the basis of all-night pleas from two engineers to postpone on the eve of the launch. But NASA and Thiokol, under pressure, said go—for money, for glory, and to please the boss: our President. And seven Americans died.

There is, fundamentally, only one kind of pressure—*internal* pressure, the value system *you* have constructed within yourself, that allows or prompts you to do or not to do, to say or not to say, as you will. No one and nothing on earth can make you do *any*thing you really don't want to do—so long as you are willing to pay the price of refusal: inconvenience, ostracism, economic ruin, or death. In other words, so long as you invariably hold your*self* accountable.

For the fact is that ethics, or accountability, comes in two decorator colors: black and white. Gray is the color we impose, or hide beneath, to rationalize indecision or failed standards—*all* of which are *internal*. The society does not impose gray upon us; *we* impose gray upon ourselves. And each of us, alone, is responsible for the conduct of our society, our business, ourselves.

Now, of course, there are exceptions, as there are to everything. But in ethics, and in personal accountability, those exceptions, those grays, should be close to one-in-a-lifetime, to be avoided by all possible human efforts. Take a journalist's gray. Our first amendment protection allows us to tell all we know quickly, without favor and without fear. But if a confidential source (who may be culpable himself) risks death or ruin to reveal a key fact in an investigation of national chicanery such as Watergate, do you name and betray him?

Or, if the date is June 1, 1944, and you learn that the Army is going ashore in Normandy four or five days hence, do you put it on page one? And here comes the Luftwaffe with those 350 fighters Hitler held in the East? And there go thousands of our guys? No, you withhold it. But you are accountable for that withholding—the right thing in this not very gray case. Just as NASA-Thiokol are accountable for withholding the knowledge of those lethal flaws in *Challenger*'s O-ring seals, surely the wrong thing in that case with *no* gray whatever. You know when what you are doing is right or wrong.

Or, as I witnessed some time ago, a young cancer surgeon was asked, urgently, by a resident, for a drug dosage for a woman in screaming pain. He replied, and I heard him: "She'll have to scream. I have one dosage, and if I don't give it to Mr. Hirshkowitz, he'll be dead tomorrow." He saw no gray. He did what he believed was right.

We return, now, to the Dishonor Roll, to people who choose to live in a gray world, who do not hold themselves accountable. People who seem to have been educated for narrow competence, self-aggrandizement, and surely not for the public good. White House Aide Lyn Nofziger, one of the Wedtech family, it turns out. Deputy White House Chief of Staff (and these all should be positions of high honor) Michael Deaver—tried for perjury and violations of ethical statutes. Attorney General Edwin Meese, guardian of our laws, who said, while attacking the Miranda decision, "You don't get many suspects who are innocent of a crime." Wonder how he feels now?

Anne Burford resigned as EPA administrator after disclosure that she bent environmental regulations to favor certain industrial polluters. William Casey, late of the CIA and this world—suspected of lying to the Congress, the representatives of *We* the People, about CIA involvement in the Iran-Contra affair. Ivan Boesky, fallen dean of Wall Street arbitragers, a financial realist, confessed inside trader. And good old Victor Posner, industrialist, corporate raider, convicted of evading $1.2 million in taxes. And if you think that's all Ol' Vic did, you just haven't been paying attention.

These men and women, clearly, have been possessed of high degrees of narrow competence. Narrow, self-serving, and, apparently, dishonorable. Among other things, whether they be public or private executives, they have violated the model oath for America's top executive, our president: "He shall take care that the laws be faithfully executed." Is there *anything* gray about that? Can *any*one claim it is not the *right* way, the winning way, the most *realistic* way to operate? And does it not speak entirely to personal accountability?

You know, it continually astounds me, as I read and attend ethical discussions, how little reference is made to the Constitution and the ethical/philosophical base from which it grew. For me they are the most potent ethical imperatives that we possess. In fact, I believe they may be the most potent that have ever been cast to guide and govern the affairs of *We* the People. As we grope for guidance, why do we seek so much from dead Greeks, dead Germans, and dead Frenchmen, and so little from our own genius?

As a final example of what people may do with literacy, with the ethical imperatives that suit their purpose, let me mention two Princeton graduates:

One, Princeton Class of '71, a philosophy major with a minor in Hebrew ethics. James Madison.

The other, Princeton Class of '57, a philosophy major with, I believe, a minor—certainly some course studies—in Hebrew ethics. Carl Icahn.

Carl Icahn made money.

James Madison made America.

The question is what will business make now?

# 12

# Business Ethics, Literacy, and the Education of the Emotions

## Robert C. Solomon

At Harvard University the business school is separated from the rest of the university by the Charles River. The symbolism is unmistakable, and it is expressed with some vengeance on both sides. At the University of Texas, through accident rather than wisdom, the Business Administration-Economics Building is less than 30 feet or so from Waggener Hall, which houses some of the liberal arts departments. And yet, for the amount of commerce between them, they might as well be at opposite ends of the state. It could easily be argued that ordinary merchants or businesspersons have never been known or thought of themselves as particularly well read, that the busy life of business has never left much time for books (even books on management), and that "book-learning" has never done very much to prepare the aspiring manager or executive for the tests, trials, and tribulations that corporate life has in store. What has changed, however, is that the separation of business and literacy has been institutionalized, reflected in our educational policies and the divisions in our schools. The average business student is so steeped in finance and management courses that he or she rarely gets the chance to take more than one or two (usually required) liberal arts courses, and, of course, the usual liberal arts student wouldn't be "caught dead" in the business building. The result is a kind of social schizophrenia, a fragmentation of sensibilities that all too often gets recognized only in the unflattering terms of mutual abuse that each side throws (from a safe distance) at the other.

Ezra Bowen has raised a pithy question for those of us who split our lives—and it does feel very much like a "split"—between the liberal arts and the business world. Coming to the aid of those who try to teach literature to business students and executives, he has brought the argument for literacy into the heart of the business world, pointing out—correctly, I think—that the cost of illiteracy to businesses, in terms of their own "bottom line," is enormous. The inability to read and write, he argues, costs billions of dollars every year, and add to that the loss in productivity, the numerous causes for embarrassment, and examples of bad taste. Bowen distinguishes three kinds of literacy, (1) functional/technological literacy, (2) cultural or civic literacy, and (3) ethical literacy, which he defines as "the use of language to articulate and achieve high purpose." It is not altogether clear how he intends to spell out this third category, which is the one I want to talk about in this commentary. Nor is it clear that the second category adequately transcends "the ability to absorb and transmit ideas and information" to include questions of value. Indeed, I would argue (and I think he would too) that an adequate conception of "cultural or civic literacy" already embraces and presupposes ethical literacy. (Both, of course, presuppose some degree of functional literacy, although there are cultures—certainly not this one—in which reading and writing may not be necessary.) The question of categories is complex, but I think that some such division is essential to any discussion of "literacy"—which all too often tends to shift its meaning from one category to the others, and I believe that ethical literacy—though not exactly as Bowen describes it—lies at the very heart of business ethics.

What's wrong with illiteracy? That is, perhaps, a strange question in a society that is losing billions of dollars because people can't read and is, or knows that it should be, devoting millions of dollars to wiping out functional illiteracy. But the question regarding business, in particular, is not why an employee or an executive should be able to read but rather why he or she should read, not labels or contracts, but books, "good" books, novels and political treatises, and scientific adventure stories. The routine defense of the fight against functional illiteracy casually slips into a defense of the liberal arts. There are multiple confusions here. The need to know how to read and write is not yet the need to read Sinclair Lewis or *The Federalist Papers*. Moreover, literacy is routinely defined as "the ability to read and write" e.g., *The Random House Dictionary*,[1] but it is more precisely (and etymologically) restricted to reading. Of course, on the level of functional literacy the necessity and utility of the two go together, but, to put the point bluntly, to insist on a person's literacy (meaning that he or she reads certain kinds of books and knows what is going on in the world) is quite different from insisting that he or she is also capable of writing down his or her ideas in any satisfactory way. Literacy is not the same as articulateness or the authorly virtues. Writing well is a kind of power; it can also be a profession. But what about reading, what are its virtues? Or, specifically, why should a busy executive take time out of her hectic schedule to read a novel or a treatise that has nothing to do with her business? If on a flight between New York and Chicago she has nothing else to do, is there any reason why she should read one of the classics rather than the latest who-dun-it from Dick Francis?

There is a category of literacy that Bowen has left out, perhaps out of kindness, but that is the rather snobbish notion of literacy that has more to do with credentials and class than it does with "getting on in the job" or keeping up with the newspaper. Some people would choose Nathaniel Hawthorne over Robert Ludlum or Jackie Collins for no reason other than "class"; it "looks" better and one thinks better of oneself. And if that's the answer to the question, "Why read (good) books?", the democratic response is surely, "Who cares?" But this, too, is more complicated than at first it might seem. The same great books that edify, educate, and inspire their readers are the ones that get used as a kind of social litmus test. Thus the easy slippage in the public mind from the well-publicized problems of higher education in general to William Bennett's insistence on the classics to the purely snobbish sophistries of Allan Bloom. Taking the importance of functional literacy for granted, both for the sake of even the most minimal success in our increasingly technical and symbol-saturated society and as the presupposition of more advanced notions of literacy, I want to consider what Bowen calls "ethical literacy," redefining the terrain a bit, trying to get a bit deeper into questions of ethics and its teaching and taking account of the "gray areas" of ethics that he too quickly dismisses. He talks nobly of "the use of language to articulate and achieve high purpose" but I am afraid that such aspirations are more appropriate to a Madison or a Jefferson or a Socrates than to the average executive or college professor. Between knowing what is going on and grand pronouncements of purpose lies the real stuff of ethics, that "gut-level" sense of values that Bowen refers to but does not seem to include in his account of ethical literacy as such. What is missing from that account is this ordinary, democratic sense of ethics, something less than "high purpose" but something more than mere information and keeping up with the news. What is missing is that sense that literacy doesn't just inform us but moves us, prepares us for experience as well as allows us to understand experiences that we ourselves will (most often happily) never have.

## THREE LEVELS OF LITERACY, REVISED

I don't mean to argue over taxonomy, but to understand the very special role of reading good books (and, I would add, watching good movies) in the ethical education of the ordinary business executive (and all the rest of us), I think that it is important to divide the topic a bit differently, collapsing cultural and ethical literacy and filling in the gap between them and recognizing the sometimes effete and class-divisive purposes that these arguments about literacy can take. Like Ezra Bowen, I want to begin by distinguishing three kinds of literacy, and the first, like his, is the ability to read (and write)—the nuts-and-bolts part of literacy—the skills that everyone in this society MUST learn if they are to have any chance at decent jobs and fair treatment and protection. This is "functional" literacy. It has to do with being able to read a simple contract. It has to do with being able to write a letter of application, or to read a warning label of an advertisement. Its practical importance is unquestionable.

Second, there is "intellectual literacy," meaning "well-read." This is the sense defended by liberal arts college presidents, for this is the commodity they sell. It is the sort of literacy that is paraded across the pages of the *New York Review of Books* and is displayed by readers thereof. It is having read not only *Moby Dick* but also *Typee,* having Nietzsche and Eliot quotes at the tip of one's tongue, and being able to recite lines of Chaucer or Shakespeare without pausing for even a moment in one's conversation. Such literacy is unabashedly elitist—given the educational privileges that (usually) make is possible. It is often competitive (if not intrinsically so) and a mark of social superiority (which is not, I hasten to add, an argument against it). This sense of literacy might also include—but need not—Bowen's "ethical literacy," "the use of language to articulate and achieve high purpose." Can one do better, in articulating high purpose, than to quote Jefferson, or Rousseau, or perhaps John F. Kennedy? But there are always those eloquent moral appeals and deep-cutting social critiques that have nothing behind them, whose claim to honor is nothing but their own eloquence. We seem subject to an easy confusion between a sense of ethical self-righteousness and a sense of ethics, as if the vigor and intelligence of our moralizing were itself the equivalent of being moral. In Bowen's terms, there can be more than a gap between articulation and achievement, and sometimes the former is intended to replace rather than lead to the latter.

Between the "functional" and the "highfalutin" is a third kind of literacy, which is what concerns me here. To call it either "cultural" or "ethical" is much too narrow, for what it serves is nothing less than the education of the whole personality, the visualization and delineation of the world one lives in.

This third kind of literacy is too often thought of as "knowledge-ability," but that word smacks too much of mere information and know-how and too little of the affective, the ethical, and the experiential, which are crucial to it. It is a type of literacy that is concentrated in but not exclusive to books, which—today—also involves film and (as it always has) the other arts. It can come from conversations on the street, lectures, and political rallies, but, for a variety of reasons that I would like to discuss here, it centers on the printed word. It has to do with participating in certain basic or even essential experiences, knowing, if only vicariously, how a form of life touches on our own, "living through" tragic or horrible or joyful situations that are central to human experience, even if we may never go through them "actually" ourselves. In this sense, reading *The Iliad* is not just an exercise in reading (which is what it too often becomes in high school) and it is not a matter of being able to say you've read it or occasionally drop learned allusions. There is a sense in which living through the Trojan War is an essential part of the "Western" experience, expected of all of us, if only in the safe and bloodless form of ever newly translated Homeric verses. Reading Einstein or Darwin is not just getting knowledge; it is sharing intellectual adventures that lie at the heart of our civilization. In this sense, literacy is a kind of love, not an ability or an accomplishment. It is participation, education in the classical sense—being brought up to be part of something, not just successful in a career. Much of the misunderstanding about business ethics has to do with the erroneous idea that ethics is something imposed upon business. The truth is, rather, that business is a way of life that is part of a larger way of life and ethics is the fabric that holds the whole together. Literacy is familiarity with and being part of that fabric, its myths and legends as well as its theories and self-images. Literacy and business ethics, in other words, are not so much two different disciplines but one. (This is why the narrative form of "case studies" has become so prominent in business ethics courses, and some of the best cases are taken straight from the classics.)

Discussions of literacy slip among its three levels with disconcerting ease. Sometimes literacy is compared to utter illiteracy, the inability to write even one's own name. Sometimes illiteracy is ignorance, sometimes social incompetence. Sometimes it is compared in a scholarly way with what is called the "oral" tradition in literature, and then accused of a kind of cultural imperialism: why do we think that books are better, say, than the shared experience of sitting around a campfire? But, of course, what one says about literacy and what one compares it to depends entirely on what one means by it. The third kind of literacy is often confused with a kind of escapism or merely "vicarious" involvement in life. The experiences one gains from books are said to be not "real" experiences but purely formal, detached, isolated from life rather than a part of it. I think that this is basically wrong, but to show this, I will have to turn to my concern for the emotions in literature. The question of what is a "real" experience and what is not is not nearly so simple as the critics of "vicarious book experience" make it out to be. To say that one is "illiterate" is not necessarily to say that he or she cannot read; it is, much more often in business circles, to say that he or she has not read, and accordingly has missed (albeit "vicariously") one of the essential experiences with which every member of our civilization is expected to be familiar.

## THE IMPORTANCE OF LITERACY

If you haven't read *War and Peace*, what have you missed? What have you missed if you haven't read Dickens, or Camus, or Borges? Or, for that matter Galbraith, Marx, Mill, or Einstein? One might respond that you've missed a certain pleasure in life, or an evening's entertainment, or, in the case of *War and Peace,* a couple of weeks' engrossed involvement. Then there are the more practical replies: "You may have missed some important information" or, perhaps, there is the possibility of blowing a job interview or a surprisingly high-flying lunchtime conversation. And then there are the political answers (rarely presented as such): not reading certain books excludes you from the literary elite, which in many corporations happens to be the power elite—with all the opportunities and status thereof.

I find all of these answers to be inadequate. Some are self-congratulatory, some are vulgarly pragmatic; most are false in fact and some are just resentment. And yet, the literature on literacy does not always make clear just what a good answer to such a question might be.

Spokespeople for the humanities, full of self-congratulation, often give lectures, invariably reprinted in alumni bulletins if not also in the local newspapers, insisting that the liberal and literary arts will make a person a better human being, solve the world's problems, and enlighten "developing" countries to the wonders of Western life. Indeed, one gets the impression that a student who reads becomes something of a saint in this day of television movies, video games, and drive-in blood-and-gore horror films. And if this pronouncement proves to be without foundation (Nero, Mussolini, and the Borgias were all well read), the same spokespeople will retreat to the contradictory idea that reading is good in itself and "its own reward." (I have philosophical doubts about anything being "good in itself," but let's let that pass.) But, in any case, however well such speeches succeed in attracting funds for the annual giving campaign, they surely fail as defenses of literacy.

So why books? The arguments I hear these days, from some very literate and book-loving theorists, make it sound as if the love of books is nothing but self-serving, not just for writers and publishers but for the "elite" who maintain their political superiority with the pretensions of "culture." In other words, nothing but our second level of "intellectual" literacy. Literacy is a capitalist device to separate out the advantaged, some Marxists say (on the basis of very wide reading). Literacy is the ploy of a white, English-speaking elite to render "illiterate" peoples from a different culture, with a different language and a different history, say some very learned educators. And, indeed, there is something very right about these arguments: whatever our clumsy attempts at democratic education, there remains a drastic difference in class and racial mobility, a difference that is easily and often measured in precisely those tidbits of knowledge that come from a literary education. Much of what is called "literacy" is cultural pretension, and it is not hard to argue that in a nation with a non-white unemployment rate of well over 20 percent, literature is a luxury that is practically, if not culturally, restricted to the relatively leisured upper-middle class.

On the other hand, there is a clearly practical problem of literacy in our public schools, which has little to do with the self-congratulatory advantages of a liberal education. Students with high school diplomas can't date the Civil War, the Vietnam War, World Wars I or II. In the best schools, students haven't heard of the Oedipus complex or read the classics, or even classic comic books. Christopher Lasch writes in his *Culture of Narcissism* of students who don't know what the Russian Revolution was about or when it was, and in a survey I carried out a few years ago for the *Los Angeles Times* I found that a majority of honors college students didn't know the names of Faulkner, Goethe, Debussy, Virginia Woolf (almost everyone knew the phrase "who's afraid of . . .", but didn't know where it came from). They didn't know who Trotsky was or Niels Bohr or Spinoza or Kafka. A small but frightening percentage didn't know who Hitler was.

So, on the one hand, we have the self-congratulatory speeches about the liberal arts; on the other, an admittedly desperate educational situation. Between them, we can see the battle between "the basics" and the need for "elitist" education developing, with the inevitable consequence that the question of literacy becomes a political problem; literacy becomes status and the basics become the focus of an education that is conscientiously devoid of anything more than the basic ability to read and write. And on the corporate level, the busy businessperson is taught to treat reading books as something of a dispensable luxury, as if one's daily experience at the office and during the commute home (together with exhausted evenings at home and an occasional weekend in the country) is quite enough for a full life, without the additional experience that (for most of us) only literature can provide.

What I want to argue here is this: Books, despite the pervasiveness of television, remain the primary vehicle of our culture, and not just as the source of our concepts and our ideals and our heroes. It is no accident that most of our best movies and television shows are derived from books, or that the ideals and heroes that endure are the ones that appeared long ago in the classics. But what is more difficult to show, though just as important, is that books are an important source of shared emotions as well as a means of understanding emotions in other people and providing a safe and central vehicle for *having* emotions. In other societies, there are other vehicles, and, one might argue, some of them are superior. ("For what ?" needless to say, remains the crucial question.) But for most of us, a literacy-deprived life is too often an emotionally limited life too, for good substitutes are hard to find.

A second part of this answer is that the activity of reading books, again as opposed to watching television or any number of intellectual more passive entertainments, requires an exercise of the imagination and the use of a critical faculty that is forcibly suspended through the continuous onslaught of TV programming. Or for that matter, through the continuous onslaught of words and images from almost any source—lectures and films, for example—that do not demand our critical and imaginative participation. Emotions are not just reactions; they are social imaginative constructions. Here is the key to what Daniel Boorstin calls a "free people," a "nation of readers" who know how to enjoy the privacy of a book, in which the wheels of their imaginations can spin at will and their private conversations and commentary can be perfected silently with or against the greatest minds of our history. But here, too, is an often unappreciated key to a rich and meaningful emotional life, for emotions, as I shall be arguing, are part of the imagination and both exercisable and educable through reading as well.

## THE EDUCATION—AND THE IMPORTANCE—OF EMOTIONS

Literature, I want to insist, is vital to the education of the emotions. One very difficult question concerns what is to count as literature— just *Moby Dick*, or *Treasure Island* too? And for that matter, what about the TV shows "The Simpsons" and "Miami Vice"? But an equally difficult question, if literature is said to serve the emotions, is just how emotions—which are generally considered to be unlearned, instinctual, visceral responses—can be educated at all. Perhaps, one might argue, literature can serve to provide models of self-restraint and control of the emotions—but this hardly counts as the education *of* the emotions. Perhaps, in the modern version of an ancient debate between Plato and Aristotle, it can be argued that literature provides an "outlet" for emotions, which might otherwise have their dangerous expression in real life. But as we know from the endless debates about violence and pornography, it is not at all clear from the evidence (and the evidence seems to be one of the lesser considerations) that such literature does not motivate and inspire such behavior instead of sublimating or defusing it. Whether inspiration or sublimation, however, the obvious effect might argue that some literature stultifies and numbs the emotions, but this hardly helps make our case for literature and the emotions either.

What we need, first of all, is a new and better conception of emotion. If an emotion is a physiological response, no matter how complex, then it will not do to talk of education, though we might talk in some limited way of cause of effect. William James, who wrote a classic treatise on the nature of emotions and came back to the theme many times in his career, defined an emotion as the sensation of visceral change, prompted by some unsettling perception. But this also means that one can change one's emotions by way of changing one's behavior, one's thoughts, and one's outlook—in other words, by educating them.

James's retreat from the physiological view of emotions to a view both more flattering and more pragmatic led him and leads us to a realization that is not readily forthcoming so long as one thinks (as James did in his essays) of an emotion as an emergency secretion of adrenalin, as in panic, sudden anger, or "love at first sight." Such emotions are indeed blatantly physiological (though this is surely not all that they are) and difficult to control—much less advise intelligently—given the urgent nature of the circumstances. But the emotions that mean most to us are not those transient moments of panic, fury, and infatuation; they are such enduring passions as lifelong love and righteous indignation, which are clearly learned and cultivated with experience and which prompt and inspire us to actions far more significant and considered than a start of panic, an "outburst" of anger, or the often embarrassing first flush of love. Here, too, we can appreciate the importance of emotions and their education. It is not mere "control" that concerns us; it is cultivation, development, refinement. Love and respect are not just "natural"; they are also taught, and learned. Moral indignation is nothing less than the end result of a moral education. Indeed, even fear—the most primitive of emotions—is more often learned than not, and the supposedly obvious examples of "inborn fear" do not make the general education of this emotion any less essential to life. Without such emotions, there can be no ethics and no business ethics, whatever the rules and the policies, the corporate codes and fine speeches from company headquarters.

The most significant emotions are those that play the largest roles in the structuring of our lives. Philosophers sometimes talk as if reason can and should direct our lives but no novelist or poet could or would try to define a theme or a character through reason alone. The structures of literature as of life are grand emotions: love, patriotism, indignation, a sense of duty or honor or justice, and the less admirable passions of jealousy, envy, and resentment. One might try to teach such emotions and establish such strictures, through general principles or slogans ("love thy neighbor" or "*écrasé l'infame*"), but one is much more assured of success teaching by example, or better, through experience itself. And where direct experience is not available—as it often is not and is not wanted—so-called vicarious experience will do the job. Thus the heart of literature is and has always been *stories*, narratives that provide not only examples of virtue and vice but also the opportunity to enter into a shared and established emotional world. There is and always will be considerable debate about the place of "morality" in literature. Literature is—whatever else it may be—the communication of emotion. But this need not depend on plot or narrative; it can be conveyed through form as well. Indeed, one is tempted to suggest that there may be as much emotion in the formalism of William Gass as in the moralizing of John Gardner. Business ethics is as likely to be inspired by the ethereal writings of Gurdjieff as it is by the horror stories in Upton Sinclair's *The Jungle*.

What is an emotion, that it can be educated? If I may summarize a theory and three books in a phrase, I would say that emotions are essentially a species of judgment. They are learned and intelligent, even if they are not always articulate. They contain essential insights—often more accurate and more useful, even more "true"—than the much deliberated truths of reason that contradict them. (If reason tells us that our petty loves and desires are of no importance while our emotions proclaim them magnificent, it might well be foolish to be reasonable.) "Every passion," wrote Nietzsche, "has its own quantum of reason." Indeed, more than a quantum; it is its own reason. "The heart has its reasons," insisted Pascal, "that reason does not fathom." Every emotion is a way of constructing the world. It is a measure of place and importance in which we and all things of significance get that significance. Love creates its love, as anger indicts the accused. To enter into an emotion is not to "enter into someone else's brain." It is to participate in a way of being in the world, a way in which things matter, a way charged with shared understandings and obsessions.

To educate the emotions is nothing like the stimulation of a physiological state, though to be sure that can and sometimes does follow hard on certain emotional experiences. To educate a person is to provide him or her with an opportunity to have that emotion, to learn when it is appropriate—and when inappropriate—to learn its vicissitudes and, if the term isn't too jarring, its *logic*. To learn to love is to learn to see another person in virtually infinite perspective, but it is also to learn the dangers of love, the disappointments, the foolishness, and the failures. Some of this one learns firsthand, but it would be a tragic lovelife indeed that had to go through the dozens of stories of love, lust, and betrayal in the first person illiterate. Not to mention the various wounds and greater injuries that one would have to suffer to learn even a chapter of *War and Peace,* firsthand.

In a rather different context, Israel Scheffler has discussed the breach between emotions and reason as utterly destructive of education.[2] He caricatures the standard view of emotion "as commotion—an unruly inner disturbance." The "hostile opposition of cognition and emotion," he says, "distorts everything it touches: mechanizing science, it sentimentalizes art, while portraying ethics and religion as twin swamps of feeling and unreasoned commitment." Education, he goes to say, "is split into two grotesque parts—unfeeling knowledge and mindless arousal."

And emotion, we might add, gets lost, for it is neither unfeeling nor mindless, though it is both knowledge and arousal. It is knowledgeable arousal, one might say, educated through experiences in some sense not one's own, through shared stories, through literature.

## LITERATURE AND THE EMOTIONS

The influences of literature on the emotions can be catalogued into four groups, over and above the brute stimulation of passions that—while dramatic and often effective—should not really count as education. A well-wrought example or story may inspire feelings of the strongest sort—of sympathy or compassion, of anger or indignation, but education means learning something, not just repeating a familiar feeling on the basis of an equally familiar stimulus.

1. Literature tells us what other people feel. The great significance of the increasing (if still largely unread) availability of foreign lit-

erature, for instance, is that it informs English readers about the circumstances and expressions of passion in people unlike ourselves. The sense of shame in Indian family life; the sense of honor in Samurai Japan. In one sense, such information does not educate our emotions at all, but rather allows us to get some glimmer of understanding about the emotions of other people. But if emotions are judgments about the world, they are also influenced—and partially constituted—by knowledge about those judgments and their context. It is of no small value to our own emotional perspective to learn that romantic love is very much a "Western" emotion, for instance, or that other societies have conceptions of family intimacy and attachment far stronger than our own.

2. Literature not only lets us know *that* other people have such and such emotions; it also tells us *how* they feel. It lets us imagine "how we would feel if. . . ." Sometimes, the circumstances are recognizable but there is good reason not to know about them first-hand. The descriptions of the battles of Borodino in Tolstoi's *War and Peace* and Waterloo in Stendhal's *Charterhouse of Parma* give us powerful portraits of "how it feels" to be on one of the great battlefields of the nineteenth century, but these are experiences most of us would gladly accept second-hand. Few of us would want to actually suffer the remorse of Emma Bovary or Anna Karenina, but it is of no small importance to our emotional education that we have, at a safe distance, understood "what it would feel like if. . . ."

3. Literature allows an actual re-creation of an emotion. This may not be true of the descriptions of Borodino or Waterloo, or for that matter, of Emma or Anna's final despairing moments. But tales of injustice—such as *Les Misérables*—do something more than inform us "what it feels like when. . . ." Our sense of outrage and injustice *is* a genuine sense of outrage, not just an understanding or a reflection of it. The Northern sense of moral indignation on reading Stowe's *Uncle Tom's Cabin* was not a vicarious emotion but, in every sense, the real thing. Emotions are not isolated feelings but world views, and worlds, unlike sensations, require structure, plot, and details. Literature provides that structure, the plot, those details, and once we have been submerged in them, the emotion is already with us. (It does not follow as a mere effect.)

4. Literature helps us articulate emotions we already have. Zola's descriptions of a harsh reality give us a language in which we can express our own sense of discontent, and examples for comparison. Marx is, whatever else, a powerful writer, who gives any sympathetic reader an enormous range of metaphors, as well as facts and theories, to bolster a large sense of dissatisfaction and give it

expressions. So too Rousseau. Literature gives us examples, models, metaphors, new words, carefully crafted descriptions as well as whole structures in which and through which we can understand and express our own feelings. The education of the emotions is, in part, learning how to articulate them, learning what to expect from them, and learning how to use them.

It should be clear from the above four categories of "influences" that the education of emotions is at least as involved in learning to appreciate other people's passions as it is in molding one's own emotions. This seems odd—or merely "empathetic"—only so long as we cling to the idea that emotions are our own "inner" occurrences, the private domain of each individual and exclusively ours, not to be shared (at most expressed or confessed) with anyone else. But emotions are public occurrences. Not only are the expressions and the context of emotion evident to a sensitive observer; the structures and values of emotion are also an essential part of a culture. One feels this most dramatically in a mob at a political rally or in a large crowd at a sports event. The emotion is not just "in the heads" of the hundreds or tens of thousands of people present; it is literally "in the air," with an existence of its own, in which the people participate. But much the same is true of more modest emotional gatherings. One sits around with one's own family and feels the complex of loving, defensive, and competitive passions fill the room. Or, one sits around while visiting with someone else's family, sensing the passion in the air but feeling quite "out of it." Visiting a strange culture sometimes gives one the overpowering sense of being present in the midst of emotions that one not only fails to share but fails to understand. Accompanying visitors to one's own society who feel similarly throws into perspective our own emotional atmosphere, which, like the (unpolluted) air, is so familiar and so essential to us that we take it for granted and do not notice it at all.

Emotions are public in the sense that they are shared views, with shared values, based on shared judgments. Such judgments depend, to an extent rarely appreciated, on the particular language of the culture. A culture without an emotion word is not likely to experience that emotion. Certain Eskimo cultures lack a word for anger, for example, and it can be persuasively argued that they do not get angry. One might say that the lack of a word indicates a lack of interest, just as a multiplicity of words suggests an emotional obsession. The French have a multiplicity of words (and distinctions) for romantic love; the Russians have numerous words for suffering; Yiddish abounds in words of despair. American English, it is worth noting, has a high proportion of its emotion vocabulary dedicated to the identification of different kinds of anger, and Oxonian English has a remarkably flexible vocabulary for contempt. Cultural generalizations may always be suspect, but it is worth noting the distribution of emotion words in peoples' own language. Not coincidentally, the language circumscribes values and judgments, and these, in turn, determine a distinctive outlook on the world.

How does one learn to participate in an emotional culture? In a word, by becoming literate. Not necessarily in the nuts-and-bolts sign-your-name read-a-contract sense, perhaps, although it cannot be denied that much of our emotional culture is defined and communicated by the written word—in newspapers and street-corner pamphlets as well as best sellers and subway and highway advertisements. And not necessarily by being part of that elite literary culture that proclaims itself the bearer of the better emotions. To participate in the emotions of a culture is to speak its language, share its value judgments, participate in its stories, its history, and its heritage. To have an emotion—even the most exquisitely private and personal emotion—is to be part of an emotional culture. A teenager in love fervently believes that he or she alone feels a passion all but unknown in the history of the world—and shares this feeling with a million other teenagers (and post-teenagers). They are all part of the world of romantic love, a world promulgated and advertised with a ferocity unprecedented in the history of emotional propaganda. Orwell tried to be terrifying by imagining a society brain-washed by "the Anti-sex league." Far more terrifying may be the present reality of an entire society, awash in love-and-sex sentimentality and so comfortable with it that it even seems "natural."

Romantic love is but one example of an emotion that, no matter how private and personal, must nevertheless be understood as a public, cultural phenomenon. Love is something learned—from every movie and toothpaste advertisement, from a hundred romances, street-corner gossip, and our whole cultural apparatus of chance meetings, dating, and unarranged (not to say inappropriate) marriages. But love is not love; it can be vulgar (mere possessiveness, for example) or it can be exquisite, and the latter, like the former, is something learned. It is one thing to love someone; that in itself is learned in a society where (romantic) love is considered essential—more important, for example, than established family or community ties and obligations, more important than duty and honor (though not necessarily incompatible with them). But *how* one loves is something more, and this too is learned. What literacy does to love is nothing less than to make it possible. Love—every love—is a narrative that follows an embarrassingly small number of plots, but they are and must be well-known plots, for they define the emotion. A young couple need not share the tragic consequences of young Montague and Capulet to recognize in their own situation—feuding families, necessarily clandestine love—a story that is a classic of the genre, and a set of emotions that defines so much of our social structure. (Just suppose that we did not consider love to be legitimate unless it was sanctioned and encouraged by our parents.) Learning the desperation of clandestine love, and the sense of heroism that goes with it, is one of the lessons of literature. (Learning the legitimacy and the heroism of unrequited love is also one of the classic and more curious dimensions of our emotional cultural life.)

Learning that love can be tender is obviously one of the more essential lessons of literature. A moment's thought should establish that such tenderness is by no means "natural" and requires a social emotional structure of considerable strength to maintain. Learning that love can be tragic is of no small importance, but perhaps most important is simply the lesson that love is important, even the most important thing in life (a sentiment that is by no means obvious in the state of nature). By the same token, one learns jealousy along with love—the strength of that emotion depending on corresponding lessons in possessiveness, betrayal, and the illusions of exclusivity. It is worth commenting, in this regard, that the prototype of our literature about jealousy—and the model for our emotion—is *Othello*, in which jealousy is a tragic emotion, inspired by trickery and maintained by a kind of stupidity, and, most important, it turns out to be unwarranted and unnecessary. Our lesson in envy from the same source, however, turns out to be much more mixed; Iago may not be a hero, but he does succeed in his envious designs. Our literature encourages love and discourages jealousy, but our vision of envy is not so clear. It would be a study of no small importance and enormous scope: the place of envy in American literature—and American life.

The kind of argument that is merely suggested here—the ways in which literature defines and teaches emotion—could and should be developed for a spectrum of emotions and a wide body of international literature. But the connection between emotions and literature should be getting clear: it is not just that literature inspires or illustrates emotions and provides us with examples of them. Literature—taken broadly as the shared perspectives and narratives of a culture—actually defines emotions and brings them into being. To teach literature *is* to educate the emotions, although—like any teaching—this can be done consciously or unconsciously, competently or incompetently. To teach literature is to teach how other people feel, and how we would feel if. . . . It is to teach us to feel certain emotions, and to articulate and understand the emotions we do have.

Literacy is not just good for or food for the emotions; it is, ultimately, what the emotions are all about.


## LITERATURE AND THE VICARIOUS EMOTIONS

It is one of the oldest debates in both philosophy and social criticism: do the emotions we experience "vicariously" through literature (including drama and film) have a healthy or a deleterious effect on us? Plato fought Aristotle on the desirability of "catharsis" in the theater, and long and varied traditions of moral psychologists throughout the history of Christian theology have argued the acceptability of vicarious experiences of the more sinful emotions as opposed to the actual Sins. (Vicarious faith and Platonic love presented very different issues.) Greek comedies presented deception, cowardice, and foolishness, but the question was, did these encourage or discourage these vices in their audience? Medieval morality plays had as their unquestioned intention the discouragement of lust, envy, gluttony, anger, pride, greed, and sloth, but it was a burning question then as now whether the portrayal of such passions, even unsympathetically, would nevertheless stimulate precisely the Sins depicted. Today, the argument regards pornography and violence on television. The question, as ever, is whether such vicarious experiences, even if presented or intended in a discouraging light, have a positive or negative effect on the genuine emotions.

The distinction between vicarious and genuine emotions, however, is not at all so clear as the proponents of the various traditional moral arguments would suggest. So, too, the charge that people who read books have thereby only vicarious emotions, not real experiences, does not hold up to examination. Of course, there is an obvious difference that can be granted right from the start: readers of a terrifying or bloody novel (*Frankenstein, All Quiet on the Western Front*) or viewers of a horrifying movie (*Jaws, King Kong*) have the luxury of fear, terror, and horror without the real risk of harm. The "willing suspension of disbelief" explains *how* they have such experiences. What is by no means so evident is *why* they choose to have them. Whether or not they are real, these experiences of fear are certainly emotions, and this needs to be explained. In this regard it might also be wise to distinguish—as is too rarely done—between the emotions of fear and terror on the one hand and horror on the other. What gets experienced while reading frightening books and viewing "horror movies" is properly horror, not terror. Terror, one might say, is real fear; it believes in the danger of its object. No "willing suspension" there. Horror, on the other hand, originates from an idea, one step removed. One is horrified by the idea of war, the threat of invasion by alien beings or wild animals, or the notion that a murderer or rapist could enter one's home. One does not experience genuine terror reading or viewing a "thriller," but one may well feel genuine horror on reading or viewing a horror tale. Vicarious horror, in other words, is real horror, whether or not vicarious terror is real fear. Both terror and horror should be distinguished, we might add, from mere grossness (a vivid description of an abortion, a close-up of the effects of a gunshot), which grade B writers and filmmakers now tend to employ instead of the more artful skills of suspense and true horror.

Discussions of vicarious emotions (and many discussions of emotion) tend to focus much too heavily on the emotion of fear. A reader of Stendhal, we may readily admit, does not really fear the sudden impact of a bullet in his or her back, and it is also extremely debatable that he or she can literally be said to fear for the fictional hero. But we already mentioned that the emotion of moral indignation one experiences while reading *Uncle Tom's Cabin* is the genuine emotion. Indeed, moral indignation, even in "real life" (and in what sense was *Uncle Tom's Cabin* not "real life"?), is an emotion that observes and judges rather than participates. The result of moral indignation may be real action, but the emotion itself is quite real regardless of the possibilities for action. Indeed, *Uncle Tom's Cabin* inspired very real action, even if the events depicted in the book were fictional.

What we just said about moral indignation holds of a great many important emotions. Grief, sadness, amusement, compassion, and pity are real enough whether or not the persons and events on the pages or on the screen are real. So too is the reader's or viewer's experience of romantic love. Who would deny that love is often experienced at a distance, directed at a person about whom we may know much less than we know about a fictional character with whom we have briefly shared a vicarious adventure? And who would deny that the persons with whom we fall in love are often fictional creations of our own imaginations or Freudian "phantasms" left over from more primal love experiences? What is true of love is true also of hate, and a dozen other passions besides. Indeed, once we start examining the list, it begins to look as if everything we experience while reading is real—except the story and its characters.

A proper analysis of vicarious emotions would take us far beyond the limited claims of this essay, but the essence of a theory can be sketched very briefly. It is typically argued that an emotion is vicarious and therefore not a real emotion because its object—what it is about—is not real. In this sense very few emotions are "real," since almost all emotions involve a certain subjective reshaping of their objects, whether it is love, hate, anger, or simple compassion. The object of every emotion is selective (we look for virtues in love, vices in hate). Most emotions involve a certain distance from their object, even when it seems that we have never been closer to them. Every emotion constitutes its own object, as the particular, perhaps peculiar, object of that emotion, even if that same object and emotion are shared by hundreds or millions of people—as the great books may be, with all the emotions they evoke. To say that the object of an emotion is fictional (and known to be so) is therefore not necessarily to say that the emotion is not real. To insist on this absurdity would be to either limit the range of "real" emotions to a pathetic and extremely timid group of realistic attitudes, or it would be to deny the reality of emotions almost together. The reality of an emotion may have very little to do with the reality (or lack of it) of its object.

What is critical to the reality of an emotion is the position of its *subject*, the person who actually feels the emotion. In the case of reading (seeing films, etc.) this has a triple edge; it means, to a certain extent, that the characters or situations in the book (film) already have a certain amount of emotion *in them*—a frightening situation, a lovable character, a vicious, envy-filled villain. Second, there must be some sense of inference to the emotions of the author, not by way of the infamous "pathetic fallacy" ("Dostoevski must have been really depressed when he wrote this"), but it is of no small importance that a story has been composed, or retained, by someone, perhaps an entire community. In oral traditions, the importance of the emotion in the storyteller (perhaps the entire culture) is self-evident. In modern literature, this link is none too evident, and has often been under attack. But my interest here is not the method of literary criticism; it is difficult to deny that the ordinary non-formalist reader is well aware that behind the pages is another human being. The easy separation of text and author is no evidence against this.

Third, and most important, the reader (or viewer) has emotions, and these are the passions that concern us. The emotions of the personalities in the pages are more or less given to us, and the emotions of the author(s) are for most purposes irrelevant to us. But the emotions of the readers are determined in part by the text, in part by the readers themselves. Here, perhaps, is the most important advantage of books over film (and other more determinate media): the reader of a book is free to visualize, no matter how precise the description of a character, his or her own version of that character. Not surprisingly, the envisioned figure almost always bears a striking resemblance (whether recognizing or not) to persons of importance to the reader. (Such recognition is usually rare; as so many critics have so often said, much of what Freud said about dreams is certainly true of the literary imagination, but in the reader as well as the author.) The reader can "act out" a drama in much more personal terms than the movie viewer, and through this activity of the imagination thereby learns how to experience (and re-experience) emotions of an increasingly sophisticated variety. The education of the emotions is, more than anything, the education of the imagination, learning to engage oneself in a variety of emotional roles, in a variety of situations that may never have been encountered in real life—at least, not yet.

What is critical to the education of emotions is precisely the fact that the emotions experienced while reading are not merely vicarious, not unreal, even if the situations and characters of the story may be wholly invented. It is not the reality of the emotion's *object* that is critical, but rather the reality of the emotion's *subject,* the reader. But it would be folly of a different kind to think that the reader simply *creates* his or her emotional experiences, that the emotions in the novel—including the form and structure of the novel as a whole— do not determine and *teach* emotions to the reader. That is the very importance of the great masterpieces of our literary tradition; they teach those emotions that, for better or worse, our collective culture has chosen as the temperament of our age.


## DECONSTRUCTION AND READER RESPONSE:
## A POLEMICAL DIFFERENCE

My thesis here is that one of the functions of literacy and literature is to educate the emotions. This requires a renewed emphasis on the importance of the reader as subject, but it also requires a somewhat conservative if not chauvinist respect for a literary tradition, defined by its masterpieces and its greatest authors. These two requirements find themselves in uneasy company, however, with both traditional and some contemporary theories of literary criticism. It has long been argued that the text is everything, that the reader just reads, supplying nothing but, one hopes, literacy and comprehension, and perhaps some structural analysis. Today, this nonsense is being overcorrected by "reader response" theory; the reader supplies almost everything, the book and the author are all but incidental. So, too, it has long been argued that literacy demands uncritical respect if not awe for one's own literary tradition. Today, this has been violently challenged by some of the Derridain deconstructionists, followers of Jacques Derrida, who rightly point out some insidious cultural biases in our literary tradition but also nonsensically deny the very existence of authors and masterpieces. Moreover, they reject (or "deconstruct") the very idea of the subject, of author, and of reader, an impossible dilemma. But however enticing the logical paradoxes and perplexities of such a position may be, our concern here is literacy and the emotions, and from that perspective, we may say simply that never has there been so inopportune or unfortunate meeting of literary theory and the fate of literature.

"It would be considered an act of war," warned the National Commission For Excellence in Education, if some foreign power had done to our educational system what we have done ourselves. The commission did not have just nuts-and-bolts literacy in mind. What is also at stake is our sense of ourselves as a culture and the emotions that give our lives meaning.

It is in the context of this crisis, rather than in my usual spirit of philosophical irritation, that I suggest looking at some of the latest fashions in literary criticism. One might be all too tempted simply to dismiss such teapot tempests if it were not for the fact that they impinge so directly on the current catastrophe.

If anything that I have been saying about literature and the education of emotions is plausible, then it follows that reading and taking literature seriously is essential. Literary theory is not detached from literature (nor will it ever replace it, as a few pundits have recently declared). Literary theory guides reading—and the teaching of reading. An emotionally detached theory—or one that encourages emotional detachment—dictates reading—and the teaching of reading—without emotion, or without taking the emotions seriously. Of course, the literary critic may have his or her own emotions— pride and vanity seem to be most in vogue these days—but they are not drawn from—and are typically antagonistic to—the emotions dictated by the text in question. They teach reading to college students, many of whom go on to become teachers of reading. And literary theory, while never the subject of discussion in the classroom, nevertheless circumscribes a manner, an approach to literature.

It is an approach defined, first of all, by the denigration of masterpieces. These are the books that carry our culture. They are also the books that students won't read. ("They are too long . . . they are too hard . . . they are too boring.") How do the new theories encourage these resisting readers? These "smug iconoclasms" (so called by critic Jonathan Culler, who defends some of them) entreat students not to admire great books but rather to "decontruct" them.

"Deconstruction" is the new weapon of high-level anti-intellectualism in America. It is also a devastating technique for undermining emotional involvement. It originated in the intentionally obscure style of French philosopher Jacques Derrida, but it has now infected probably half of the literature departments in our universities.

Deconstruction is, stripped of its self-promotion and paradoxes, a way of not taking texts seriously, not entering into them but undermining them, "reducing" their emotional context to petty subjectivity and thereby not taking it seriously—which is to say, not allowing oneself to feel what the book insists we ought to feel. Deconstruction is, in one sense, just criticism—but it is criticism of a particularly nasty variety. It goes after weaknesses rather than strengths, searching the margins of the text instead of trying to comprehend the whole. Of particular interest to the deconstructionists are political and cultural biases and inconsistencies and, especially, sexual hang-ups. And this is not Norman Mailer they are deconstructing, but Melville and Emily Dickinson.

Consequently, the geniuses of literature are no longer to be admired. Their texts are no longer there to be venerated but rather to be undermined. Their role as vehicles of culture is destroyed and their power to inspire emotion—any emotion except perhaps contempt or pity—is extinguished. And, concerning the general crisis in literacy, the resisting reader cannot help responding, "Why then read them at all?"

The power and the importance of literature in educating the emotions lies in literature's ability to bring to and submerge the student in a context (and perhaps a culture) quite different from his or her own. Teachers sometimes talk sympathetically about "tapping into the student's emotional experience," but, in fact, this is getting it backward. Literature does not "tap into" so much as it informs and ultimately forms students' emotional experiences. It is essential that the book (or film, etc.) provides the student with something that he or she does not already have—a situation, at least. The core of the emotional experience is in the book (film, etc.) and the student enters into it. It is thus with particular alarm that we should look at the new theories of criticism, which as a genus have attracted the title "reader response theories," of which deconstruction is one marginal example.

According to reader response theory, the new heroes of literature—replacing authors and masterpieces—are the barely literate readers, and, of course, their English professors. It was Geoffrey Hartmann of Yale who notoriously proclaimed that the creative baton has passed from the author to the literary critic (which, given the readability and intelligibility of current criticism, philosopher John Searle rightly calls the reductio ad absurdum of the movement). But from an emotional point of view, one can only dimly imagine what our passions might be like if we depended upon literary theories to inform them.

Consider, for example, this recent comment from one of the more distinguished professors of literary criticism in America:

No longer is the critic the humble servant of texts whose glories exist independently of anything he might do; it is what he does, within the constraints of the literary institution [i.e., tenured English professors] that bring texts into being and makes them available for analysis and appreciation.[3]

In other words, *Moby Dick* is not the masterpiece. Indeed, Melville's masterpiece would not even exist if it were not being taught and written about by English professors. Melville, we now learn, in fact contributed very little; the true creator of the work is the student: "the reader . . . supplies *everything*."[4]

In other words, any emotions involved in literature are simply supplied by the reader. He or she does not learn. The reader simply supplies an emotion—any emotion presumably, without regard for the text. If one wants to be amused by Anna's suicide or giggle through *Cry, The Beloved Country*, the text has lost its authority to insist otherwise. (Any relation to a society where teenagers occasionally gun down a stranger "for fun"?)

Literature, I have argued, also teaches us to articulate our emotions. What practical advice do the new theories have to offer today's student, trying to express an emotion in a proper sentence with at best insecure command of English vocabulary and grammar?

"Deprived of a scenario, [they are] left with a page on which it is impossible to write an incorrect sentence." (The author calls this "freedom.") The same professor of literature goes on to say:

> Since language can no longer produce meanings that allow us to think contemporary experience, we have to look elsewhere—to mathematics, or abstract art or superrealism, or movies, or, perhaps, new languages created by random selection of words.[5]

One need not denigrate mathematics to doubt its ability to express emotion. And one would not have to look further than some student papers to find such a "random selection of words," but it is not at all clear that what is expressed thereby is "contemporary experience"— or any emotion whatever.

And finally, what could be more detrimental in the current situation than to give into the worst form of student resentment—perhaps at least honorable of all emotions—and the fact that they despise their texts (unread) just because they are required. And, they blame the author for this injustice. But consider a well-known Marxist literary critic, who, whatever his political views, is also employed to teach students to admire and enjoy literature. This one celebrates "the revolt of the reader," who has been "brutally proletarianized . . . by the authorial class." He encourages "an all-out *putsch* to topple the text altogether and install the victorious reading class in its place." It seems not to bother him that the class of readers is quickly becoming a null class. "We don't need the authors," he insists, leaving open the question whether we need any readers either. And against the tyranny of literature, he encourages "political intervention . . . if necessary by hermeneutical violence"[6] (by which he means deliberate misreadings of books—another timely bit of advice for students who don't know how to read carefully in the first place).

Now it might be objected that education is not just ingesting books and forming emotions; it is also learning to criticize them. Heroes are to be scrutinized. Emotions are to be evaluated.

But there is a difference between criticism with respect and criticism that undermines the very possibility of enlightened understanding and emotion. It is one thing to question a book or a passion as an ideal; it is something quite different to reject all ideals.

It might also be objected that it is important to encourage individual interpretations and the application of one's own emotional experience to the text. There is no doubt that a nineteenth century New England reader of *The Scarlet Letter* inevitably interpreted that book very differently from a contemporary student in Los Angeles. But it is quite different to claim, as it is now claimed with a bravado appropriate to its absurdity, that "there is no text," that there are only readers' individual interpretations and emotions. Hawthorne certainly has something to do with our feelings about Hester, and it is not very likely that her experience has already been duplicated by a typical Beverly Hills sophomore.

It might also be objected that most of our "masterpieces" and consequently our emotions are "ethnocentric," the product and property of a very narrow segment of the world's population. Deconstruction and its allies deflate this pretension. But the answer to this objection is to broaden the curriculum, add more books from Africa, Asia, and South America. It is not to eliminate the best works of "Western" literature and pretend that they are of only negative value. To appreciate the emotions of others—including negative emotions caused by one's own society—is extremely important, but it does not necessitate disclaiming or demeaning one's own emotional experience.

Emile Durkheim wrote, a century ago, that education is primarily concerned not with careers and techniques but with passing along a culture and, we may add, the emotions that are deemed proper to it. Literature is a primary vehicle of that culture and those emotions, and theories of literature are tools to service that vehicle. They help teachers to focus and to criticize, to interpret and to make literature accessible and exciting to students. Inevitably, they will also provoke an entertainment of their own—featuring battles between warring factions of faculty that may make the sectarian disputes in Lebanon seem civilized by comparison. But when fashions and fury among the faculty undermine the very purpose of education, literary theory ought to teach and learn a new emotion—humility, for if literature teaches us anything about the emotions, it is that whatever we learn to feel, it's all been felt before.

## NOTES

I am grateful to Cambridge University Press for permission to reprint some paragraphs from my essay in *Literacy, Society and Schooling*.

1. Random House Dictionary: Concise Edition (New York: Random House, ed., s.v. "literacy." 1980).

2. Israel Scheffler, "In Praise of the Cognitive Emotions," *Columbia Educational Review* 79, no. 2 (December 1977).

3. Stanley Fish, *Is There a Text in This Class?* (Cambridge, MA: Harvard University Press 1980), p. 368.

4. Fish, "Why No One's Afraid of Wolfgang Iser," *Diacritics* 11, no. 1 (1981): 7.

5. O. B. Hardison, Jr., "The De-meaning of Meaning," *Sewanee Review* 91, no. 3 (1983): 404.

6. Terry Eagleton, "The Revolt of the Reader," *New Literary History* 13, no. 3 (1982): 449–452.

# 13

# Business Ethics as Moral Imagination

## Joanne B. Ciulla

Business ethics would be a dull subject if ethics came in two off the rack colors, black and white. Most of us aren't lucky enough to have such simple ethical tastes. We're stuck with designer ethics, the decorator variety of moral puzzles that come in gray or spectacularly mixed tones of competing claims and conflicting duties. Gray is the color that thoughtful people often see when they initially confront an ethical problem. And gray problems seldom surrender to lily-white solutions. Sometimes we aren't quite sure we did the morally right thing. So, business ethics embraces much more than simply cultivating the ability to "Just say no" or "Just say yes" to clear-cut alternatives. It includes the discovering, anticipating, encountering, and constructing of moral problems, some of which are bona fide dilemmas, and the creating of workable solutions.

This requires what Ezra Bowen calls cultural or civic literacy and ethical literacy, or the ability to use moral language effectively.[1] But it's not what literacy is but what literacy does that is important. By opening up other possible worlds of business and morality, literacy stimulates imagination and gives us a new way of seeing. Traditions can be assessed and reapplied and moral language can be woven into contexts and situations in ways that actually transform them. Business ethics shouldn't just add a chapter to the book of business education—it should re-write it. We can do more than just heighten moral awareness or produce obedient employees—we can develop moral imagination in our students. By exploring the moral grays of business life, students must be inspired to use their creativity

212

and technical know-how to produce workable multicolored solutions.

Ethical behavior can be seen to encompass prescriptive and creative functions. The prescriptive side says, "Do no harm" or "Thou shalt not" or "You ought to always do X" (i.e., always tell the truth) or "Promote the good." It is explicit and seeks to put certain limits on human behavior. The creative involves inventing ways to live up to moral prescriptions, given the practical constraints of the world. A student once asked me, "Does acting ethically mean that if I work in the loan department of a bank and a poor person can't make his mortgage payment, I shouldn't foreclose on it because it would put him out on the street? You can't run a bank that way." Some people would just do their job and foreclose on the mortgage, others would try to come up with creative financing, and a few would invent a system for humanely dealing with such problems. Educators should ask themselves, "Which response do we want our graduates to have?" Moral commitment comes in many hues, some of which demand that we go out of our way to make the world better. This takes imagination, vision, maturity, and technical know-how. While teaching business ethics to undergraduates generally requires more emphasis on the prescriptive side of ethics, teaching it to adults requires greater emphasis on the creative side. The study of ethics should lead them to think about new possibilities for business. In this respect a course in business ethics overlaps with courses on leadership and innovation.

## THE SUPERIORITY OF THE REAL WORLD

As essayist C. K. Chesterton points out in his essay on ethics and imagination, the businessman prides himself on pragmatism not idealism.

> When the businessman rebukes the idealism of his office-boy, it is commonly in some such speech as this: "Ah, yes, when one is young, one has these ideals in the abstract and these castles in the air; but in middle age they all break up like clouds, and one comes down to a belief in practical politics, to using the machinery one has and getting on with the world as it is." [2]

One of the first things you hear upon entering a business school is references to something called the "real world." This "real world" consists of concrete, contingent things, current business practices, rules of the market, black-letter laws, and statistics. It dictates what you can and can't do. Some students enter business school infatuated with this world. They want to live in it and don't want it to change in any fundamental way. It smacks of certainty and promise and appeals to those who pride themselves on having their feet planted squarely on the ground. Neither immoral nor amoral, the real world does not preclude morality—it just has a hard time making it fit in.[3]

Because of this reverence for the "real world," the most damning indictment of business ethics is that it's not practical. Here one needs to look critically at a variety of business assumptions concerning economics and consumer behavior. As Chesterton goes on to point out in his essay, he never gave up his childlike ideals, but he did give up his childlike faith in practical politics. You can't teach ethics to business students without first forcing them to confront their childlike faith in things like the rules of the market. This may sound a bit harsh, but as anyone who has taught business students knows, if you don't come to class armed with some pretty good reasons and counterexamples to show why the market alone is not a sufficient force for punishing and regulating the behavior of people, you will have a pretty hard time getting them to appreciate what Kant has to say. I'm not saying that students have to reject everything that they have learned—on the contrary. Rather they have to dampen their enthusiasm for the certainty of these presuppositions. One has to learn to think critically before one can think creatively.

## MORAL LANGUAGE

Business students have a basic understanding of right and wrong and general agreement on the merits of honesty. They possess the right moral concepts or linguistic tools but have not mastered them in the environment of business and the culture of particular organizations. If we take the view that thought is embodied in language and language is embedded in a shared form of life, then it makes perfect sense to say that experience can enrich our concept of, say, "honesty," while the concept itself remains the same.[4] On this theory of language, understanding is not reduced to definition, but expanded by experience.

The use of moral concepts by individual speakers over time is grounded in an increasingly diversified capacity for participation in a variety of social practices.[5] It takes time to understand the practices of a new culture or community. Hence, someone who is competent at solving ethical problems in his or her personal life is not necessarily good at solving ethical problems in corporate life. Ethical and cultural literacy are life-long projects. Mastery of moral language not only reveals new possible worlds but allows us to create them.

## FAIRY TALES AND REAL LIFE STORIES

Imagination does not have to lead to fantasy, but fantasy can stir imagination. Case studies are about real situations, but they can nonetheless be taught in a way that challenges students to come up with creative solutions. The only limitation is that the solutions be workable. Imaginative problem solving operates between two broad and expandable assumptions. The first is a critical one: just because business is a certain way does not mean that it necessarily has to be that way. I don't know how many times I have heard managers rebuke me, like Chesterton's office boy, with what they consider a prudent rule of business, "If it ain't broke, don't fix it." This phrase is symbolic of both competitive and moral mediocrity—the idea that we only confront problems when we are forced to. Hence we only worry about making better cars after the Japanese do, and we only worry about our accounting practices after we are convicted of fraud.

The second assumption, borrowed from Kant, is a practical one. It rests on the old adage "ought implies can," or you are only morally obliged to do that which is possible for you to do (or you are free to do). This assumption needs to be critically explored and constantly expanded. Students often think that taking a moral or socially responsible stand requires either individual or corporate martyrdom—i.e., you lost your job or your market share. They feel powerless and sometimes prefer to mortgage their ethics until they are the CEO of a company because they think that only those at the top can effectively take a moral stand. However, the really creative part of business ethics is discovering ways to do what is morally right and socially responsible without ruining your career and company. Sometimes such creativity requires being like the cartoon mouse who outsmarts the cat.

Perhaps it wouldn't be a bad idea for people to go back and read fairy tales. In his book, *The Uses of Enchantment,* Bruno Bettelheim says that the main message of fairy tales is that the struggle against severe difficulties is a fundamental part of life, but "if one does not shy away, but steadfastly meets unexpected and often unjust hardships, one masters the obstacles and emerges victorious." He stresses the fact that fairly tales impress because they are not about everyday life. They "leave to the child's fantasizing whether and how to apply to himself what the story reveals about life and human nature."[6]

Fairy tales teach children an inspiring lesson—they can use their wits to resolve insurmountable problems. Take, for example, "The Genie and the Bottle." In it, a poor fisherman casts his net three times and brings up a dead jackass, a pitcher full of sand and mud, potsherds and broken glass. On the fourth try, he brings up a copper jar. When he opens it, out comes a giant genie. The genie threatens to kill the fisherman and the fisherman begs for mercy. Then, using his wits, the fisherman taunts the genie by doubting the ability of such a large genie to fit into such a small jar. The genie goes back into the jar to prove the fisherman wrong. The fisherman closes the lid, casts the jar into the ocean and lives happily ever after.[7]

Now this may not be the best case for your business ethics class. Getting students to talk about literature that doesn't refer directly to business can be an uphill battle. Yet, just as most adults remember their fairy tales, students tend to remember the unreal literary cases long after they have forgotten the real ones.[8] I've found that some of the stories my students tell about their work experiences pack the same punch as "The Genie and the Bottle."

In a class on international business ethics, an Indian student explained that, before enrolling at Wharton, he had worked for a steel company in India. His company bid on and won the contract for a $20 million project in Venezuela (the first of its kind for an Indian steelmaker). However, the transaction could not proceed until the Indian government approved the deal. When the government official met with the student the official indicated that all would go well if a $2,000 bribe were paid. The student halted his story there and the rest of the class then discussed what they would have done in this predicament. A majority of students felt the bribe request posed an insurmountable barrier to closing the deal. They saw two incompatible possibilities—either you paid the bribe and got the contract, or you didn't pay the bribe and lost the contract. Arguments for paying the bribe rested on commonality of bribes in various parts of the world, the size of the transaction, its benefits to India, and the relatively small size of the agent's request.

As the discussion heated up, some students got frustrated and said, "Ethics is one thing, but this is the real world." They then asked the Indian student if he had gotten the contract and he said, "Yes." Satisfaction fell over the room. Order had been restored to their real world. Morality hadn't interfered with business. The class, half of which consisted of foreign students, assumed that the bribe was paid. But then the Indian student said, "Now, let me tell you what I did. That day, I just happened to have my Walkman in my pocket. I switched it on and put it on the table. Then I said to the government official, I'm sorry, but I forgot to tell you that we tape all of our official conversations with government officials and send them to the appropriate supervisors." Like the quick-witted fisherman, the Indian had tricked the evil genie back into his bottle. He avoided doing evil and won the contract. Unlike his classmates, he saw more than two ways to solve the problem.

Most important, morality entered the real world and altered it. The student's behavior, based on rejection of bribery as wrong, offered a novel solution to a common and serious problem. At this point, a clever moralist might raise the questions, "Is it right to lie to a briber? Is blackmailing a briber like breaking a promise to a terrorist? Do two wrongs make a right?" But for a businessperson this story might prompt thinking about how a company can protect itself in such situations—perhaps taping transactions is a good policy. Sometimes the act of an individual opens up a new repertoire of action for others in like circumstances.

According to Bettelheim, some stories demonstrate why self-interest must be integrated into a broader notion of the good in order for people to effectively cope with reality. For example, the Brothers Grimm story, "The Queen Bee," tells the tale of a king's three sons. The two smart sons go off to seek adventure and lead a wild and self-centered existence. Simpleton, the youngest and least intelligent son, sets out to find his brothers and bring them home. The three brothers finally meet up and travel through the world. When they come to an anthill, the two older ones want to destroy it just to enjoy the ants' terror. But Simpleton will not allow it—later, he also forbids his brothers to kill a group of ducks or set fire to a tree in order to get honey from a bee's nest. Finally the trio comes to a castle where a little gray man tells the oldest brother that if he doesn't perform three tasks in a day, he'll be turned into stone. The first and second brothers fail at the three tasks. Then Simpleton is put to the test. The tasks—gathering 1,000 pearls hidden in the moss in the forest, fetching from the lake a key that opens the bedchamber of the king's daughters, and selecting the youngest and most lovable princess from a room full of identical sleeping sisters—are impossible. Simpleton sits down despondently and cries. At that point the animals that he saved come and help him. The ants find the pearls, the ducks volunteer to find the key, and the Queen Bee settles on the lips of the youngest princess. The spell is broken, Simpleton's brothers are brought back to life, and Simpleton marries the Princess and gains a kingdom.[9]

"The Queen Bee" might well be the child's version of stakeholder analysis. It highlights the interdependence and reciprocal relationships between individuals and groups. Most important, it shows that, contrary to some economic assumptions, decisions based on the self-interest, and not the interest of others, may not be the most profitable way to meet the challenges of life.

Our view of what is possible in the business world comes from personal experience and the media. We are bombarded with reports of unethical behavior. These reports create both outrage and cynicism. It is, however, interesting to note how the business community responds to morally responsible behavior that bucks conventional wisdom. Think for a moment about the impression that Johnson and Johnson made when it recalled Tylenol because someone had put poison in some of the bottles. It took morally responsible action at a high cost for something that wasn't the company's fault. Johnson and Johnson was later rewarded by the market for its responsible behavior. This story offered the business community a new paradigm for responding to a problem. It was a real life story of what we had hoped to be true in fairy tales. Doing the morally right thing may be difficult and costly, but in the end, you win back the kingdom. People have always needed to believe that ethical behavior will bring about some good even if the good is simply self-respect and peace of mind.

## MORAL DILEMMAS

There are, however, a variety of moral conflicts that don't seem to bring about the good. Moral dilemmas are situations in which two equally important obligations conflict. You morally ought to do A and morally ought to do B, but can't do both because B is just not doing A, or some contingent feature of the world prevents you from doing both. Tragedy and drama sometimes focus on such conflicts. Often cited is the conflict in Sophocles's play *Antigone*. Antigone wants to bury her brother but Creon won't let her, because her brother was a traitor and his burial could stir up unrest in the city. Her obligation to the State conflicts with her obligations to her family and the gods. Antigone is in a fix. She's damned if she buries her brother and damned if she doesn't. With real moral dilemmas we never feel quite happy with our decision. Some students mistakenly believe that all moral conflicts are unsolvable and draw the conclusion that there are no answers to ethical problems, only opinions.

Recently there has been a lively debate over whether moral dilemmas exist. Many philosophers have denied that bona fide dilemmas exist (lest they be put out of business). Kant, Ross, and Hare offer levels of analysis and hierarchies of duties that serve as tiebreakers in what at first glance appear to be moral conflicts, but turn out to be sloppy or inadequate descriptions and analysis. Hare, for example, approvingly quotes a message posted on a sign outside of a Yorkshire Church. It said, "If you have conflicting duties, one of them isn't your duty." [10]

Bernard Williams argues that moral conflicts are more like conflicts of desire than conflicts of belief about facts. If, for example, you believe that Camden is in Pennsylvania, and you believe that Camden is in New Jersey, unless there is something to explain how both of these beliefs can be true, you must give up one belief in favor of the other. So by accepting belief B, it is logically necessary for you to reject belief A. Williams says that we respond much differently to conflicting desires. For example, the desire of a man to be a loyal husband may conflict with his desire to have an affair with another woman. When it comes to strong conflicting desires, we usually try to imagine ways to satisfy both. Often this isn't possible. Yet, choosing to act on one desire does not logically eliminate the second desire in the same way that choosing one fact necessarily eliminates another. The husband may choose to act on his desire to remain loyal to his wife, but still desire to have an affair with the other woman. Williams says, in this kind of case, a person may believe that he "acted for the best" but the case is not closed as it is in a factual dispute. What is left, or the "remainder" of the conflict, Williams calls, "regret," or the "What if?" question.[11]

While I wouldn't draw a relativist conclusion from Williams's argument, I think he has put his finger on an extremely important point of moral psychology. We feel different when we reject a moral claim than we do when we reject a factual one. In serious moral conflicts, our desire, like the desire of the married man, is to satisfy both. Ambivalent feelings about a particular moral decision do not necessarily mean that it is a bad one. Regret is the emotion we try to minimize when we construct solutions to moral problems. We do this by imagining how we will feel about different possible outcomes. In serious dilemmas, both outcomes may appear equally attractive or unattractive, just as conflicting moral obligations may carry equal weight. The hallmark of this peculiar species of moral problem—the true dilemma—is that regret is built into the problem.

## CONCLUSION

Philosophers throughout the ages have offered tiebreakers or means for resolving conflicts. Their insights offer a window on the rich complexity of moral reasoning. Snappy case studies and engaging stories are a key part of teaching business ethics, but equally important are the powerful ways of seeing provided by the legacy of moral philosophy. People who think morality is black and white and believe that all we have to do is teach values in our schools may not like the idea of imaginative ethics. As I have tried to show, it isn't theories or values alone that will change business, but rather the critical perspective and creative actions of our students. Companies that want ethical employees but business as usual are bound to be disappointed.

## NOTES

1. Ezra Bowen, "Literacy—Ethics and Profits (The Centrality of Language)," Ruffin Lectures, 1988.

2. C. K. Chesterton, "The Ethics of Elfland," *Collected Works,* Vol. I (San Francisco: Ignatius Press, 1986), p. 249.

3. Business schools still suffer from the legacy of positivism, which stipulated that facts are subject to truth conditions while values are not. Hence, facts are objective things that happen in the real world and values are subjective actions guiding things. By cleaning up language for science, the fact/value distinction muddied the waters for ethics. We were left with the problem of building a bridge between distinct categories—fact/value and theory/practice. It's no surprise that with the emergence of applied ethics there is a renewed interest in ethical realism and virtue theory. Both of these approaches offer an integrated picture of facts and values, which allows us to study what people and institutions do, because values are embedded in practices and traditions. For business ethics this theoretical approach makes the study of ethics inseparable from the study of business practice.

4. Ludwig Wittgenstein, *Philosophical Investigations,* 3rd ed. trans. G. E. M. Anscomb (New York: Macmillan, 1986), pts. 18–20 and 241.

5. Sabina Lovibond, *Realism and Imagination in Ethics* (Minneapolis: University of Minnesota Press, 1983), p. 32.

6. Bruno Bettelheim, *The Uses of Enchantment* (New York: Vintage, 1983), p. 8.

7. Ibid., p. 28.

8. See Robert Coles, "Storyteller Ethics," *Harvard Business Review* (April–May 1987).

9. Bettelheim, *Enchantment,* pp. 76–77.

10. R. M. Hare, *Moral Theory* (New York: Oxford University Press, 1981), p. 26.

11. Bernard Williams, *Problems of the Self: Philosophical Papers, 1956–72* (Cambridge: Cambridge University Press, 1973), pp. 166–86.

# INDEX